IMAGES
of America

GRAND CANYON'S TUSAYAN VILLAGE

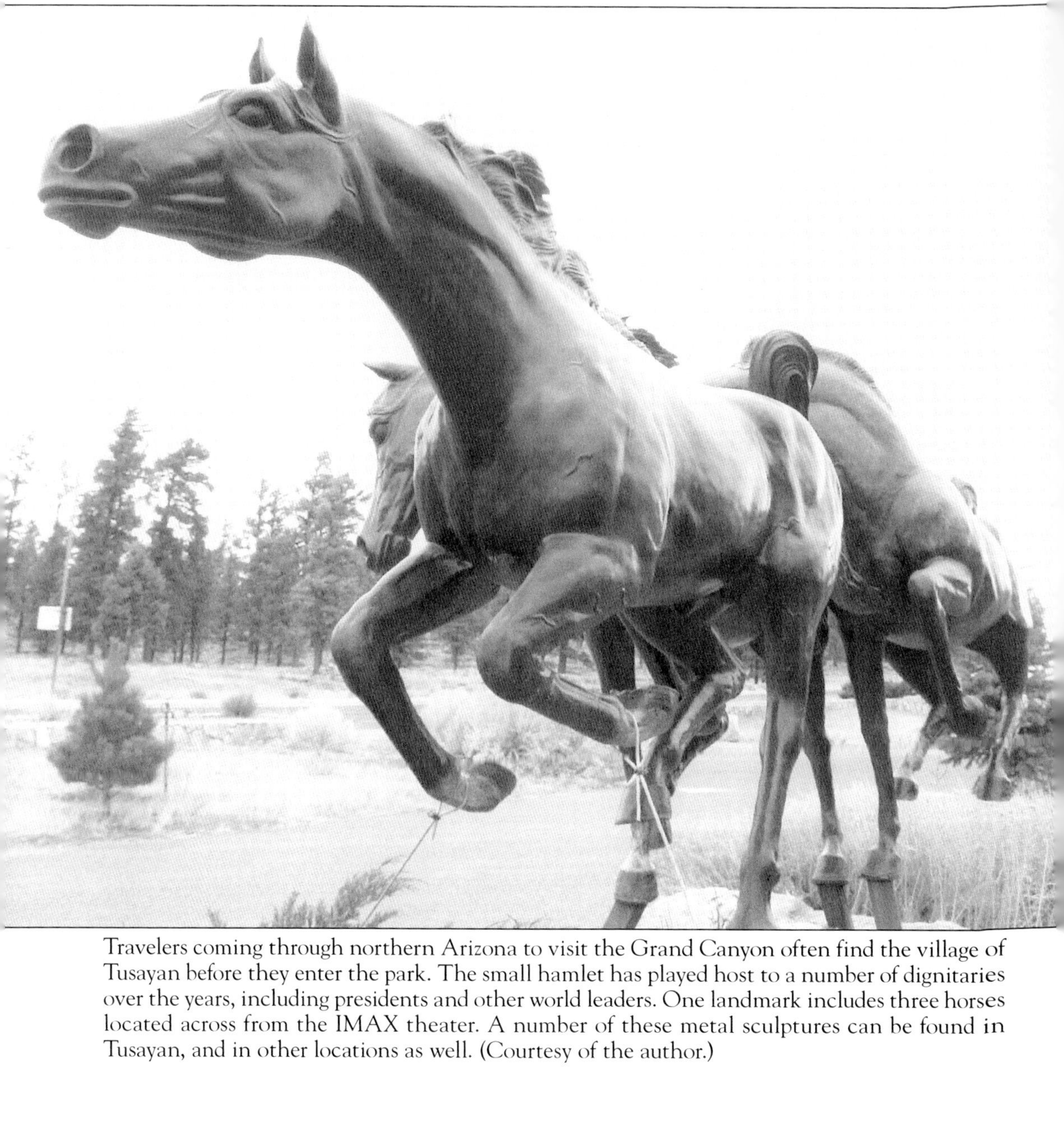

Travelers coming through northern Arizona to visit the Grand Canyon often find the village of Tusayan before they enter the park. The small hamlet has played host to a number of dignitaries over the years, including presidents and other world leaders. One landmark includes three horses located across from the IMAX theater. A number of these metal sculptures can be found in Tusayan, and in other locations as well. (Courtesy of the author.)

ON THE COVER: Ellsworth and Emery Kolb are pictured on a fishing trip sometime between 1900 and 1910. The two are based near the Supai camp within Grand Canyon. Besides their many interests in the area, the famed brothers also documented Tusayan village and the Grand Canyon in photographs. (Courtesy of Clarinda Vail.)

IMAGES
of America

GRAND CANYON'S TUSAYAN VILLAGE

Patrick Whitehurst

ARCADIA
PUBLISHING

ISBN 978-0-7385-7890-3

Published by Arcadia Publishing
Charleston SC, Chicago IL, Portsmouth NH, San Francisco CA

Printed in the United States of America

Library of Congress Control Number: 2009941019

For all general information contact Arcadia Publishing at:
Telephone 843-853-2070
Fax 843-853-0044
E-mail sales@arcadiapublishing.com
For customer service and orders:
Toll-Free 1-888-313-2665

Visit us on the Internet at www.arcadiapublishing.com

For Clarinda Vail—a true Tusayan icon

Contents

ACKNOWLEDGMENTS

This history of the Tusayan area would not have been possible without the help of numerous individuals living in and around the Grand Canyon area. Photographs documenting the rich history of Grand Canyon's Tusayan village came from private collections, libraries, the John Ivens Post of the American Legion, the National Park Service, and many others. Quite simply, there would be no history of Tusayan without all of these great folks—many of whom continue to make history in the area to this day.

Special thanks goes to Clarinda Vail with Tusayan's own Thurston family, Mary Hoover with the Grand Canyon American Legion, John Thurston, Michael Quinn with the National Park Service, Clay McCauslin of the Williams Rotary Club, author Thomas Ratz, Dan O'Connell, Margaret Hangen with the Kaibab National Forest, Ryan Williams and Lynda Duffy with the *Williams-Grand Canyon News*, Al Richmond, historian Ronald Warren, and librarian Betty Upchurch with the Grand Canyon National Park. Thanks also goes to Jared Jackson, Hannah Carney, and everyone else at Arcadia Publishing for continuing to produce their wonderful Images of America series, bringing the past to life for old and young historians alike.

Like all great adventures, developing *Grand Canyon's Tusayan Village* has been nothing short of an investigative journey. While there are many families who remain fixtures of the small community, there are many others who have since moved on, as is the nature for many small communities with a transitory population. Some live as close by as Flagstaff or Williams, while others have moved out of Arizona altogether.

Gathering information, therefore, proved to be a tasking endeavor, but with the help of many in the community of Tusayan and within Grand Canyon National Park, as well as notices in the *Grand Canyon News*, that challenge was answered. The book you now hold in your hands is the result of that journey.

INTRODUCTION

Tall pines bend slowly under a gentle northern Arizona wind. Elk, mule deer, Kaibab squirrels and other indigenous creatures go about their business under a wide blue Arizona sky. While the winters do spread snow across the area at certain times of year, and summer monsoons can bring streaking lightning and drumming thunder to the vicinity (creating their own special magic), sunny skies are the prevalent force throughout most of the year. The forested terrain backs up to one of the world's most glorious treasures, the Grand Canyon, also one of the most visited locales on the planet. Millions make the pilgrimage to the inspiring South Rim each year, passing through the forest and a certain small community on their way.

There is nowhere in the world quite like Grand Canyon's Tusayan village. Very few communities can claim the noble distinction of being at the front door to one of the world's natural wonders. But Tusayan is much more than simply an entryway to the Grand Canyon National Park; it is a living, thriving community with borders that do not end at the entrance to the South Rim.

Part of what makes Tusayan so special is its unique ties to the national park. Tusayan's children and children living at the Grand Canyon attend the same school, the only K-12 school located within a national park. Residents of Tusayan go to the Grand Canyon's library, many are buried at the Grand Canyon Cemetery, seek medical services at the Grand Canyon Clinic and so on. As such, there is no true distinction between the two communities in the eyes of those who live in the area. For them, the lines between Grand Canyon's South Rim and Grand Canyon's Tusayan village are blurred.

The entrance to the national park is a well-known landmark in the area. And like the south entrance to the canyon, which has moved around quite a bit over the years, the village of Tusayan continues to change to this day. The area plays host to numerous hotels, restaurants, stores and other attractions, including the IMAX theater. Tours are a common sight in the canyon community, both on Highway 64 (running through the center of Tusayan) and in the blue skies above. This was not the case a hundred years ago, however, when the Grand Canyon Railway brought most of the canyon's visitors to the South Rim from Williams. Early Grand Canyon pioneers, such as Emery and Ellsworth Kolb, the Hull brothers, and George Reed, had much of the area to themselves. The Kolb family would go on to have a number of interests in the area of Tusayan, including a short-lived airport, land holdings, and more. Always thinking ahead, they would store belongings in the area on the off chance of a devastating fire at their home on the South Rim.

Tusayan village did not begin with the canyon in mind, however. When former forest ranger George Reed first came to work in the area in the early 1900s, he saw potential for growing vegetables in a particularly spacious area of land near the South Rim, but far enough away to be off the beaten path. Stationed at Hull Tank Cabin during his forest service tenure, Reed eventually homesteaded the nearby land. His smart little claim encompassed 160 acres in sections 23 and 24 of Township 30. Then 40 years old, Reed, hand-in-hand with his wife, Mable, grew vegetables for their family. He sold his excess crops to the hotels, located roughly 7 miles north on the South Rim.

It wasn't long before other interested parties began to appear in the area, including Tony Galindo, who would eventually open the first Tusayan Bar. Named for the surrounding forest, which was then known as the Tusayan Forest Reserve, the bar would become a popular watering hole in the area, at least until a mysterious fire burned it to the ground a few years after it opened. A sign outside the bar, which read "Tusayan," became the name for the fledgling community. Future business leaders in the area would go on to include Ann Wren, Tom Mace, and the Rotter family. The Rotters had a number of interests in the area and were also responsible for building the Canyon Plaza Resort.

Of the many individuals who made the village of Tusayan what it is today, Williams rancher and businessman R. P. "Bob" Thurston would be at the top of the list. Thurston moved to the area in 1935 after he purchased the Reed homestead property. Thurston's wife owned land adjacent to that purchased by her husband. The family's Williams ties remain to this day.

Among his many accomplishments in the village of Tusayan, Thurston is credited with building the Red Feather Lodge between 1963 and 1964, the first hotel to be built in Tusayan. Thurston had already constructed a Shell gas station and steak house in the late 1950s with his friend Jim Kennedy. Thurston's son, Bill, and daughter-in-law, Bonnie, came to live in Tusayan in the mid-1960s. Though the couple both died in the late 1980s, their three children, Bess, John, and Clarinda, continue to be a part of the community to this day. Other Thurston relatives, including the Fain family, have kept their roots in the Williams community.

The earliest residents in the area were, of course, the indigenous peoples who called the area home for thousands of years. These included the Anasazi, Cohonina, Paiutes, Navajo, and Cerbat, from whom the Havasupai are said to have descended. The land in and around the South Rim is sacred to the Havasupai people, including the Tusayan village area, Pasture Wash, and nearby Red Butte. While their city, Supai, is located at the bottom of Grand Canyon, the tribe would winter on the South Rim, where they would hunt during the colder months of the year. The tribe summered in the canyon, where they would farm the land for their needs. Today Supai is a popular travel destination that sees roughly 30,000 visitors annually.

Like many areas of Arizona, water has also played a crucial role in the community's growth. For many years, the community had to rely solely on hauled water, which was trucked in from Williams and other areas. Many of the earliest parades in the Tusayan community featured water trucks in their festive lineups, as the trucks played a large part in the community and forest service as well. The first successful water well did not appear in the area until 1987. A sanitary district was also formed to deal with the community's wastewater. Called the South Grand Canyon Sanitary District, the area's treatment facility has been highly regarded for its use of reclaimed water per capita.

One

Havasupai Land

Indigenous peoples called northern Arizona home 4,000 years before Europeans first settled in northern Arizona. The Anasazi, Cohonina, Paiutes, Navajo, and Cerbat were among the first to inhabit the Grand Canyon. The Havasupai tribe, descended from the Cerbat, has been in the area for roughly 800 years. They are known as the only permanent residents within the Grand Canyon. While Havasupai is the tribe's common name, they are also known as the Havasu 'Baaja, which experts say means the people of the blue-green waters.

Reaching the tribe can be an arduous task, as they can only be accessed by an 8-mile hike or via helicopter. Supai, the city located within Grand Canyon, is one of only a few remote locations that still receive mail via mule deliveries. Even so, the tribe plays host to roughly 30,000 visitors each year, thanks to a number of attractions that draw visitors to the area. Gorgeous waterfalls, including Havasu Falls and Mooney Falls, are among the attractions for tourists visiting the land. Much of the land around the area was severely altered in August 2008, following a large flood that washed through the area. Navajo Falls was obliterated in the flood, and a number of new waterfalls were formed.

The Havasupai people, who would farm within the canyon during the summer and spring, once used the land on the South Rim frequently. They would spend their winters and fall hunting near the South Rim in areas such as Pasture Wash. When the U.S. government formed the Havasupai Indian reservation in 1882, made up of roughly 518 acres, the tribe was left to survive solely within the canyon. That changed in 1975, when government officials gave roughly 185,000 acres of land back to the Havasupai.

The tribe has had a long relationship with the Tusayan area. Red Butte, a sacred site for the tribe, is located just south of Tusayan and often appears as a small mountain to those traveling north on Highway 64 to Grand Canyon.

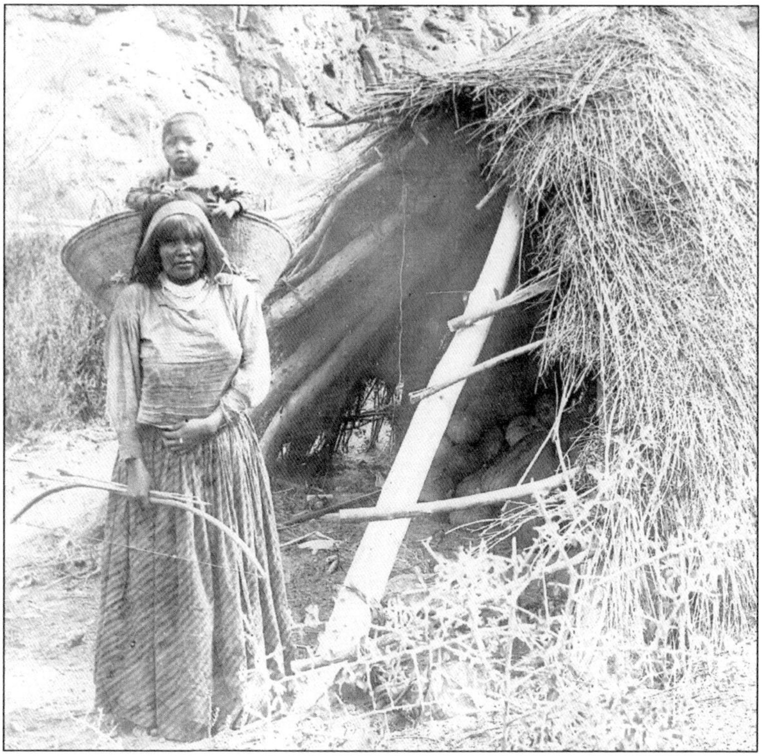

A Paiute woman is visible in this photograph taken within the Grand Canyon in 1898. The woman is pictured standing next to a "Hawe" structure with a burden basket and a child on her back. This particular member of the Paiute tribe married into the Havasupai tribe, according to historical record. (Photograph by Maude and Bartoo; courtesy of the National Park Service.)

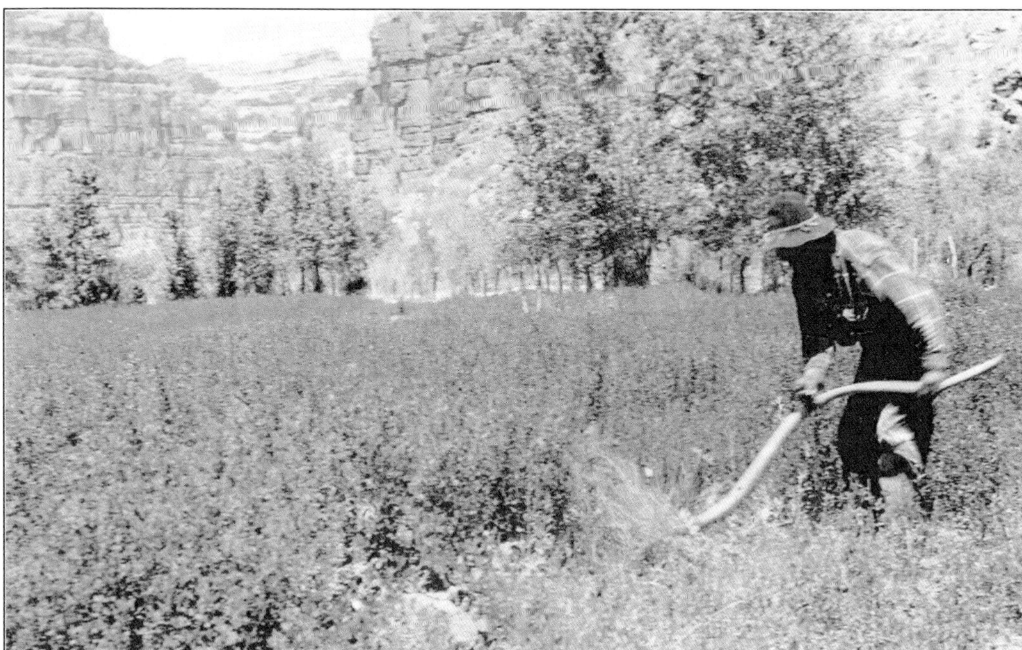

Havasupai chief Watahomagie is pictured in 1944 as he tends to a field in the Havasupai village. Watahomagie was photographed while mowing alfalfa by hand. Behind him is the Supai Formation, a popular attraction for those who make the trip to the village area each year. (Photograph by Harold C. Bryant; courtesy of the National Park Service.)

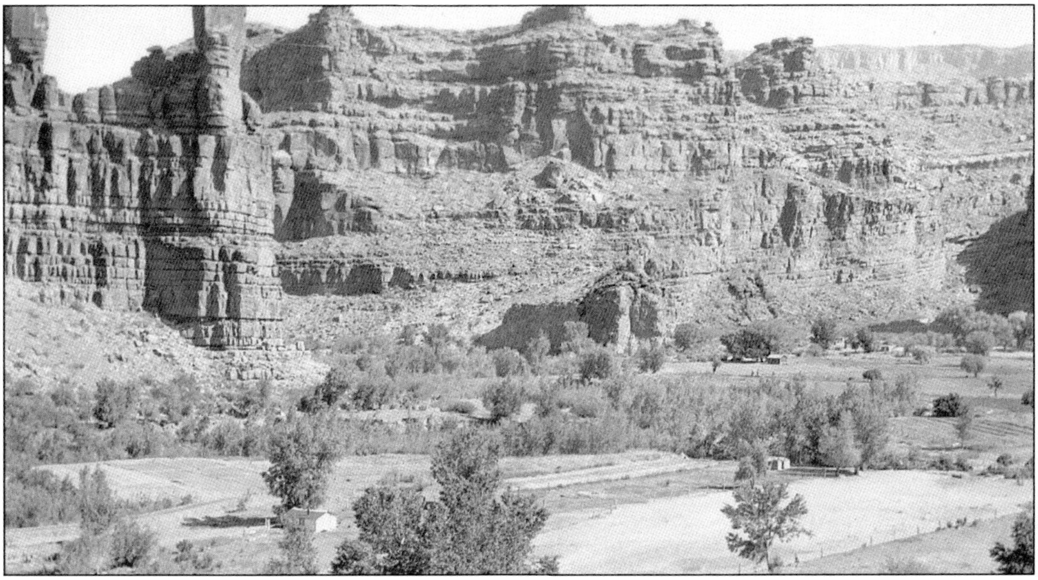

This 1944 photograph shows the magnificent view overlooking the Havasupai farmlands. In it one can see the scale of the houses and nearby animals as compared to the walls of the Grand Canyon in the background. The lands are irrigated by the Havasupai. (Photograph by Harold C. Bryant; courtesy of the National Park Service.)

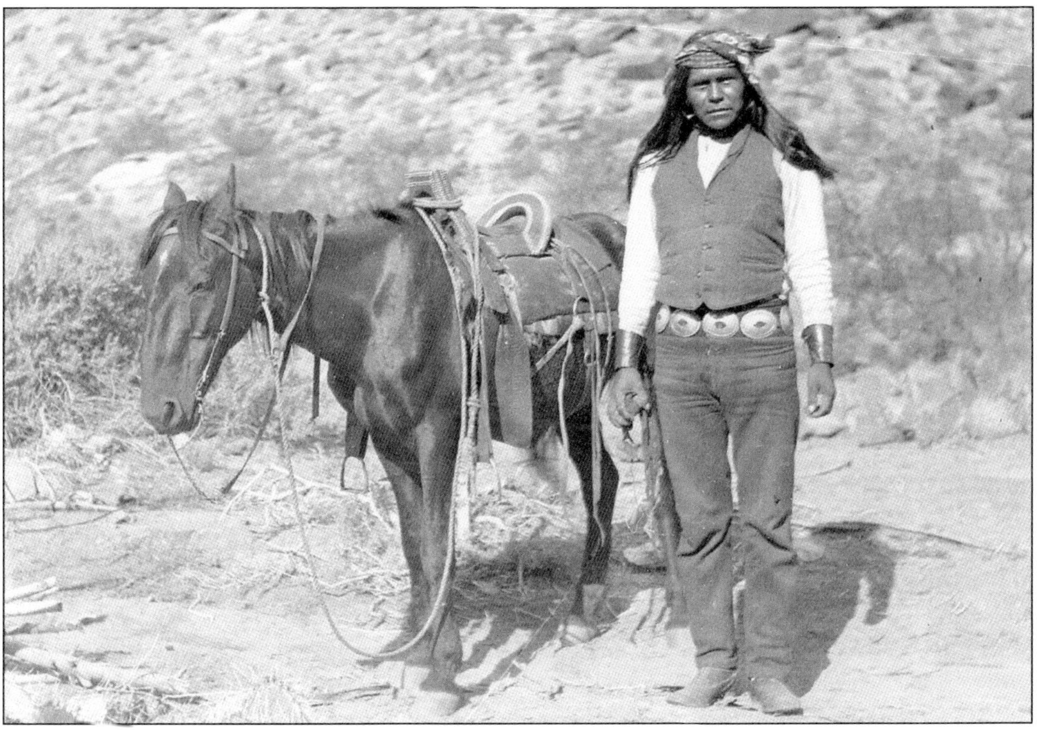

Hamteq, a young male member of the Havasupai tribe, is pictured in 1899. Hamteq, which according to national park historians means "nighthawk" in the traditional Havasupai language, is standing beside one of the tribe's ponies. This particular pony has been saddled for its journey. (Photograph by Peabody; courtesy of the National Park Service.)

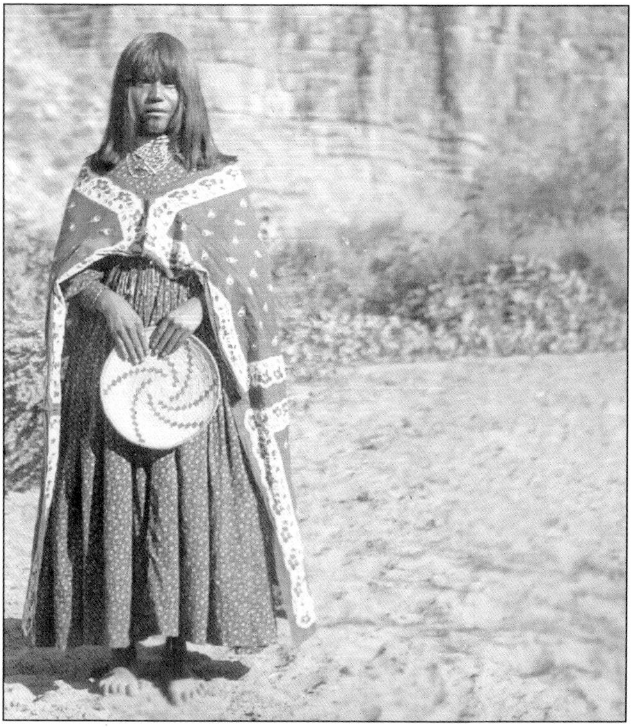

Havasupai woman Fannie Baanahmida, wearing a long dress, stands facing the camera while holding a woven basket in this 1902 photograph. Fannie Baanahmida's name means "glad man" in the traditional language of the Havasupai tribe, according to historians with the National Park Service. (Photograph by Peabody; courtesy of the National Park Service.)

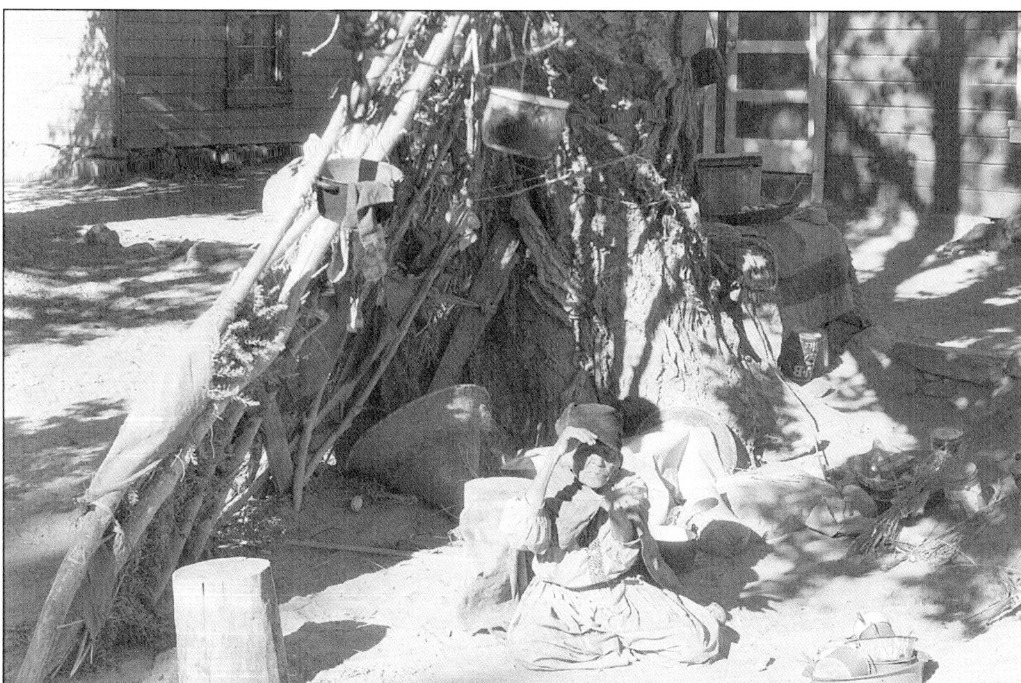

Modern buildings can be seen behind this 107-year-old member of the Havasupai tribe within the Grand Canyon. The elderly woman, the mother of well-known tribal member Allen Acappa, finds shelter thanks to a traditionally built Havasupai structure in this photograph taken on November 15, 1938. (Courtesy of the National Park Service.)

This 1938 photograph shows Mooney Falls, located within Havasupai Canyon, as water roars over the edge, dropping roughly 210 feet to the bottom. The falls are named for D. W. James Mooney, a miner who fell to his death at the falls while trying to carry a wounded miner on his back. (Courtesy of the National Park Service.)

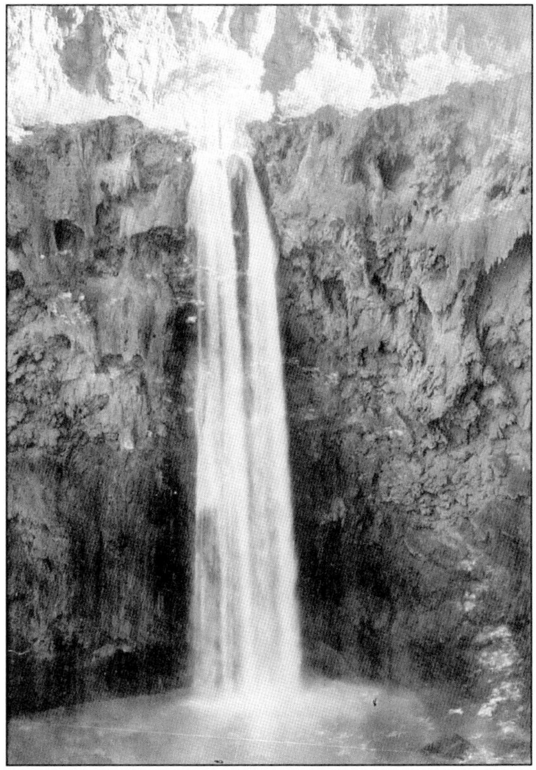

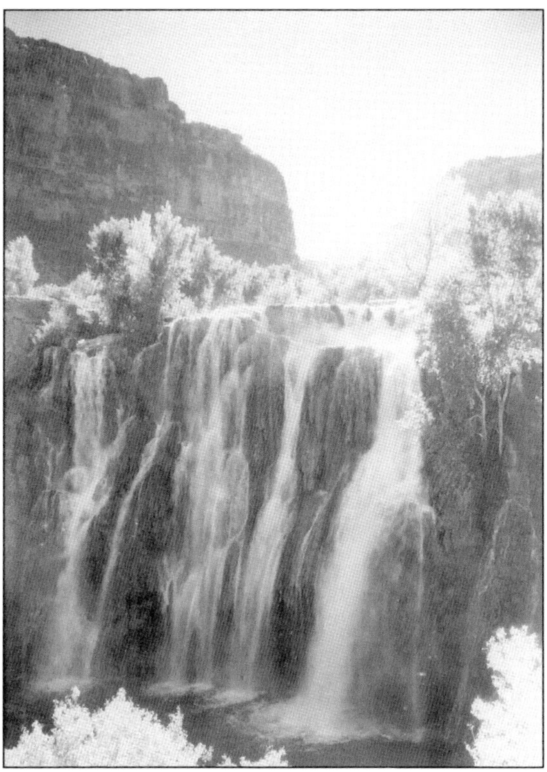

The famed Navajo Falls location is visible in all its splendor in this 1938 photograph. Like Mooney Falls, Navajo Falls was also located within Havasupai Canyon and was a popular spot for tourists visiting the area. The falls were wiped out in 2008 from a mudslide resulting from flooding in the area. (Courtesy of the National Park Service.)

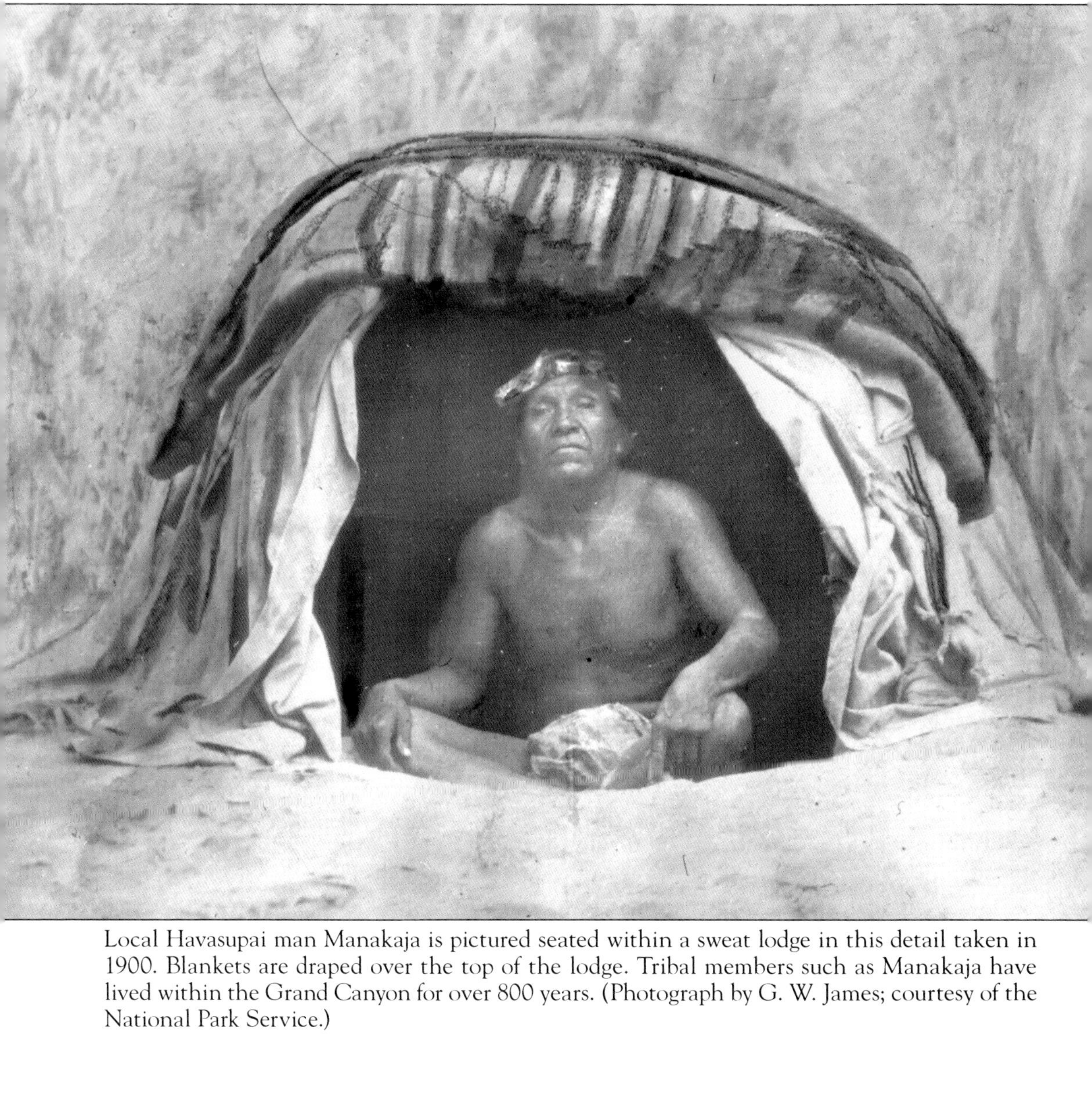

Local Havasupai man Manakaja is pictured seated within a sweat lodge in this detail taken in 1900. Blankets are draped over the top of the lodge. Tribal members such as Manakaja have lived within the Grand Canyon for over 800 years. (Photograph by G. W. James; courtesy of the National Park Service.)

This 1940 photograph paints a striking portrait of well-known canyon local Mary Wescogame as she stands at the South Rim near Emery and Ellsworth Kolb's famed studio. Wescogame was also known as "Supai Mary." The Havasupai called her "Yul Gsyoo," which means "dragging a rope." (Photograph by the Kolb brothers; courtesy of the National Park Service.)

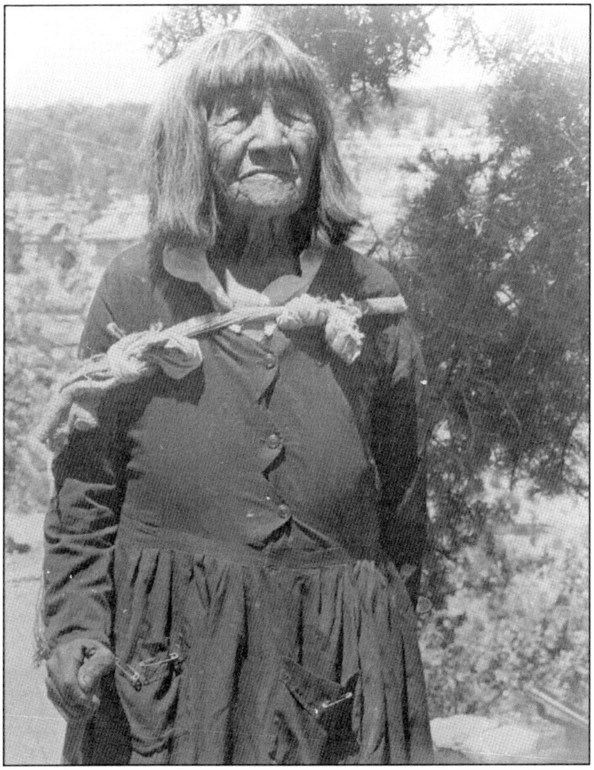

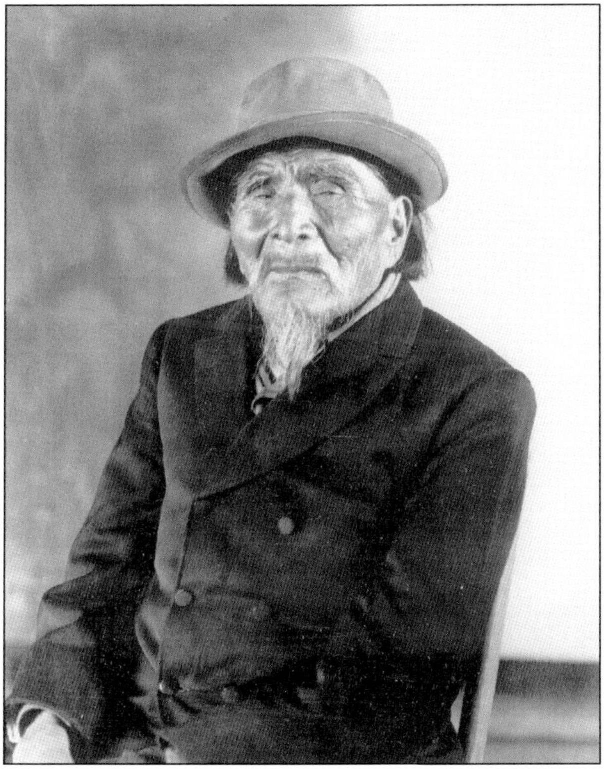

Another visitor to the studio owned by Emery and Ellsworth Kolb was Havasupai Chief Big Jim. He is pictured dressed in a preacher's coat once owned by Emery Kolb's father. A painted background can be seen in this black and white photograph, taken around 1915. (Photograph by the Kolb brothers; courtesy of the National Park Service.)

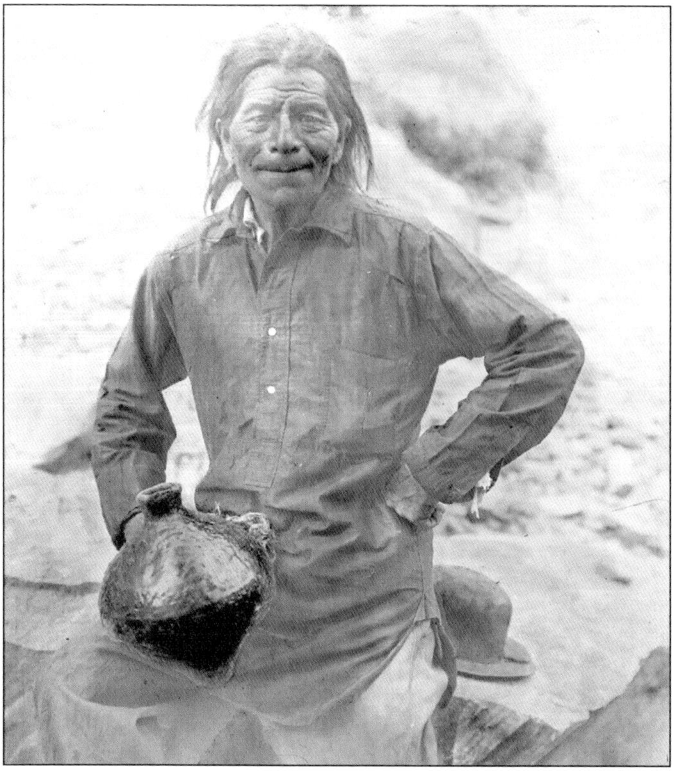

Local Havasupai man "Captain Burro" poses for the camera in this portrait taken around 1900. Burro is pictured with a pitch-covered basket canteen. It is estimated that under 1,000 tribal members live in the Havasupai area, though 30,000 are estimated to visit the land annually. (Photograph by G. W. James; courtesy of the National Park Service.)

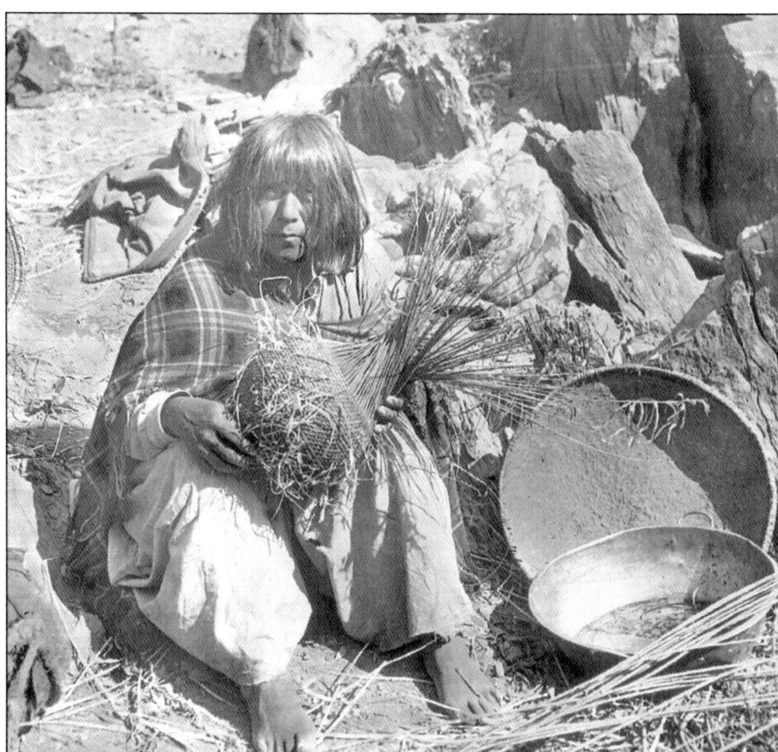

A local Havasupai woman is pictured around 1900. The woman, according to National Park Service records, was the wife of local Havasupai member Jeck-Spa-Na-Pi. Baskets can be seen near the woman as she poses eloquently for the camera. (Photograph by G. W. James; courtesy of the National Park Service.)

This photograph shows Havasupai Kohot, or Chief "Captain Navajo" around 1900. Captain Navajo is shown sitting on a blanket in front of a dwelling in Havasupai. Members of the tribe historically spent summers within Grand Canyon, while spending winters on the South Rim hunting game, a territory that includes the area now known as Tusayan. (Photograph by G. W. James; courtesy of the National Park Service.)

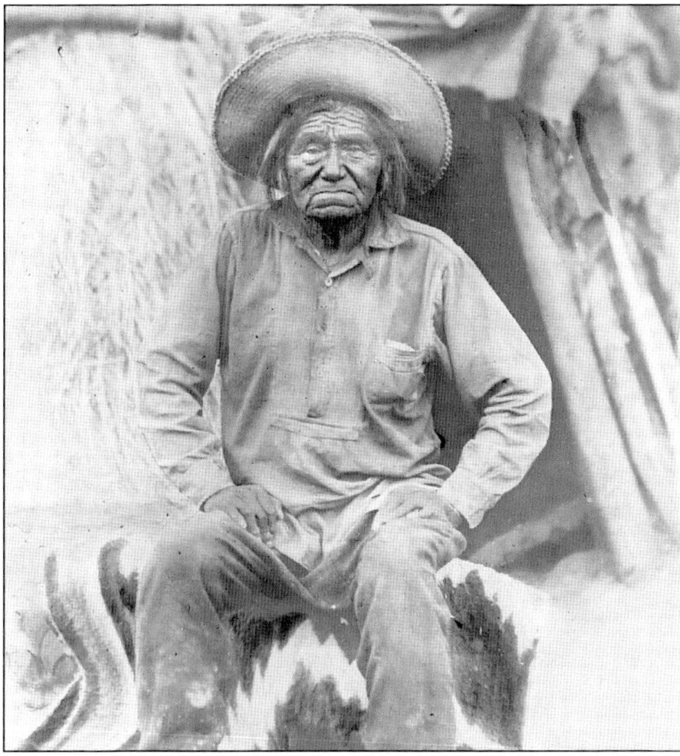

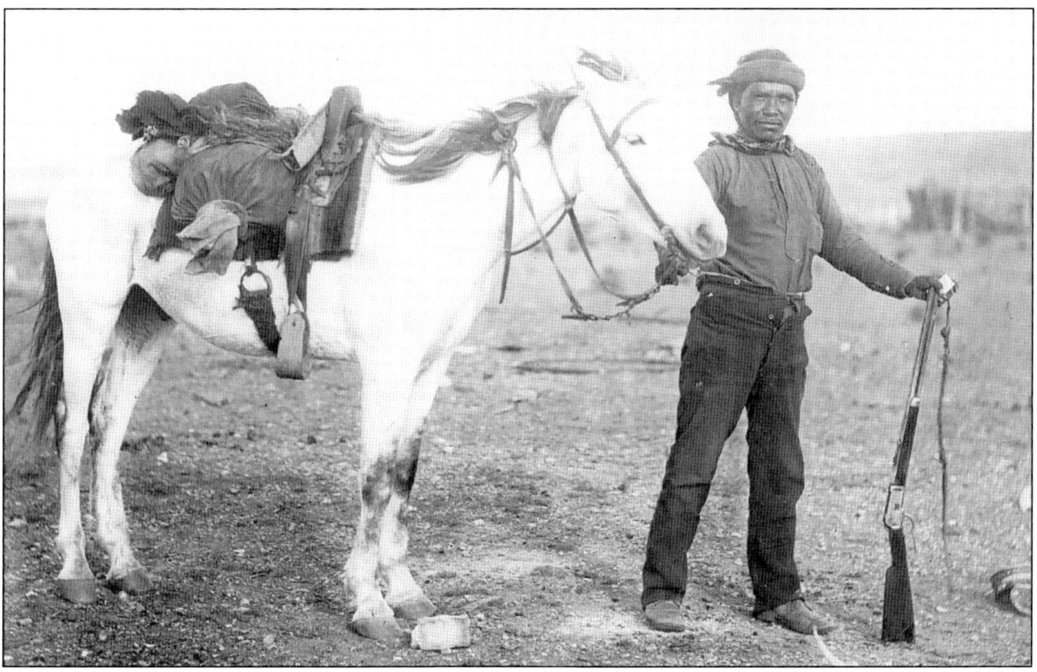

Pictured is Havasupai tribal member Chick-A-Pan-A-Gi (Jqbqnga) in this photograph taken around 1900. Chick-A-Pan-A-Gi, whose name means "hat" in the traditional language of the Havasupai, according to National Park Service historians, is shown holding a rifle while standing with his saddled horse. (Photograph by G. W. James; courtesy of the National Park Service.)

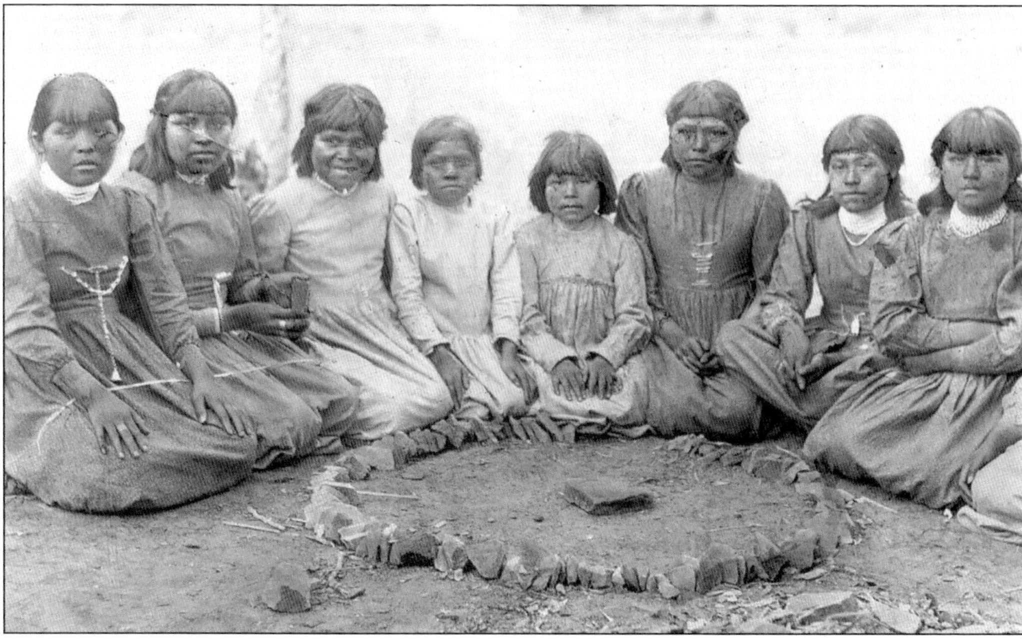

This *c.* 1900 photograph shows nine young female members of the Havasupai tribe. The girls are shown dressed in non-traditional European clothing as they play the traditional gambling game utilizing painted sticks, Hui-Ta-Qui-Chi-Ka, within the Havasupai village of Grand Canyon. Tribal members are governed by members of the Havasupai Tribal Council. (Photograph by G. W. James; courtesy of the National Park Service.)

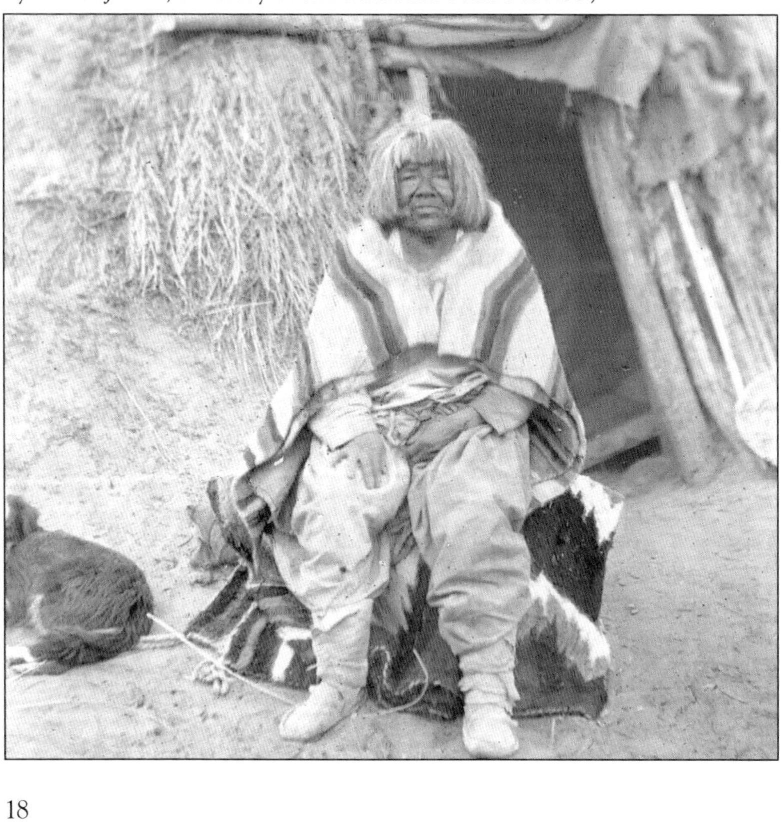

Pictured in this *c.* 1898 photograph is Ilwi', the oldest wife of Chief Navajo. Ilwi', whose name means "snake" in the Havasupai language, was the head wife of Navajo. She perished in a flood in 1910 and was counted as the disaster's only casualty. Said to have been blind in her old age, Ilwi' was unable to find her way to safety. (Photograph by G. W. James; courtesy of the National Park Service.)

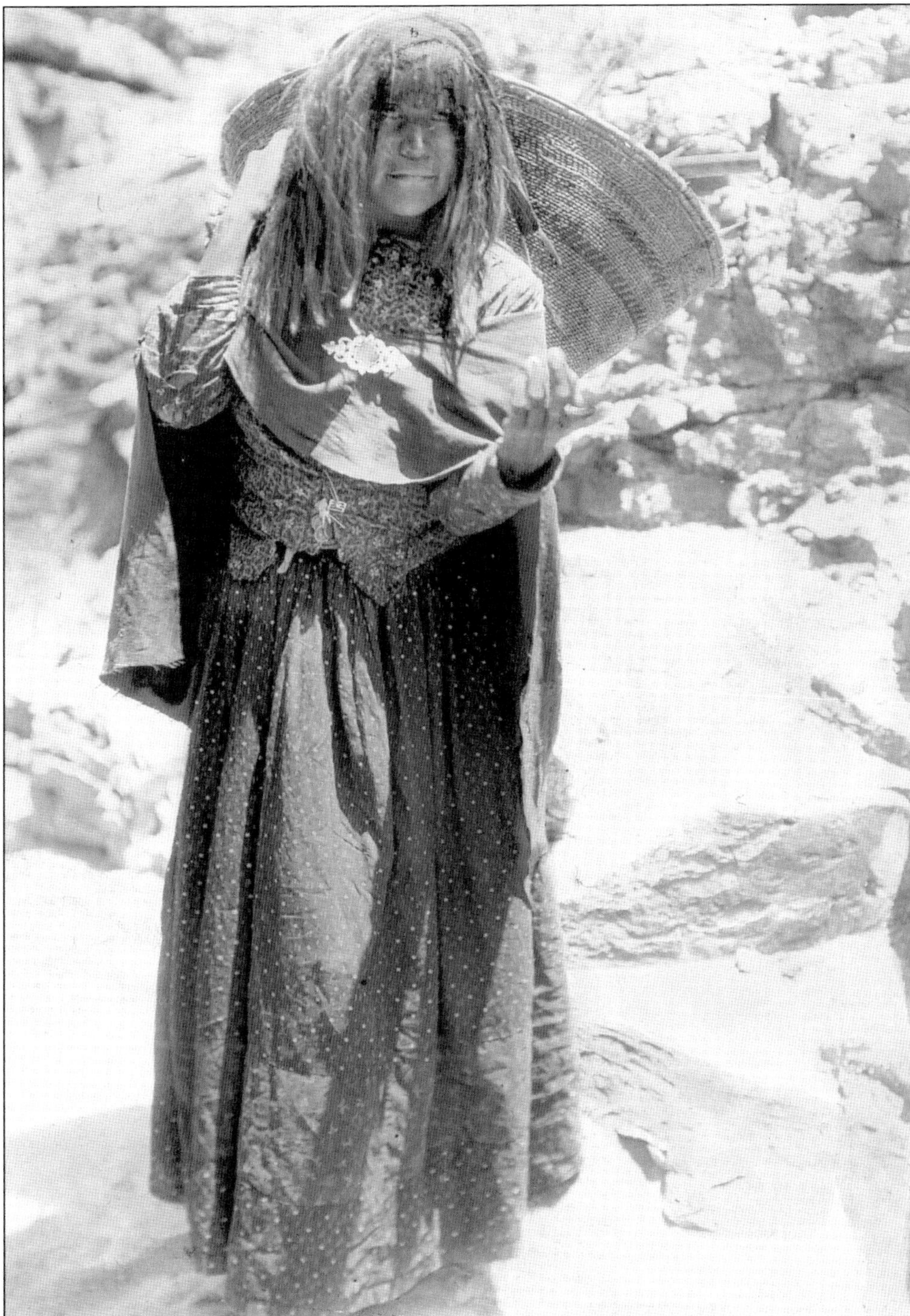

This c. 1900 photograph shows a Havasupai woman in a beautiful long dress. Mescal shoots are located in the basket the woman is wearing on her back. Members of the Havasupai tribe would often gather medicinal plants in the area now known as Tusayan. (Photograph by G. W. James; courtesy of the National Park Service.)

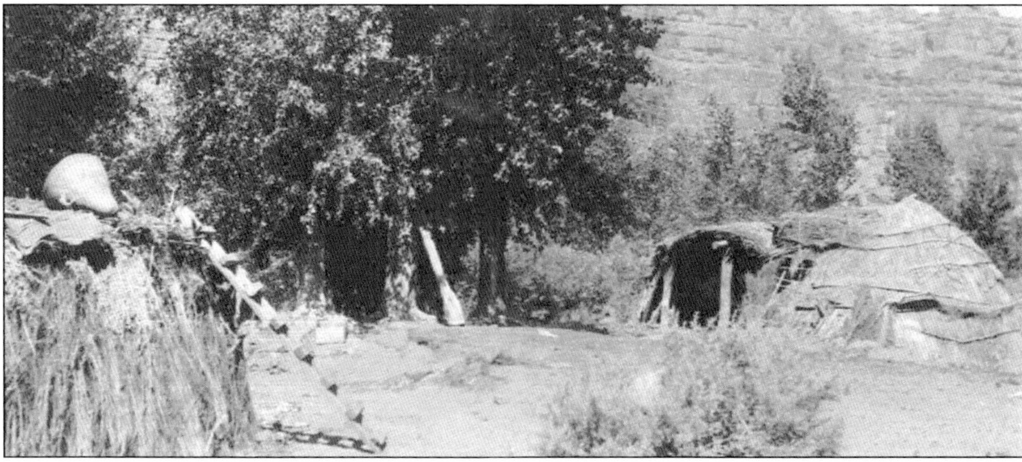

This *c.* 1900 photograph from the Thurston collection shows a structure in the Havasupai village taken around 1900. The trip from Tusayan can take up to two hours via a southern route. A northern route will also lead to trail leading down to the Havasupai eservation, but can take longer. (Courtesy of Clarinda Vail and the Thurston family.)

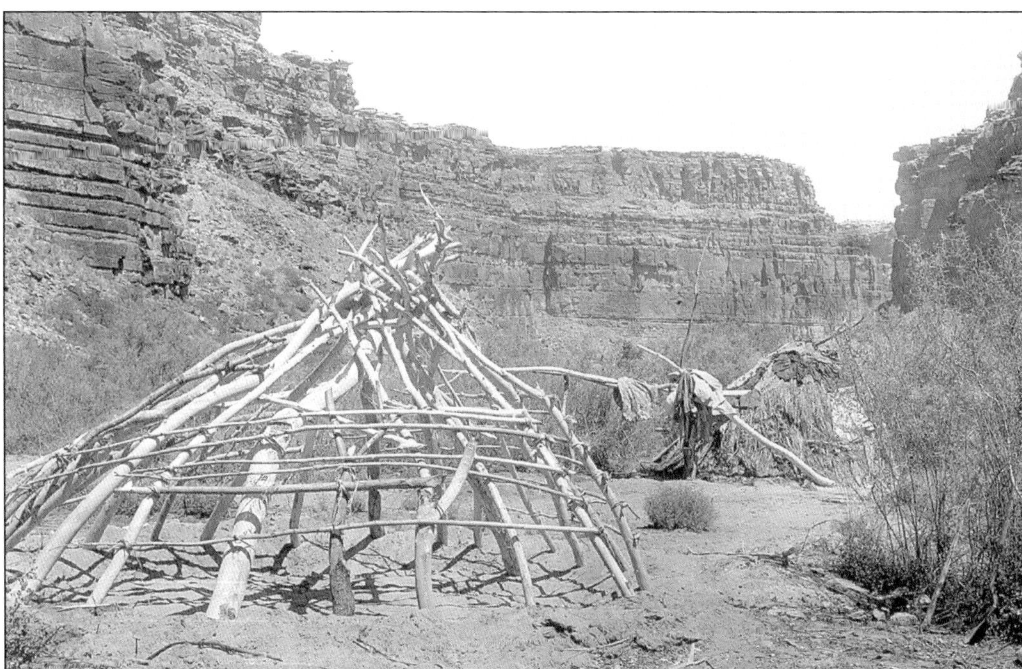

This photograph, taken around 1900, shows a behind-the-scenes glimpse of the framework involved in constructing a traditional Havasupai home, or *hawe*, according to National Park Service historians. The awe-inspiring cliffs of Havasu Canyon can be seen in the background of the photograph. (Photograph by G. W. James; courtesy of the National Park Service.)

A Supai home can be seen at Cataract Canyon in this photograph taken around 1900. The Cataract Canyon home looks down on the fields located near Havasupai village. Fruit trees can also be seen in the image. The tribe's nearby city, Supai, is the capital of the Havasupai Indian reservation. (Photograph by G. W. James; courtesy of the National Park Service.)

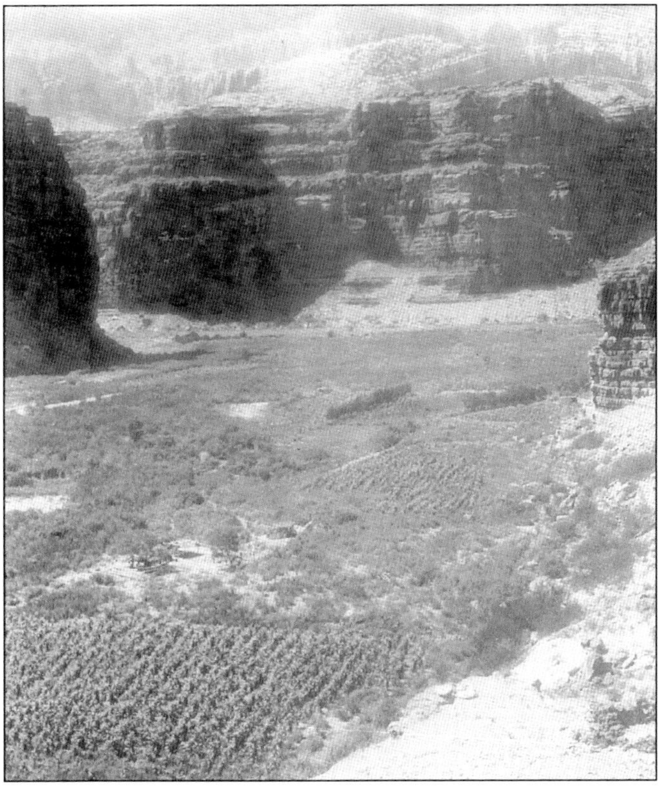

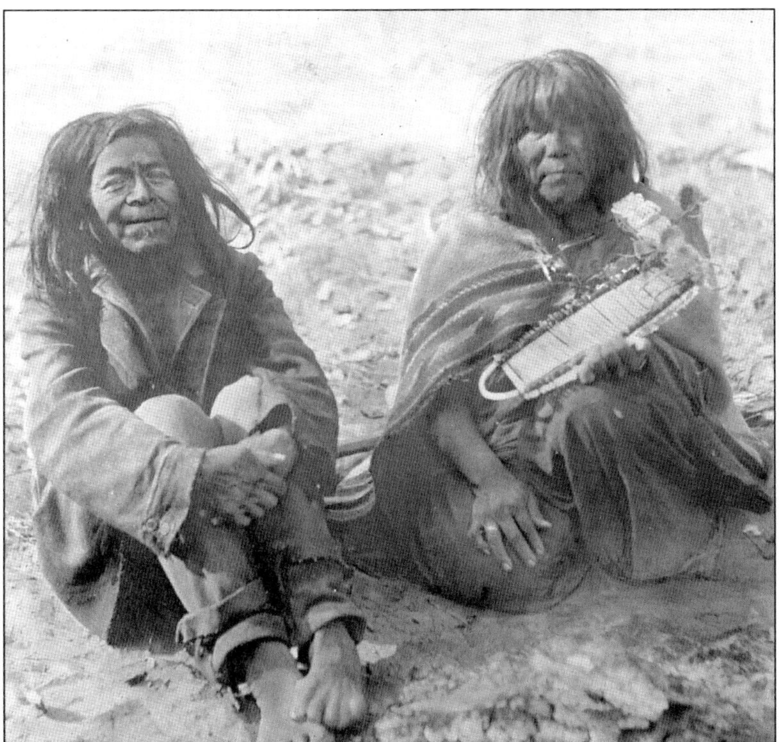

This photograph, taken around 1900, shows Mike and Sarah Mooney of the Havasupai tribe. Sarah Mooney is holding an empty infant cradleboard in the photograph. The language of the Havasupai, according to experts, is nearly identical to that of the dialect of the Hualapai tribe, though both groups are said to have very different social and political practices. (Photograph by G. W. James; courtesy of the National Park Service.)

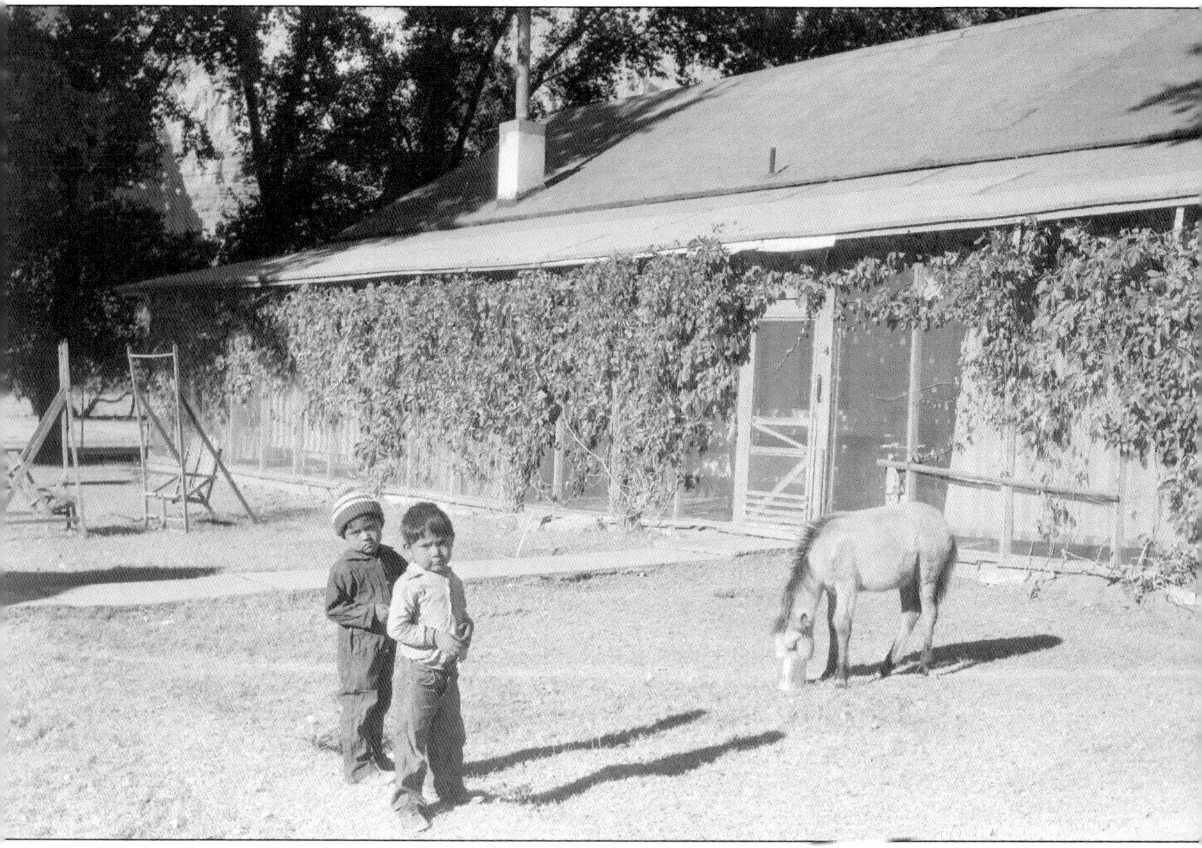

A building with modern amenities, such as a screened-in porch, can be seen in this 1938 photograph. Two local Havasupai children are also shown in the photograph as they play with a pony outside of the structure. (Photograph by Virgil Gibson; courtesy of the National Park Service.)

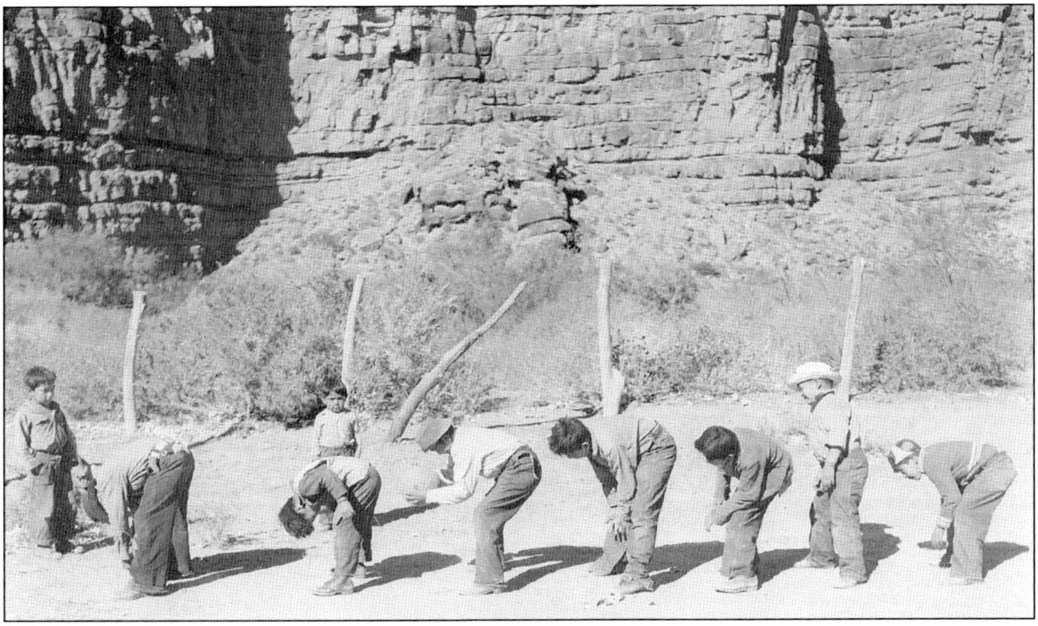

A number of Havasupai children play games during school while other students watch in this 1938 photograph. Attractions in the reservation, including numerous waterfalls and spectacular views, ensured students in the Havasupai school plenty of visitors from outside of the Grand Canyon. (Photograph by Virgil Gibson; courtesy of the National Park Service.)

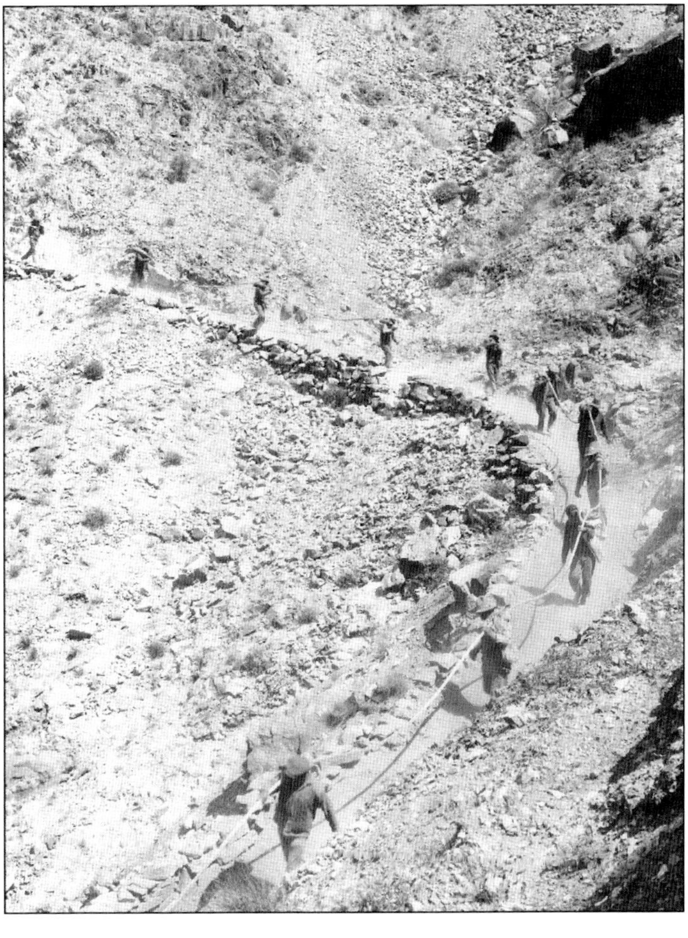

This photograph, taken around 1928, shows a number of hard-working Havasupai tribal members as they navigate a winding trail down the Grand Canyon while supporting heavy cable on their shoulders. The Havasupai workers hauled the burdensome material for construction of the planned Kaibab suspension bridge. (Courtesy of the National Park Service.)

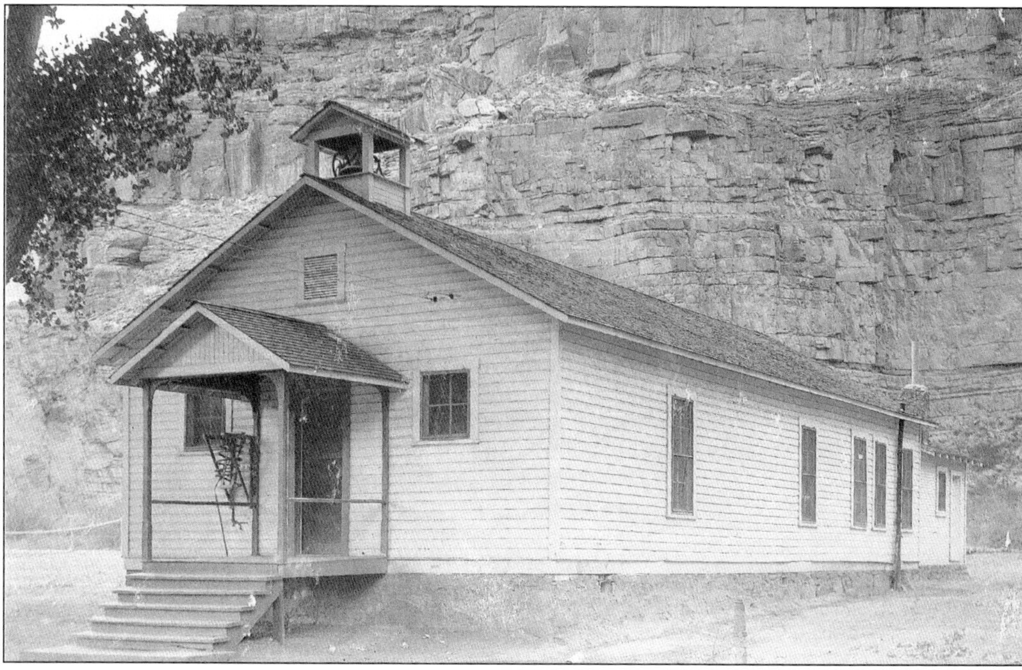

This 1938 photograph shows the front and one side of the local schoolhouse, located within the Grand Canyon on the Havasupai Indian reservation. The canyon's vast cliffs can be seen in the photograph behind the school. (Photograph by Virgil Gibson; courtesy of the National Park Service.)

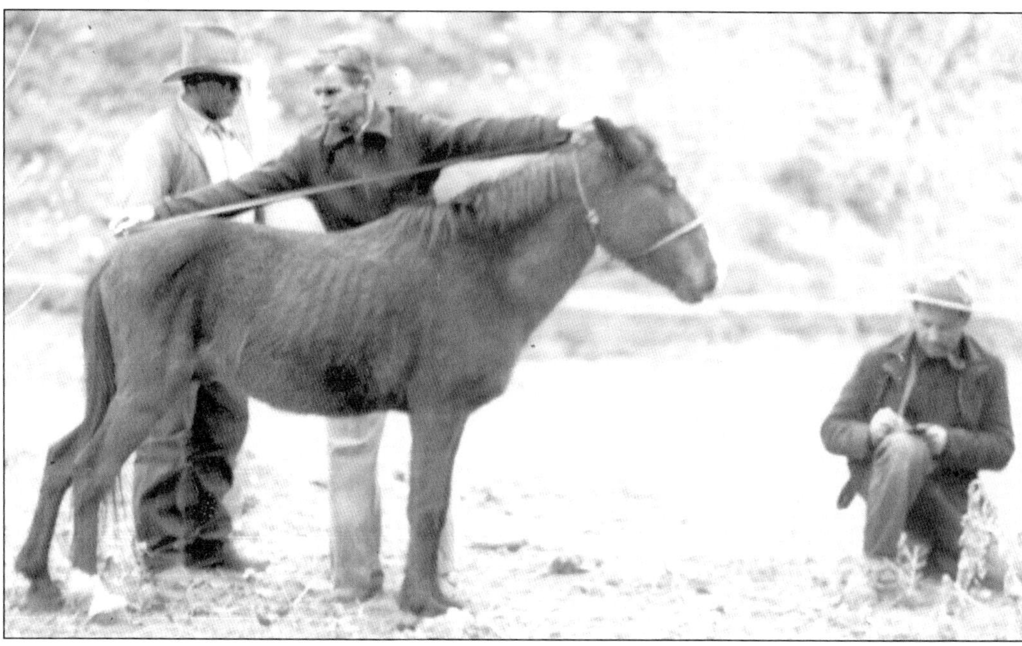

This 1938 photograph was taken during the "Little Horse Expedition," held in January of that year. Edwin McKee is pictured measuring a little horse captured very near the Havasupai village. The horses, once thought to be miniature ponies, were discovered to be merely malnourished. (Courtesy of the National Park Service.)

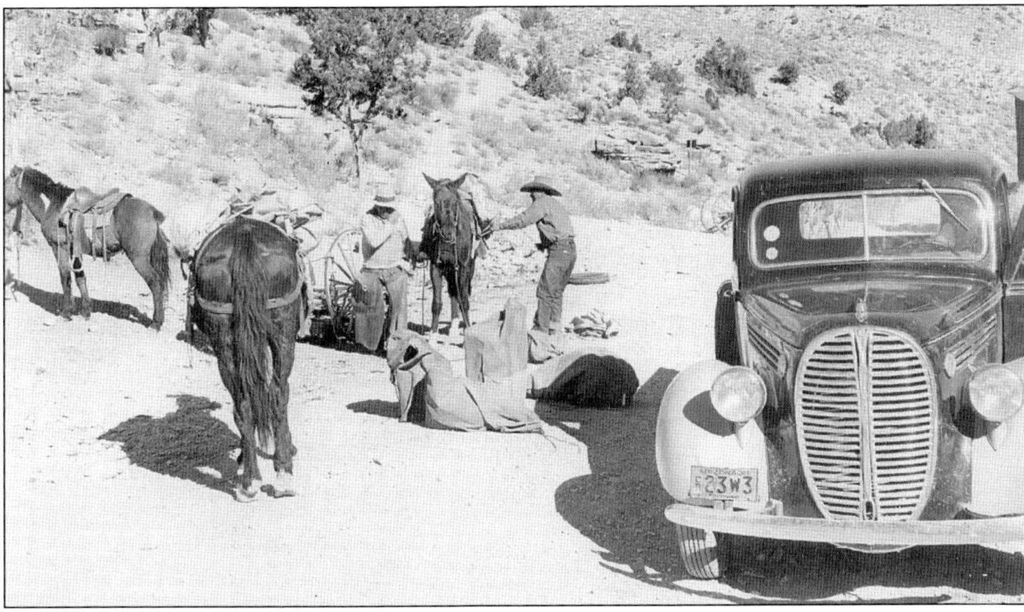

Horses are loaded with mail at a hilltop in this 1938 photograph. The horses are being prepped for an 8-mile hike into the Grand Canyon. The only other way to reach the reservation is by a short helicopter flight from the trailhead leading to the Havasupai land. Post is also delivered by mule to Phantom Ranch, also located within Grand Canyon. (Courtesy of the National Park Service.)

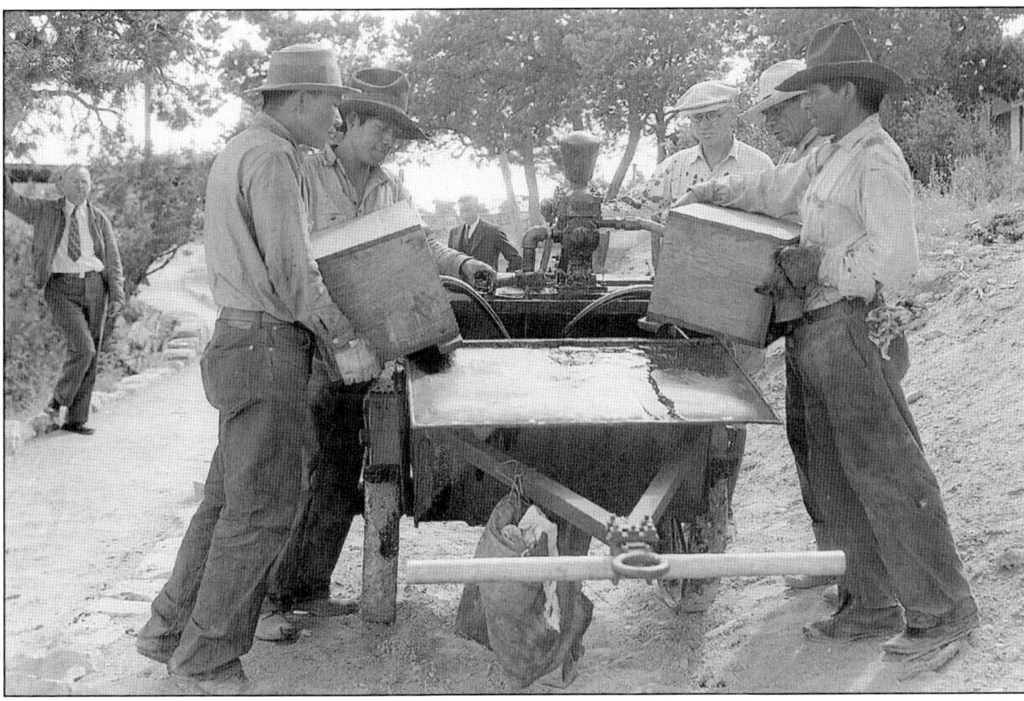

This photograph, taken around 1932, shows Havasupai workers and their equipment on the Rim Trail of the Grand Canyon. The Rim Trail is located near Bright Angel Trail. The workers are using an oiler cart in an attempt to coat the trail. The effort ultimately did very little to help the hiking picture. (Courtesy of the National Park Service.)

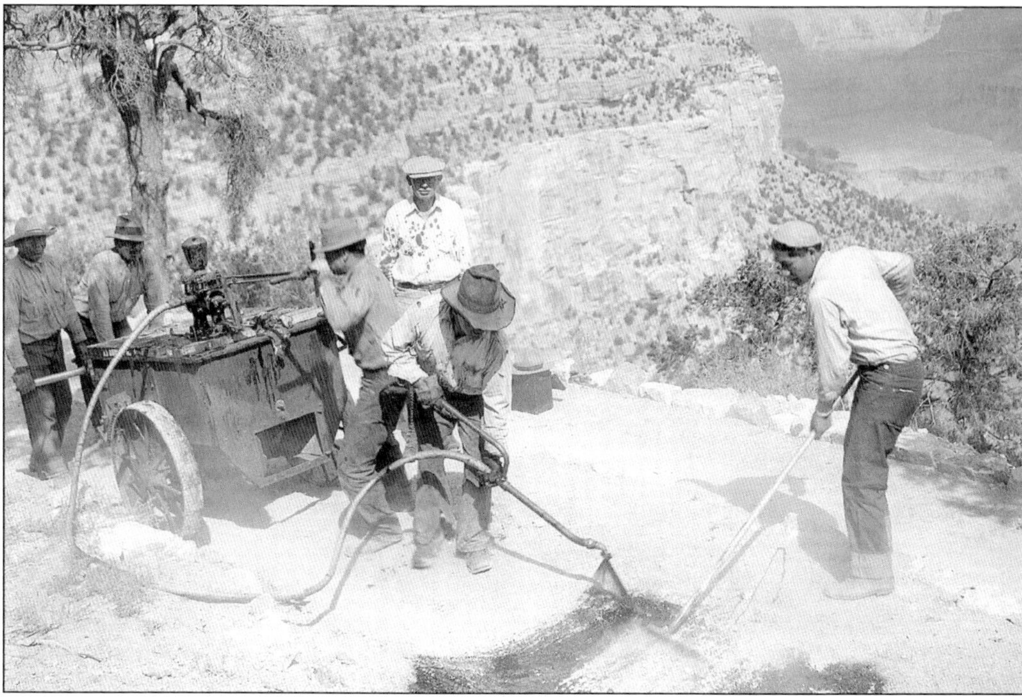

Havasupai tribal members worked to spread the oil by hand along the upper switchbacks of Bright Angel Trail along the rim. A pushcart full of oil can also be seen in this September 1932 photograph. Besides hikers, the trail has also been used by mule riders to enter the Havasupai land. (Courtesy of the National Park Service.)

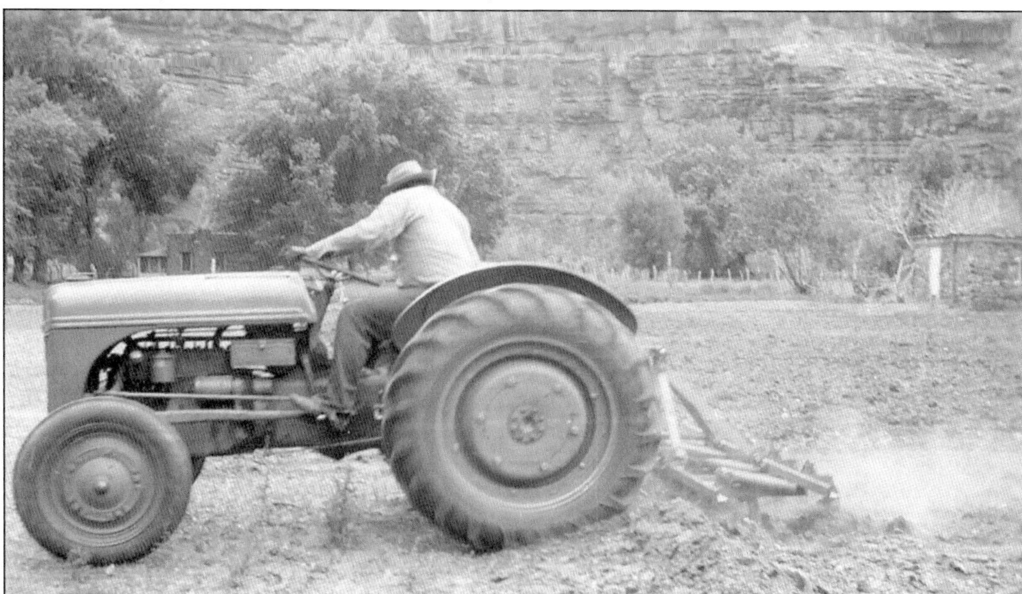

This 1948 photograph shows a tractor plowing a field within the Havasupai Indian reservation inside Grand Canyon. The tractor was dismantled prior to being hauled into the Grand Canyon. After being carried piece by piece onto the reservation land, the tractor was put back together again and put into service. (Photograph by J. M. Eden; courtesy of the National Park Service.)

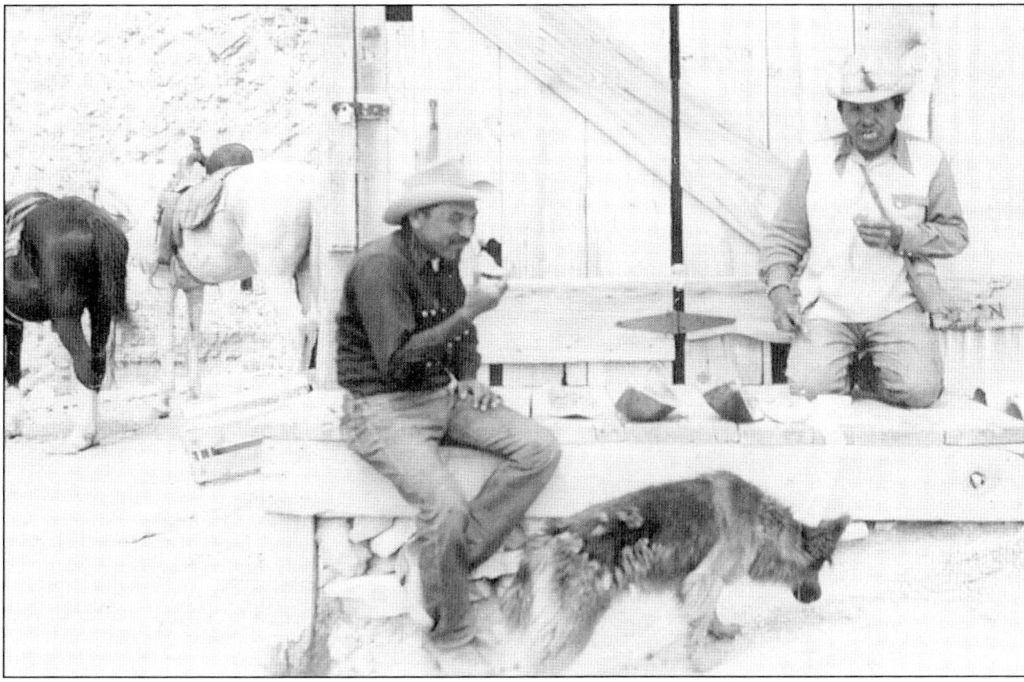

Havasupai tribal members Harlow Uqualla and Lemuel Paya are pictured here in 1950. Both Uqualla and Paya are pictured at the Hualapai hilltop. They worked as guides to the Supai for Fred Gurley, who desired to camp in the area. Gurley was president of the Atchison, Topeka, and Santa Fe Railway. (Photograph by Harold C. Bryant; courtesy of the National Park Service.)

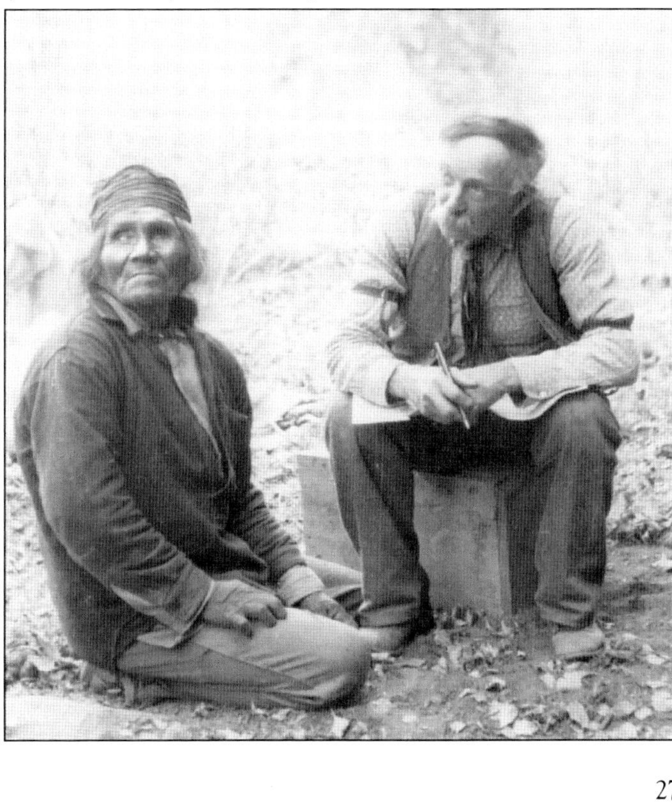

Grand Canyon notable William W. Bass is pictured here in 1906. Bass is pictured holding a pen and a piece of paper as he sits with "Big Jim" at the Havasupai reservation. Big Jim was also known locally as Chick-A-Pan-A-Gi by other members of the Havasupai tribe. (Photograph by the Kolb brothers; courtesy of the National Park Service.)

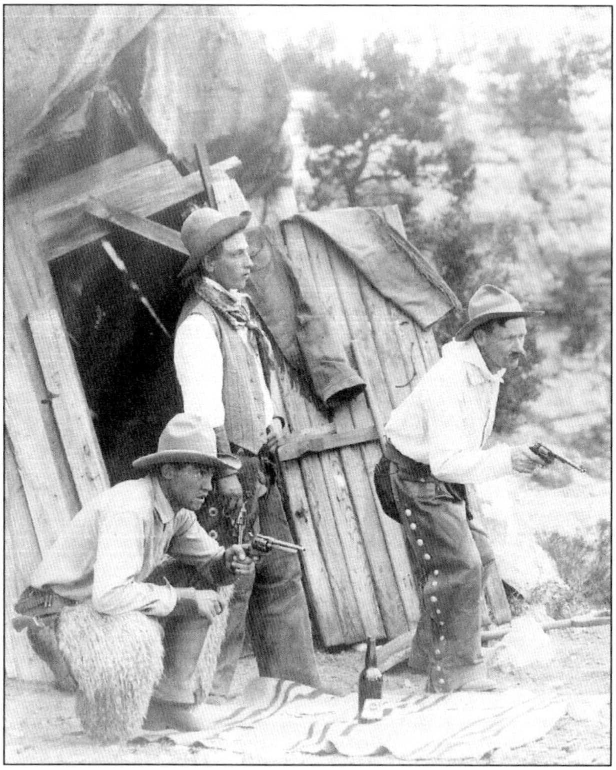

A number of local Grand Canyon "cowboys" can be seen in this photograph taken around 1911. Pictured from left to right are Bob Fix, Art Blower, and a man identified as Boulin as they pose for the camera with their guns drawn. The group is pictured near Big Jim's shelter near the rim interchange. (Photograph by the Kolb brothers; courtesy of the National Park Service.)

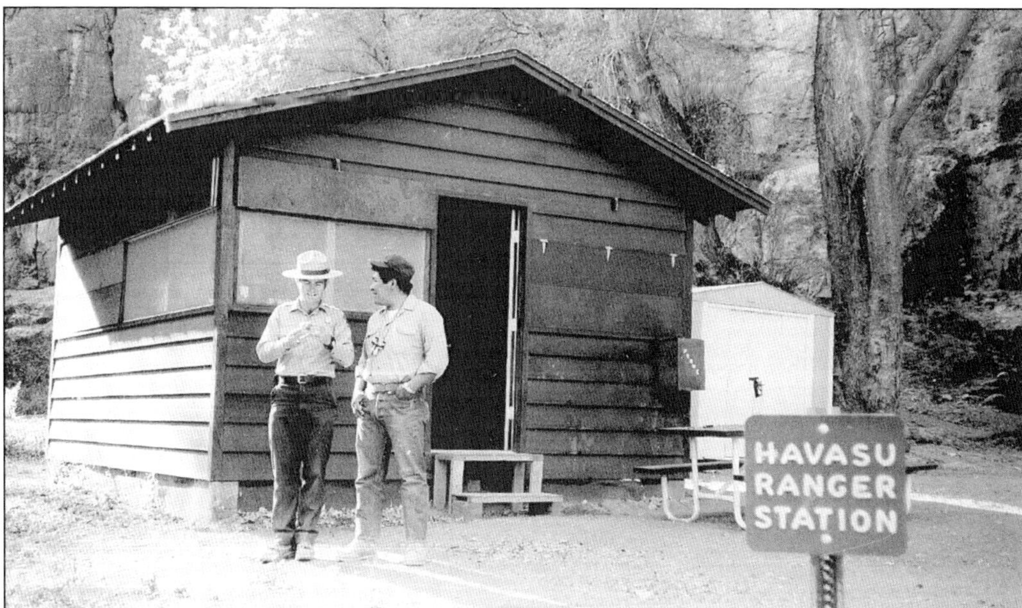

This 1977 photograph shows white and Supai rangers standing for a photograph in front of the Havasupai Ranger Station. Officials with the National Park Service served as administers for the ranger station. Tourism constitutes the tribe's main source of revenue. Reservations to camp in the area are often restricted due to sheer volume. (Photograph by Glenn Fuller; courtesy of the National Park Service.)

Clark Jack and Reverend Jenkins are shown in this July 1952 photograph. The photograph documents the opening dedication of the Havasupai village recreation hall, in which the key to the building is handed over to Havasupai tribal members for their use of the facility. (Photograph by R. S. Leding; courtesy of the National Park Service.)

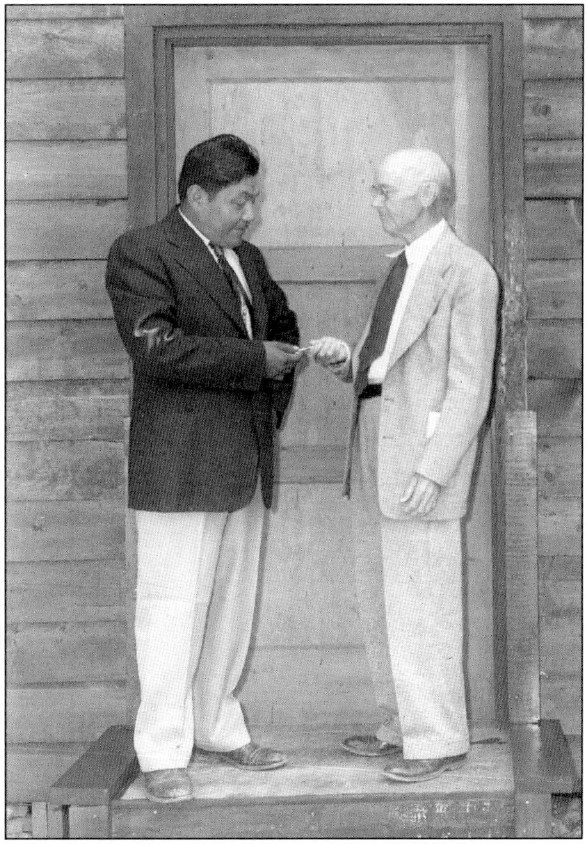

Pictured from left to right are Jim Crook, H. C. Bryant, Tom Dodge, Lemuel Paya, Reed Watahomagie, Dudley Manakach, William H. Zeh, Big Jim, L. A. Garrison, and Foster Marshall as they pose for the camera. Every member of the Havasupai Tribal Council met with national park officials in 1947 at Grand Canyon Village. (Courtesy of the National Park Service.)

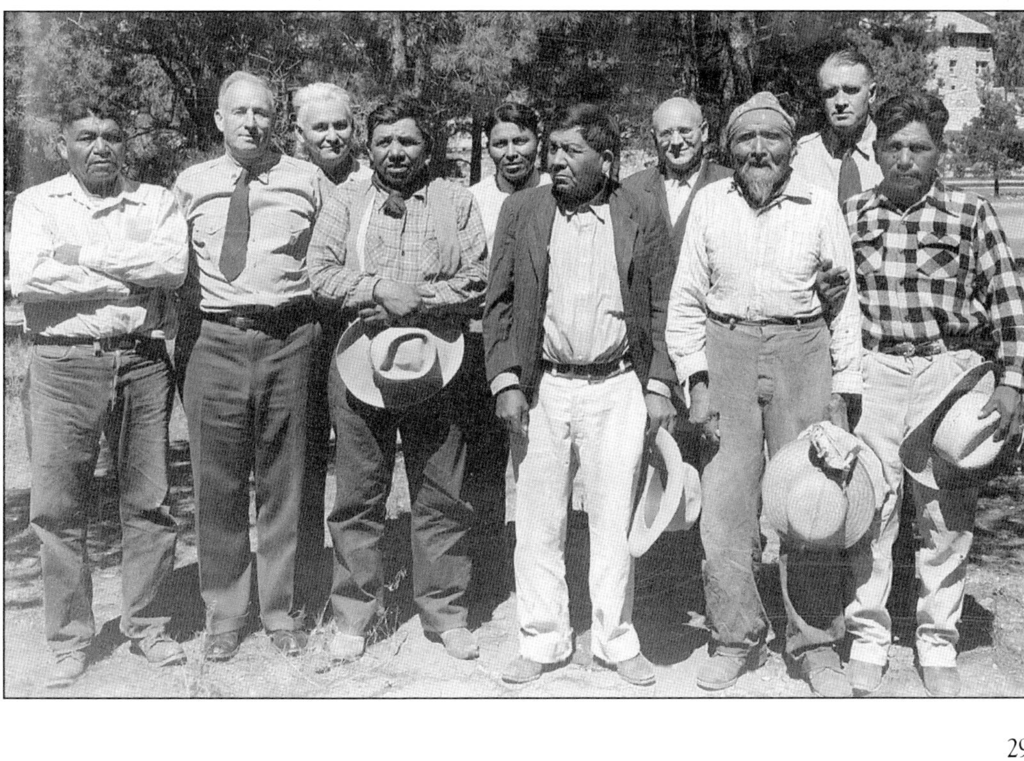

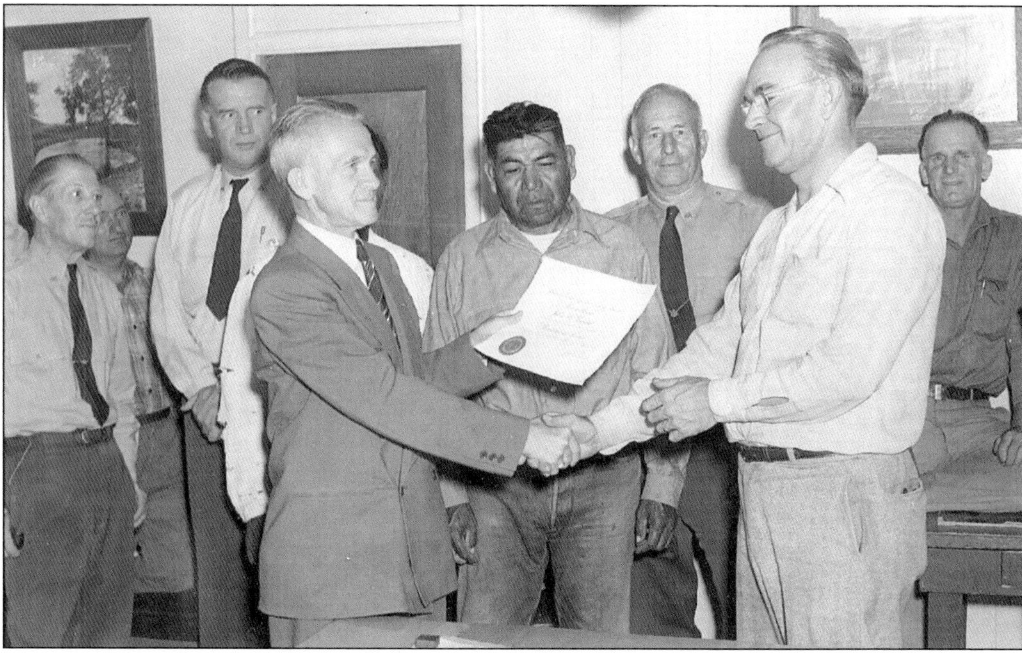

This 1949 photograph shows J. A. Gaustad as he received a Department of Interior Meritorious Service Award from Region Three director M. R. Tillotson. Gaustad was awarded the honor after he saved a park visitor from being crushed between two cars. His award included a certificate, lapel button, and a medal. (Photograph by J. M. Eden; Courtesy of the National Park Service.)

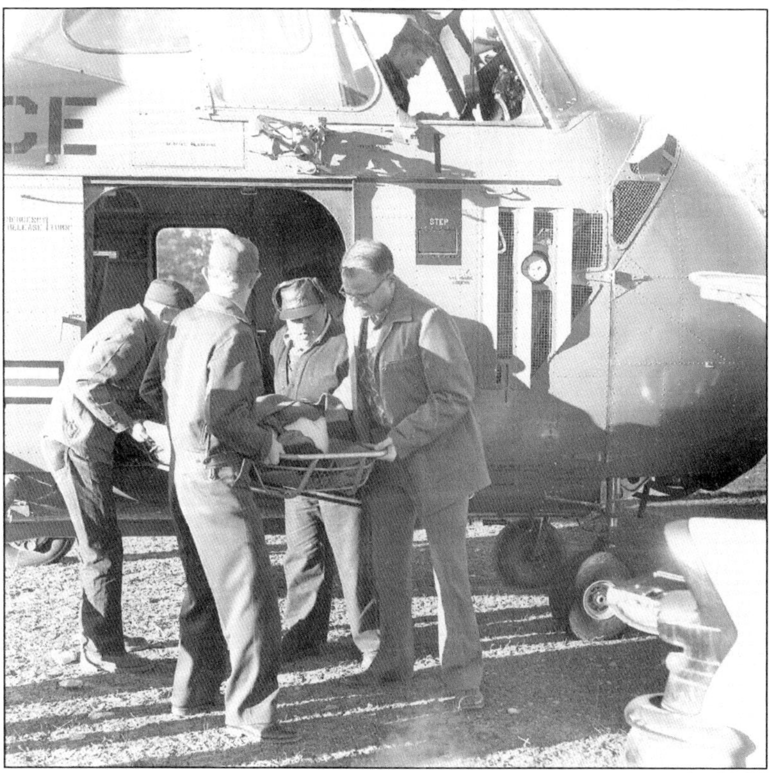

This 1956 photograph shows park personnel as they remove a seriously ill Supai woman. Pictured are ranger Dan Davis, chief ranger Lynn Coffin, Louis Farnworth, and Dr. Bill Henry. National park officials and the members of the Havasupai tribe share a close relationship, as do tribal members with forest service officials in the Kaibab National Forest. (Photograph by R. S. Leding; courtesy of the National Park Service.)

Two

Hull Cabin and Beyond

It wasn't an easy thing to get to the South Rim of the Grand Canyon in the late 1800s. Rugged terrain and long distance travel prevented most from making the long trek from the Flagstaff, Williams, and Ash Fork train stops, though a few brave souls did make their way to South Rim by horse and wagon. Once there, a number of Canyon residents helped make their stay a memorable one, including Grand Canyon legends John Hance, William Wallace Bass, and Ralph Cameron. William Francis Hull and other members of his family made their way west from Illinois around 1849, and they would eventually add their own contribution to the history of the Grand Canyon and Tusayan area.

It was around 1880, three years before the Atlantic and Pacific Railroad crossed northern Arizona, that the Hulls established a large tract of ranchland in an area roughly a mile south of the canyon's South Rim. By 1884, William and his brother Phillip Jr. operated a successful sheep ranch near the area now known as Tusayan. William led the first recorded tour of Grand Canyon that same year with the help of Hance, who worked at the Hull's sheep ranch. The two soon became partners in the budding tourism business.

By 1893, the land surrounding Hull Cabin became part of the Grand Canyon Forest Reserve. Having already lost his brother to a heart attack in 1888, William soon gave up the sheep ranch in favor of other ventures, including a mining operation, which he ran until around 1901, the same year the Grand Canyon Railroad began to bring passengers to the South Rim. The property, including Hull Tank, once used for watering sheep, soon became the property of the federal government.

Forest service ranger George Reed was one of the first rangers stationed to the cabin around 1905. In 1910, the area became part of the Tusayan National Forest. Reed stayed on at the cabin until 1919, the same year the Grand Canyon was designated a national park.

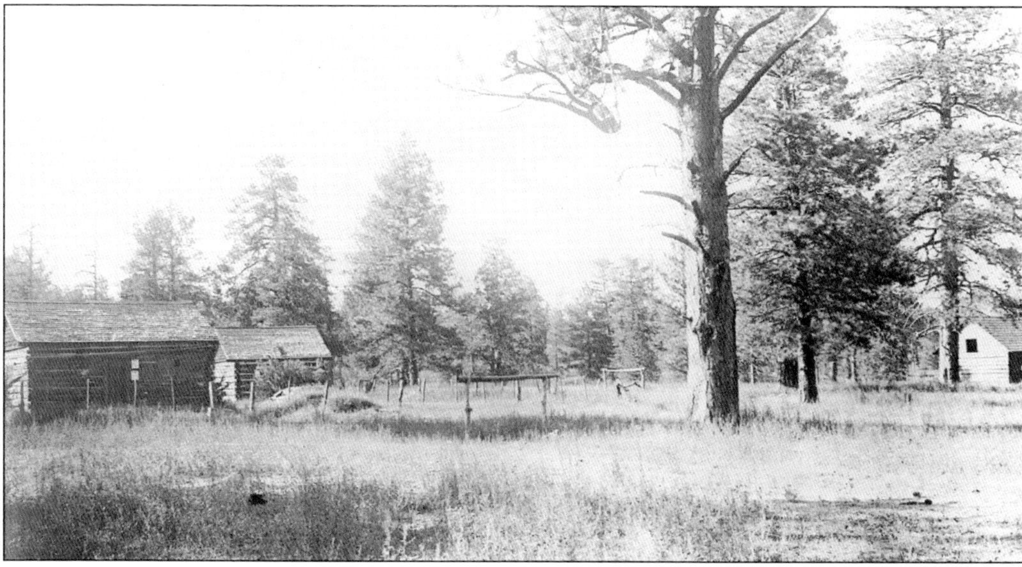

This 1907 photograph shows an overview of the Hull Cabin grounds, located within the area of Tusayan village and the Grand Canyon National Park. Shake roofs, a fence, and a barn can be seen in the image. The area was a sheep ranch in the late 1800s, operated by brothers William and Phillip Hull. (Photograph by the Kolb brothers; courtesy of the National Park Service.)

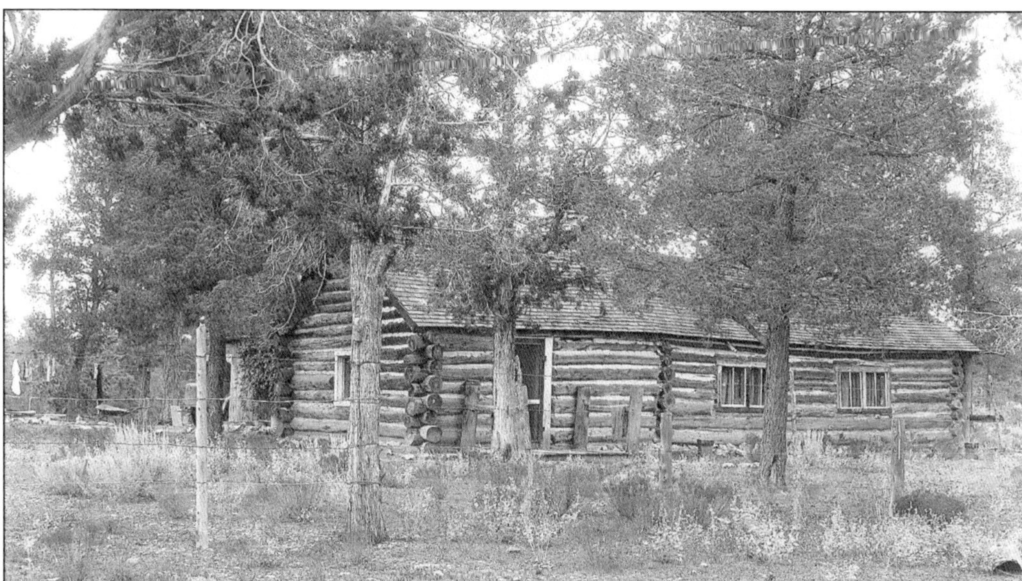

Pictured here is the old Tusayan Forest Reserve Ranger Station as it appeared in 1927. The structure, which was once located at Rowe Well, was later destroyed in 1932. The Tusayan Forest Reserve would later become known as the Tusayan Ranger District of the Kaibab National Forest. (Photograph by Ensor; courtesy of the National Park Service.)

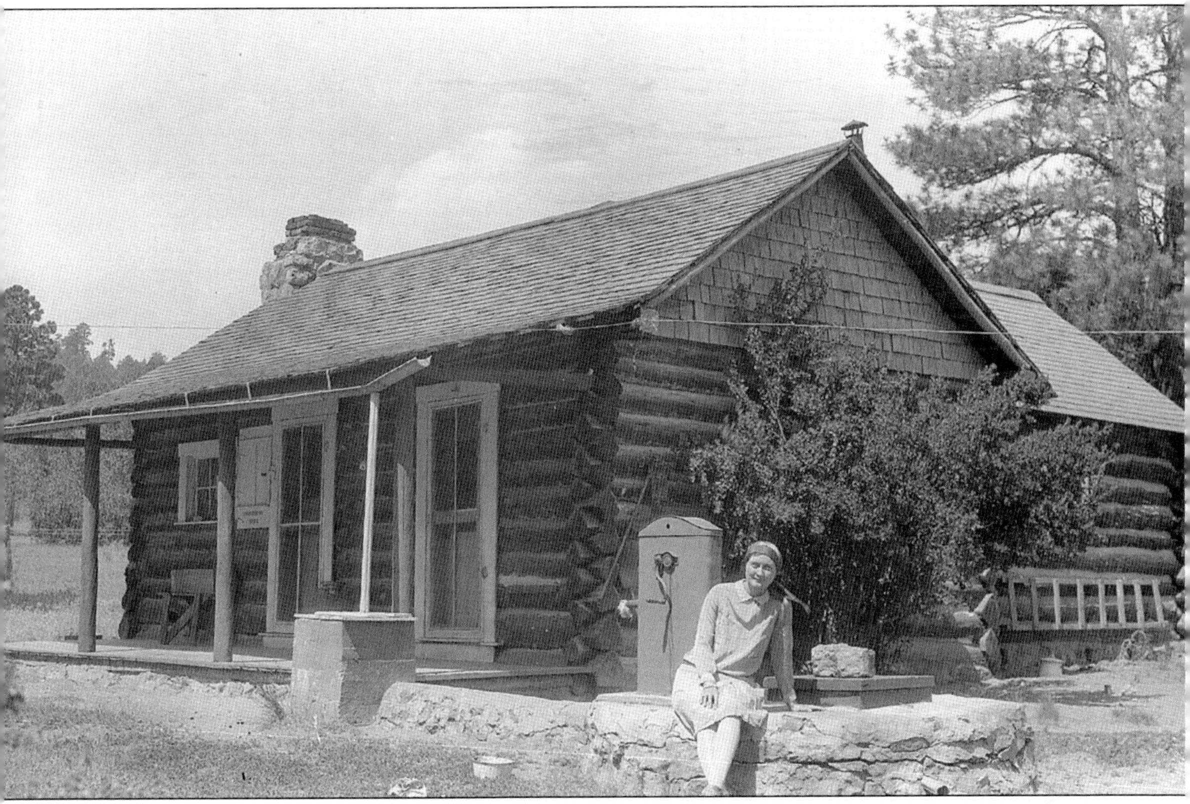

This 1929 photograph shows Barbara Hastings McKee at the Hull Tank Ranger Station. The land around the cabin was first established by the Hull family around 1800. Forest ranger George Reed, who eventually homesteaded the land where Tusayan is today, also lived in the cabin for a number of years. (Photograph by Edwin McKee; courtesy of the National Park Service.)

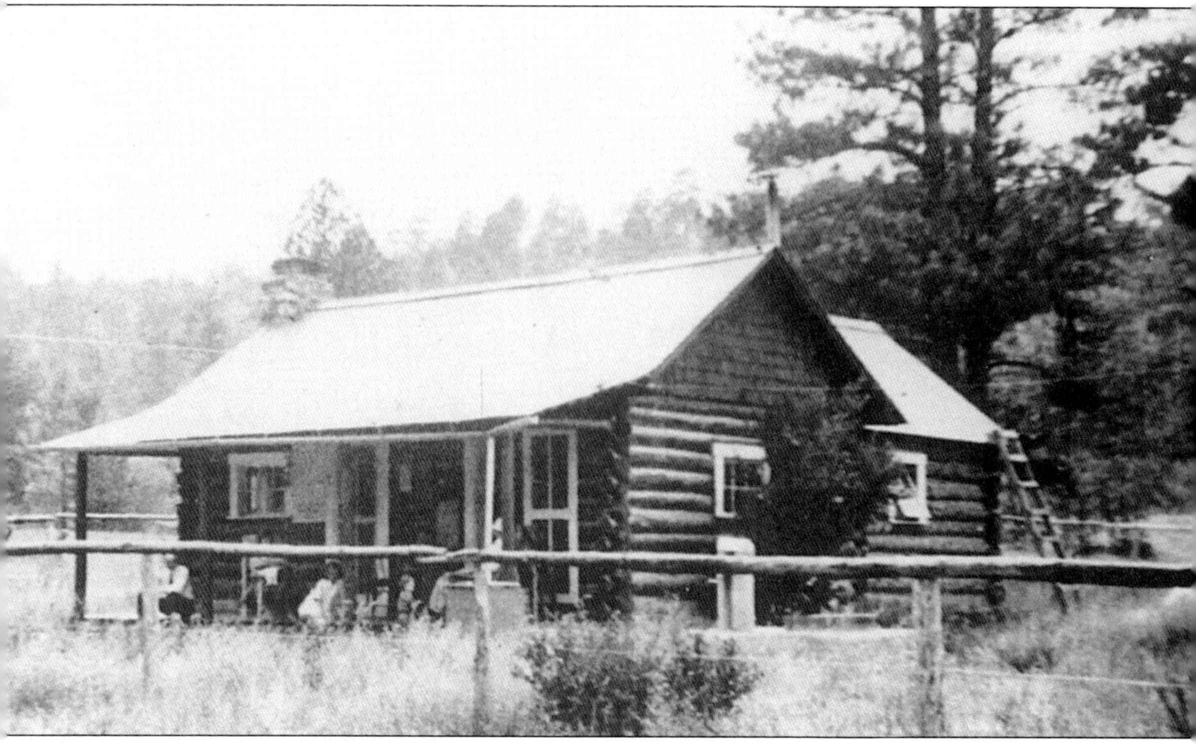

A group of people can be seen through the fence in this 1919 photograph taken by the Hickey family. The group appears to be lounging at the front of the Hull Tank Ranger Station, popularly called by the simpler name of Hull Cabin. A ladder resting against the back of the building can be seen at the back of the cabin. (Courtesy of the National Park Service.)

Three

The George Reed Influence

While a number of individuals, such as the Hull and Kolb brothers, operated around the area now known as Tusayan, no mention of the area would be complete without George Reed. Reed is often called the founder of Tusayan. He arrived in northern Arizona in 1905 and remained in the area until the 1930s. Reed initially worked as a forest ranger in the Tusayan Forest Reserve, an area now known as the Tusayan Ranger District of the Kaibab National Forest. From 1905 to 1919, the year government officials named the Grand Canyon a national park, Reed patrolled the forest from his base of operations at Hull Cabin.

During these years, Reed became well acquainted with the area. One particular spot, located along Coconino Wash roughly 7 miles from the South Rim, caught the Iowa native's eye. Reed soon homesteaded 160 acres of land with his wife, Mable. According to historical records, Reed took possession of the property in April 1920, the same month the Grand Canyon was formally dedicated as a national park.

The Reed family went on to create a lucrative farming business, where Reed grew enough fresh vegetables to provide for his family and to sell to local businesses. His crops were especially popular with the hotels along the rim. When a new highway came along in 1928, getting supplies to his hungry consumers at the South Rim became much easier for Reed. Thanks to a deal between National Park Service officials and Coconino County administrators, part of the park's acquisition of Bright Angel Trail, construction began on the first highway between Williams and Grand Canyon.

Even with the highway, located near where Highway 64 sits today, the rigors of farming grew to be too much for the Reed family. They sold their interests to the Ten X Cattle Company. By this time, however, others had moved into the area, and individuals such as Rudolph "Chick" Kirby and Tony Galindo became common names in the area. Galindo himself is credited for being the first to use the name "Tusayan" in his business, a local bar.

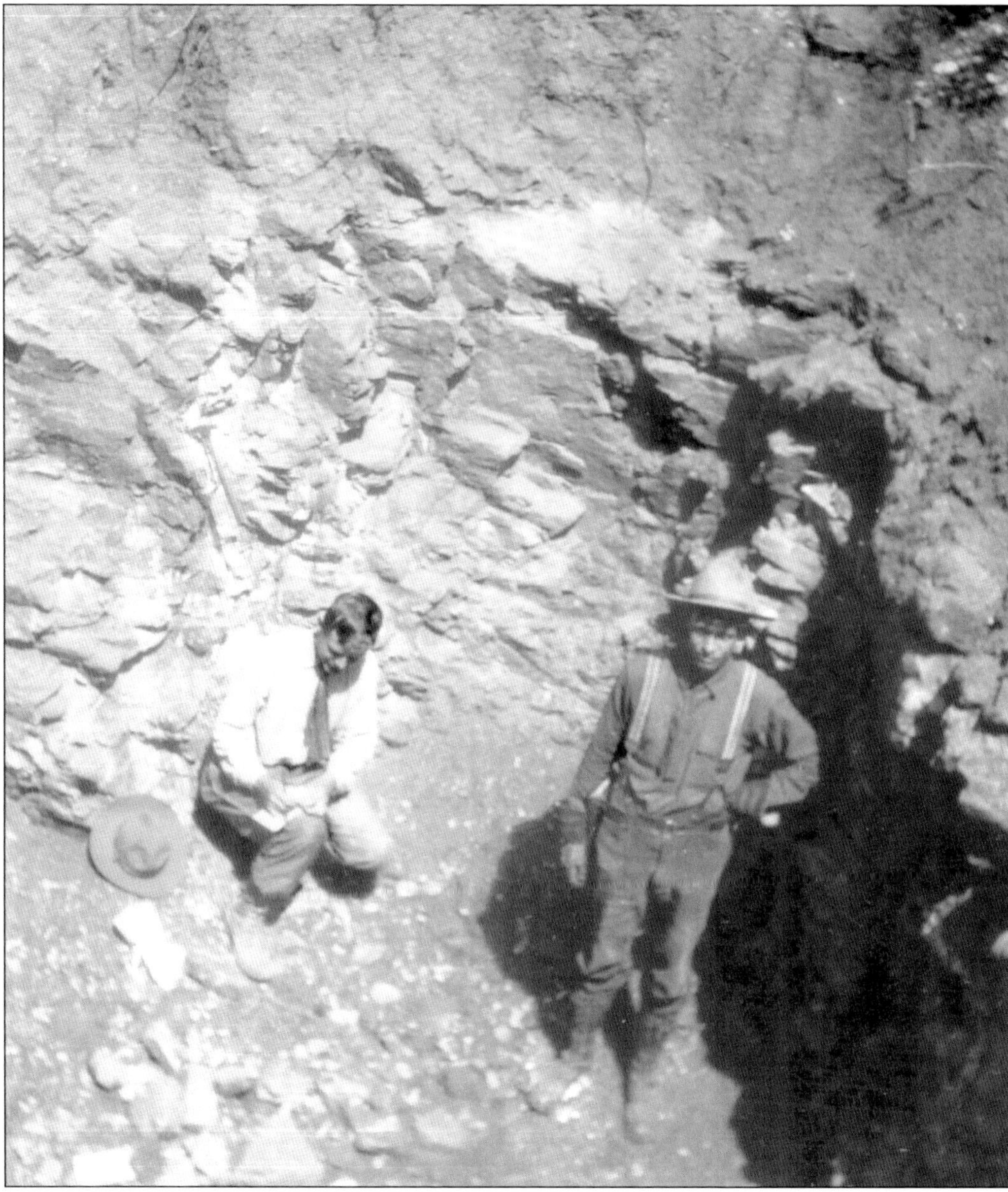

Forest ranger George Reed can be seen in this 1913 photograph as he checks on a mining claim at Grandview Point. Pictured with Reed is John Page of the Canyon Copper Company. Reed worked as a forest ranger in the area prior to the Grand Canyon's designation of a national park in 1919. (Courtesy of the National Park Service.)

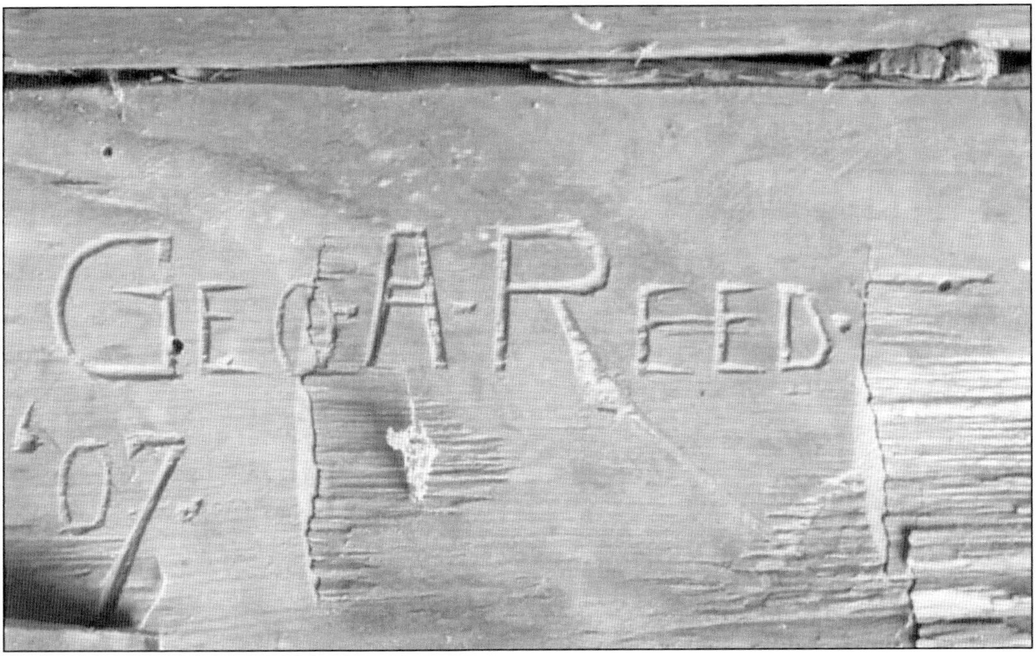

George Reed's name can be seen carved into a wall at Hull Cabin with the year 1907 identified in the photograph. At the time he carved his name, Reed was employed with the forest service as a ranger in the Tusayan Forest Preserve. (Photograph by Margaret Hangen; courtesy of the Kabaib National Forest.)

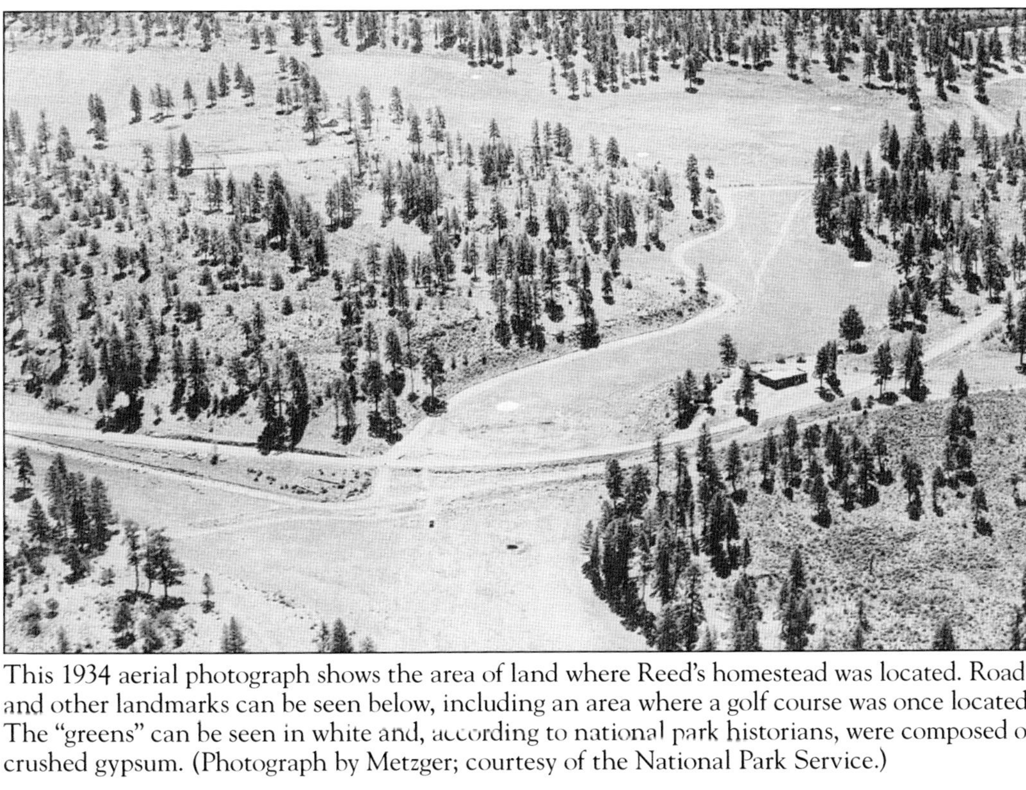

This 1934 aerial photograph shows the area of land where Reed's homestead was located. Roads and other landmarks can be seen below, including an area where a golf course was once located. The "greens" can be seen in white and, according to national park historians, were composed of crushed gypsum. (Photograph by Metzger; courtesy of the National Park Service.)

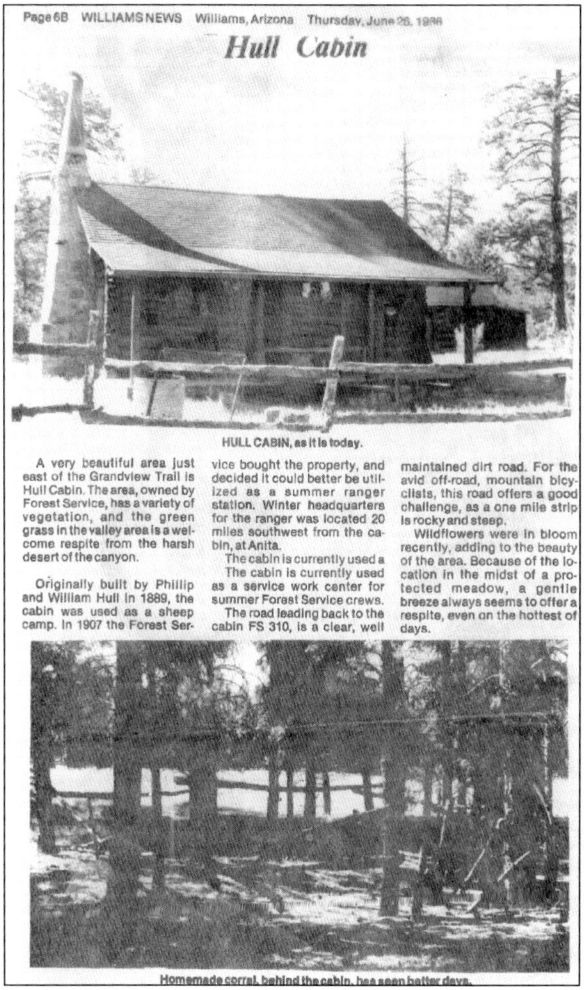

Page 6B WILLIAMS NEWS Williams, Arizona Thursday, June 26, 1986

Hull Cabin

HULL CABIN, as it is today.

A very beautiful area just east of the Grandview Trail is Hull Cabin. The area, owned by Forest Service, has a variety of vegetation, and the green grass in the valley area is a welcome respite from the harsh desert of the canyon.

Originally built by Phillip and William Hull in 1889, the cabin was used as a sheep camp. In 1907 the Forest Service bought the property, and decided it could better be utilized as a summer ranger station. Winter headquarters for the ranger was located 20 miles southwest from the cabin, at Anita.

The cabin is currently used a

The cabin is currently used as a service work center for summer Forest Service crews.

The road leading back to the cabin FS 310, is a clear, well maintained dirt road. For the avid off-road, mountain bicyclists, this road offers a good challenge, as a one mile strip is rocky and steep.

Wildflowers were in bloom recently, adding to the beauty of the area. Because of the location in the midst of a protected meadow, a gentle breeze always seems to offer a respite, even on the hottest of days.

Homemade corral, behind the cabin, has seen better days.

Hull Cabin's historical appeal has intrigued visitors to the area for a number of years, as is evident in this article on the cabin. The article illustrates a number of points, such as the cabin's location to Grandview Trail and its origins as a sheep ranch. The forest service purchased the cabin in 1907. (Courtesy of the Kaibab National Forest.)

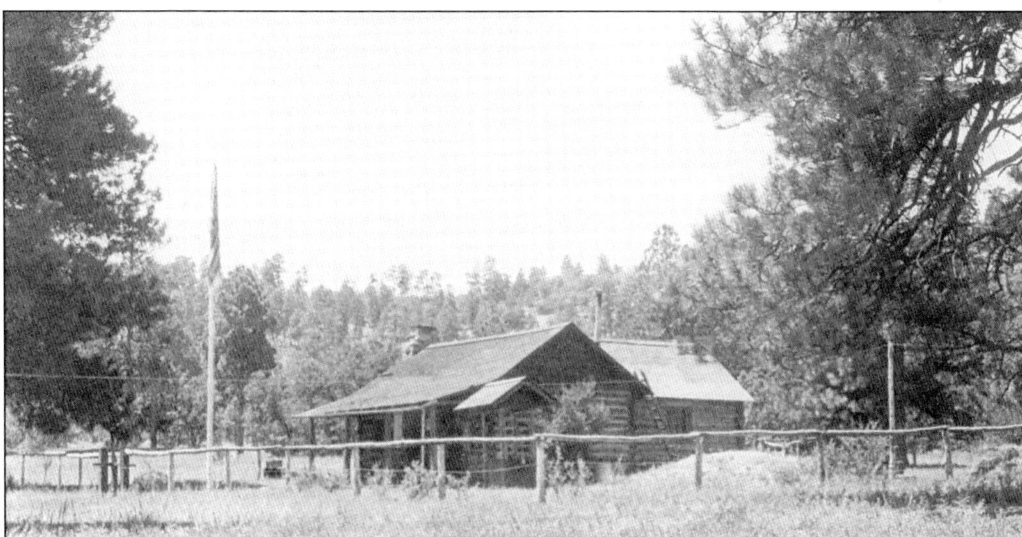

This view of Hull Cabin shows the view many would see as they approached the cabin in the late 1800s and 1900s. A number of Grand Canyon area residents worked for the Hull brothers at their sheep ranch, including famed local John Hance, before the forest service purchased the land in 1907. (Courtesy of the Kaibab National Forest.)

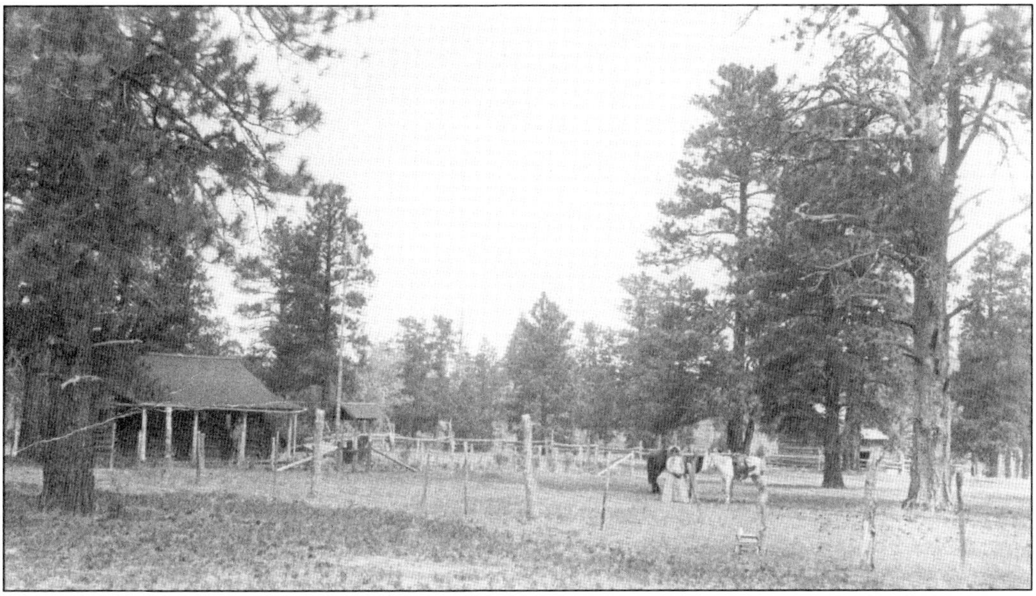

Hull Cabin, complete with a cozy fireplace, was originally built in 1889 by brothers William and Phillip Hull. Later the forest service utilized the structure as a ranger station. Rangers were typically posted there during the summer months. A handmade corral is located at the back of the cabin. (Courtesy of the Kaibab National Forest.)

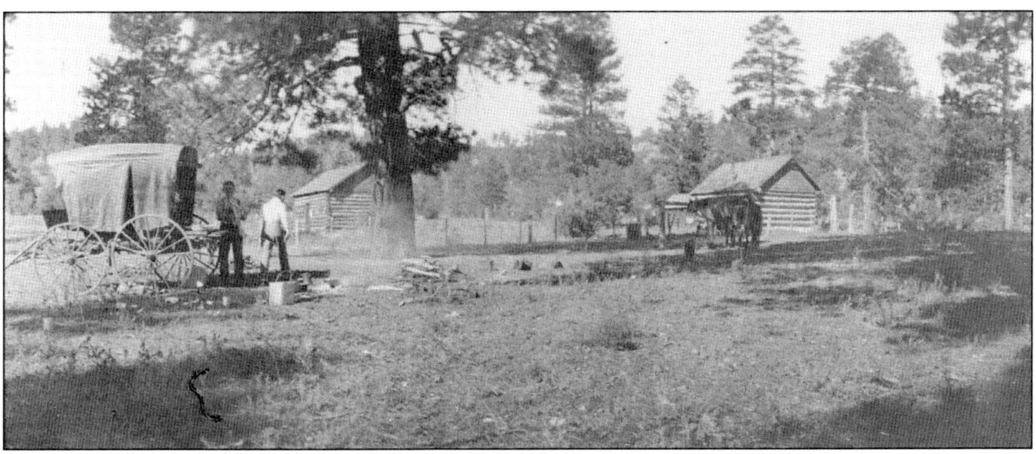

The famous cabin owned by the Hull brothers, besides being a sheep ranch, was also an important stop for visitors traveling to the Grand Canyon's South Rim. The two brothers were known as entrepreneurs in the area, and their cabin was known as an important watering hole for weary travelers. Accommodations closer to the South Rim began to appear later on. (Courtesy of the Kaibab National Forest.)

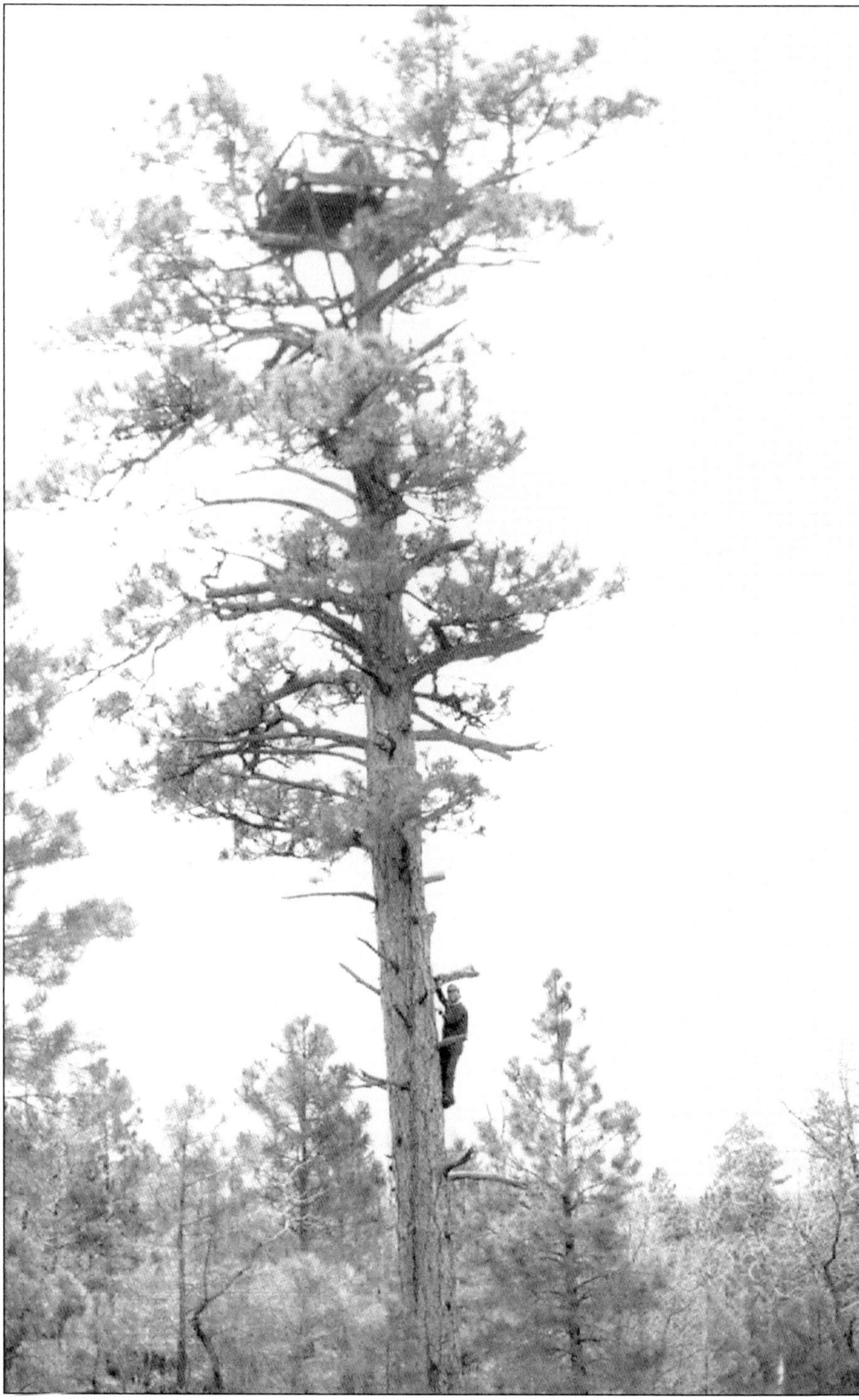

A forest ranger climbs to the top of a lookout tree in the Kaibab National Forest. There are a number of lookout trees in the Tusayan area, which was once known as the Tusayan Forest Reserve. It is now known as the Tusayan Ranger District—a part of the Kaibab National Forest. (Courtesy of the Kaibab National Forest.)

Four

A National Park Is Born

While having been the home to a number of native peoples throughout its storied history, the Grand Canyon did not feel the effects of the modern world until the late 19th century. Early pioneers in the area sought what they hoped would be a mother lode of minerals in the area in the 1880s. Most quickly turned their attentions to the lucrative tourist trade, though mining continued to play a part in the canyon's history. By 1901, the Grand Canyon Railway began transporting visitors to the South Rim from nearby Williams. By 1905, tourists found luxury accommodations in the El Tovar Hotel. The area was named a national park 14 years later by the newly formed National Park Service and Pres. Woodrow Wilson.

The boundaries set forth by the park service, as well as earlier edicts that declared the land as a forest preserve, helped shape where the village of Tusayan would eventually grow. The national park would continue to grow in subsequent years as additional lands were added to the designation. In 1975, Pres. Gerald Ford essentially doubled the size of the national park by adding more land to the park, including Marble Canyon National Monument. The park is now estimated to cover nearly 2,000 square miles.

In 1919, an estimated 44,173 visitors made their way to the Grand Canyon, but those numbers would continue to rise nearly every year. Today an estimated five million people flock the national park annually. By the 1930s, when the automobile began to surpass train travel to the park, traffic began to be more of a concern for those traveling through the Tusayan area into the park. Entrances were built on roads leading into the park, where park service employees collected entrance fees. At the South Rim, these entrances have served as a kind of marker, delineating where the national park begins and the Tusayan area ends. Once much closer to the South Rim itself, the entrance to the park is now roughly 1 mile north of the Tusayan community.

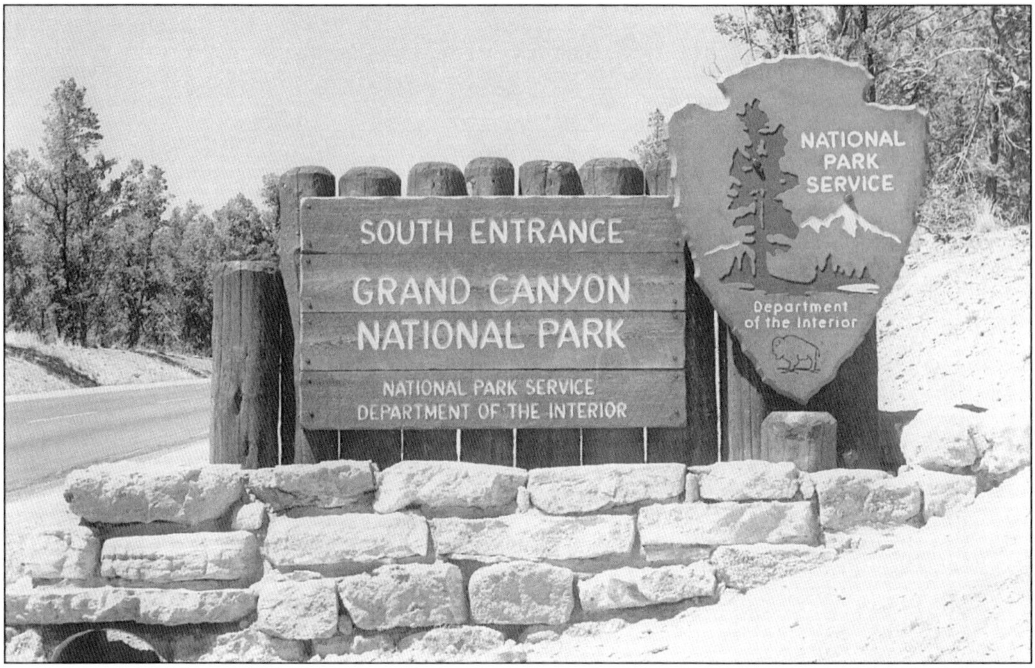

The south entrance road sign designating the boundary to the Grand Canyon National Park can be seen in this 1959 photograph. The sign was constructed from stone, logs, and planks in the hopes that it would survive what can be occasional harsh winters and severe summer monsoon activity. A culvert is also located below the sign. (Photograph by R. S. Leding; courtesy of the National Park Service.)

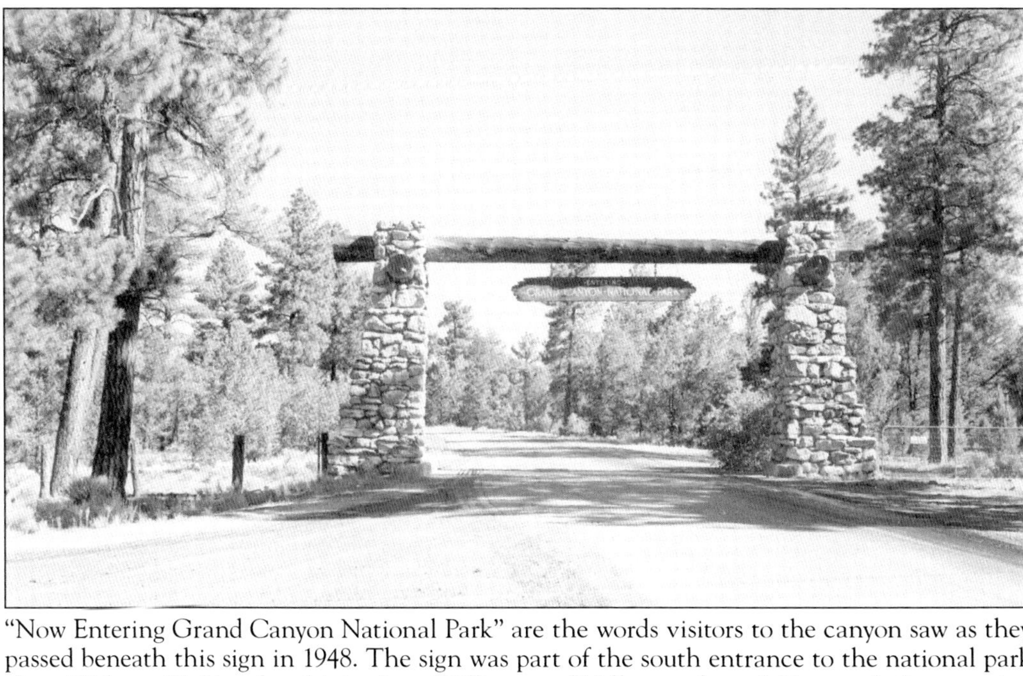

"Now Entering Grand Canyon National Park" are the words visitors to the canyon saw as they passed beneath this sign in 1948. The sign was part of the south entrance to the national park along Highway 64. Travelers driving from Williams and Valle pass through Tusayan before entering the national park. (Courtesy of the National Park Service.)

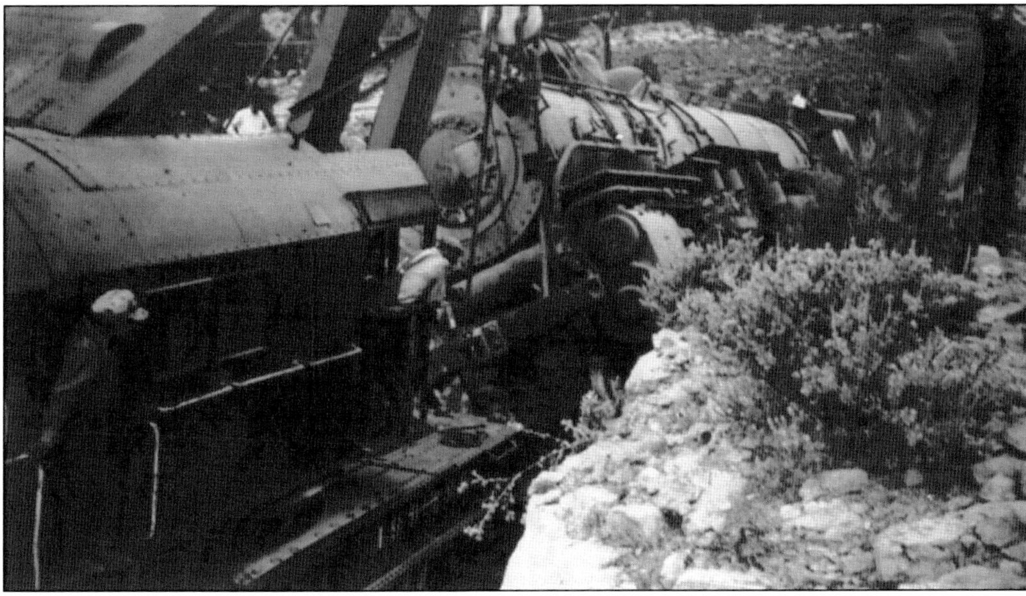

This 1939 photograph shows crews on the Needles Wrecker working to lift Engine No. 3853 from the tracks after it hit a broken rail and rolled into the wall at Tooker's Cut, which is located in the Coconino Wash. The cleanup took several days to complete before passenger service resumed to the South Rim. No one was seriously injured in the accident. (Courtesy of Clarinda Vail and the Thurston family.)

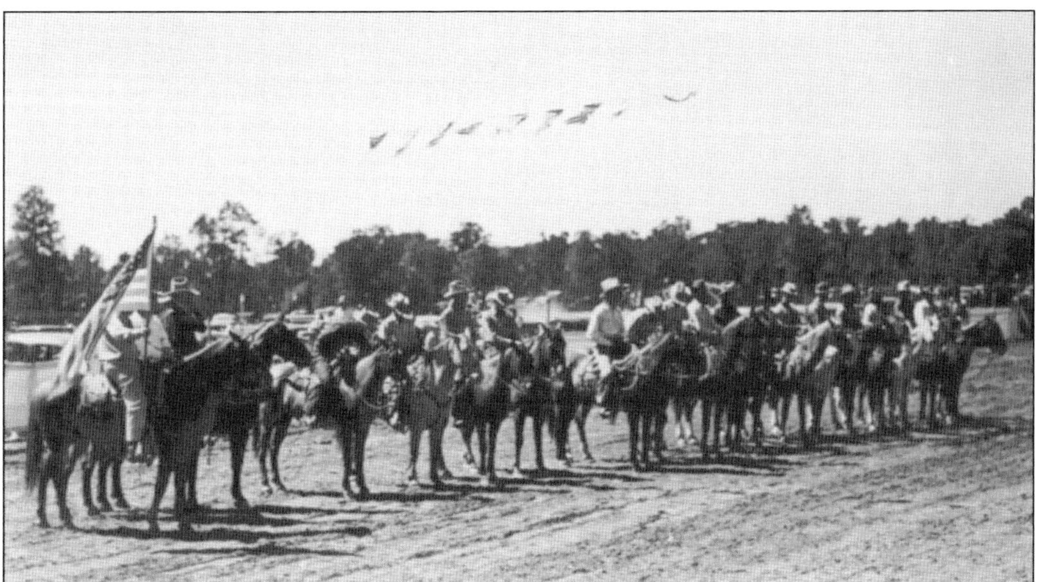

A long procession of Arizona cowboys can be seen taking part in a rodeo in this photograph taken sometime between 1930 and 1940, and R. P. Thurston competed in many of them. The Thurston family would also host rodeos on their land in the Tusayan community. (Courtesy Clarinda Vail and the Thurston family.)

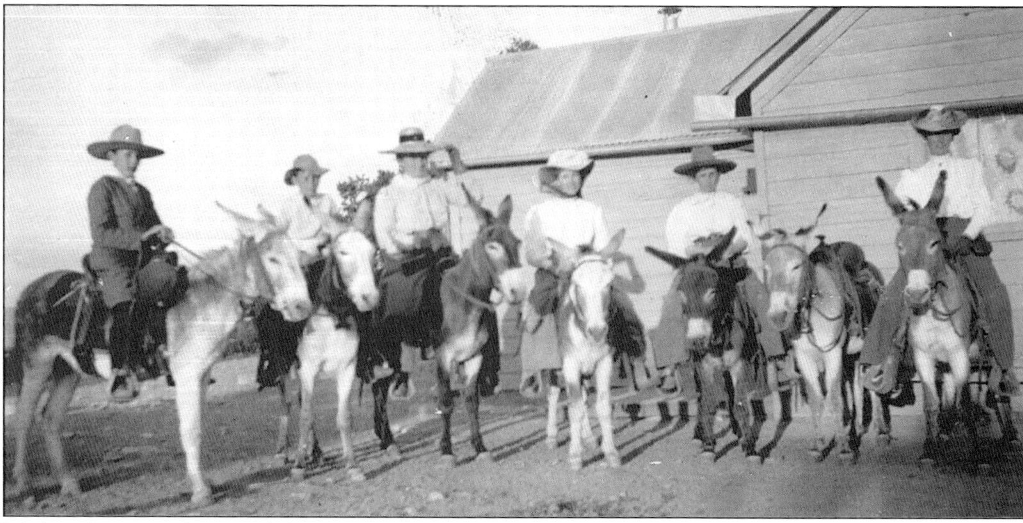

Mule rides in and around the Grand Canyon have always been a popular attraction. Rides along the South Rim, leading into the canyon from Bright Angel Trail, are often booked a year in advance. Early Tusayan resident Bess Thurston, for instance, would often meet riding groups for excursions at the South Rim. (Courtesy Clarinda Vail and the Thurston family.)

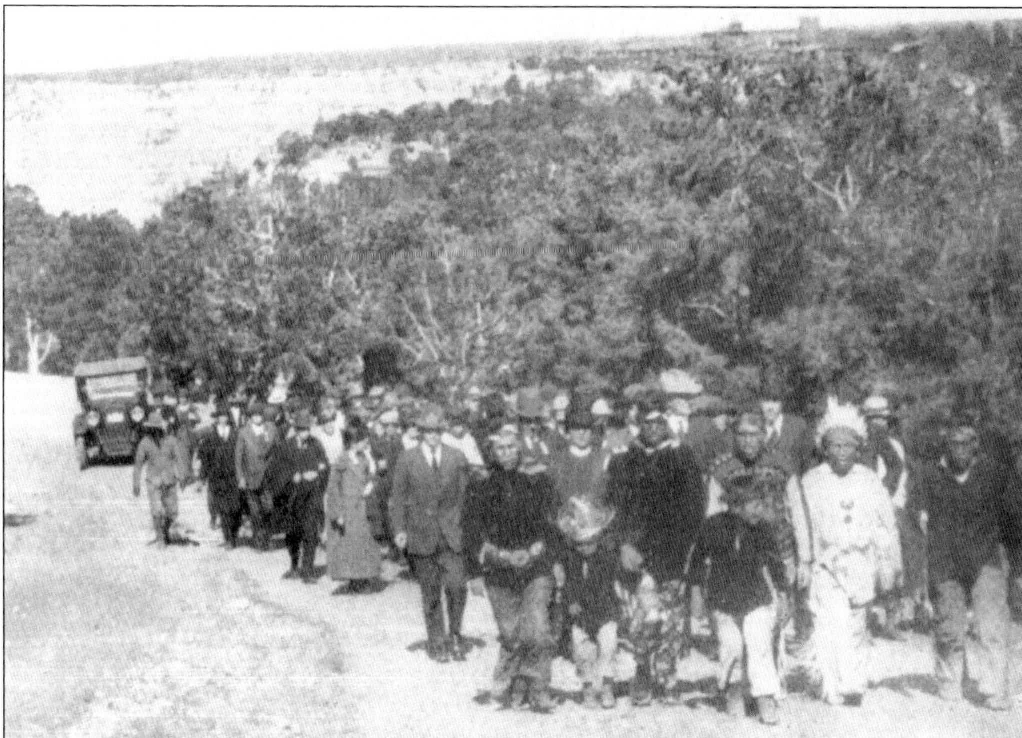

This April 30, 1920, photograph shows a procession of dignitaries, including a group of Native Americans, as they make their way along Hermit Road during the dedication of the Grand Canyon as a national park. The dignitaries can be seen in this Santa Fe Railroad photograph walking near the South Rim. Hermit Drive is also known as Rim Drive. (Courtesy of the National Park Service.)

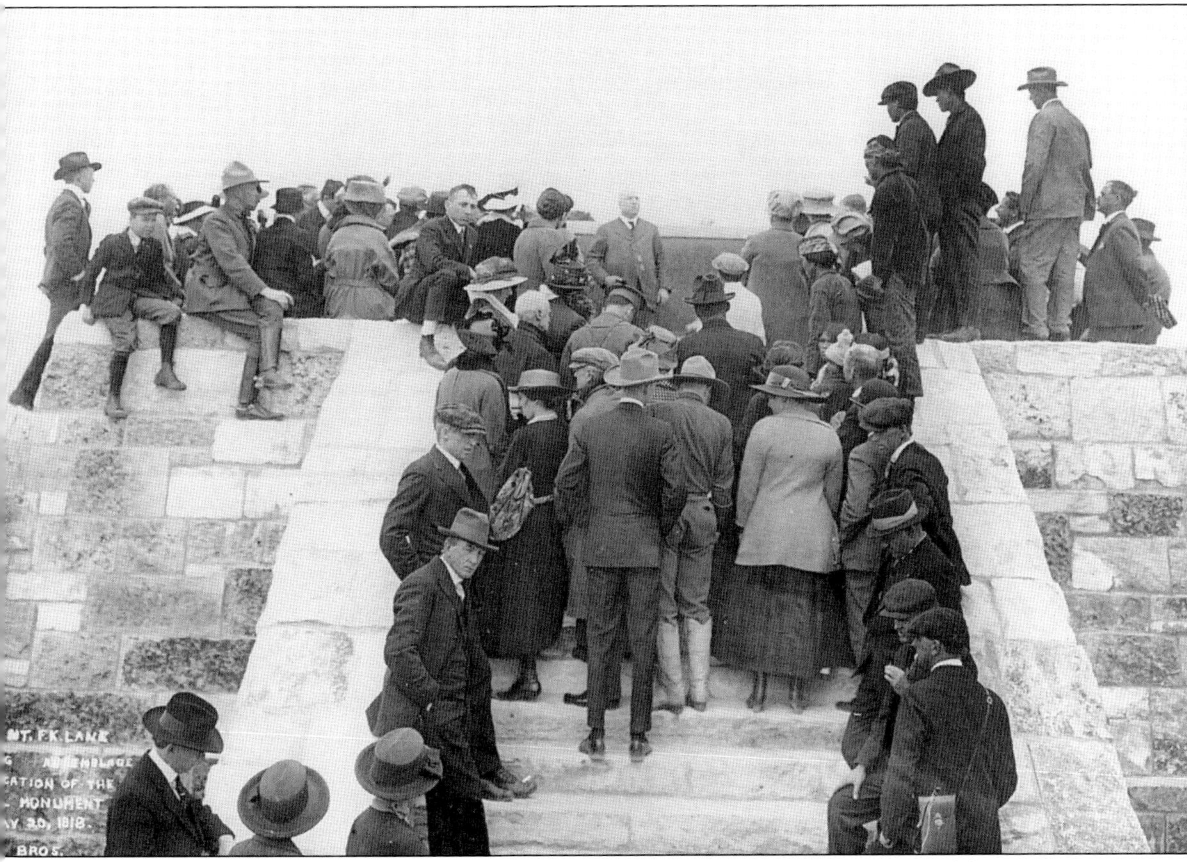

This 1918 photograph shows the dedication of the Powell Memorial by Secretary of the Interior F. K. Lane. In it, Lane can be seen addressing the audience that assembled for the memorable event. Audience members included children, park rangers, journalists, and more. (Photograph by the Kolb brothers; courtesy of the National Park Service.)

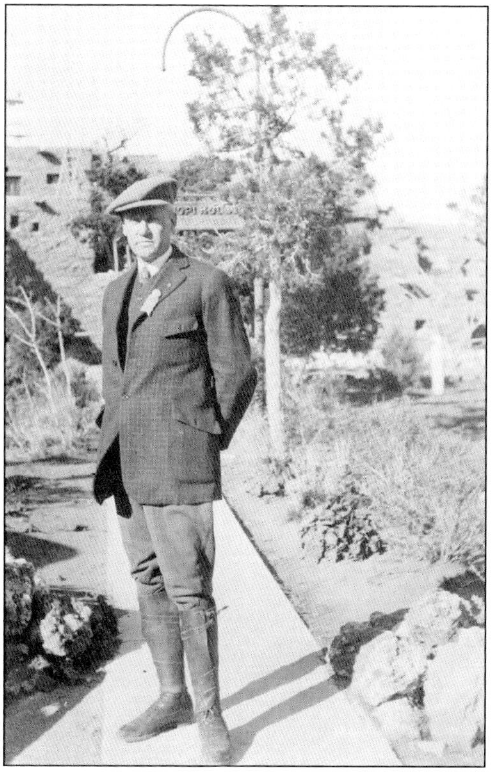

This 1920 photograph shows Steven T. Mather as he poses by the Hopi House at the South Rim of Grand Canyon. Mather appears in all his finery for the April 30 dedication of the area as a national park. (Photograph by McClintock; courtesy of the National Park Service.)

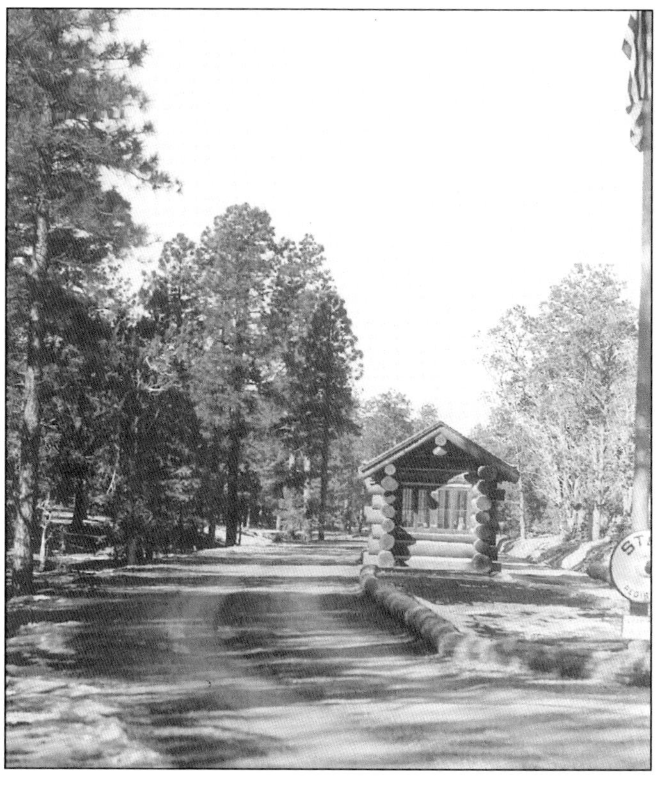

This 1932 National Park Service photographic detail shows the exit lane for tourists leaving the park after experiencing the Grand Canyon. The south entrance station, constructed from logs with large windows, can be seen to the side of the exit lane. (Courtesy of the National Park Service.)

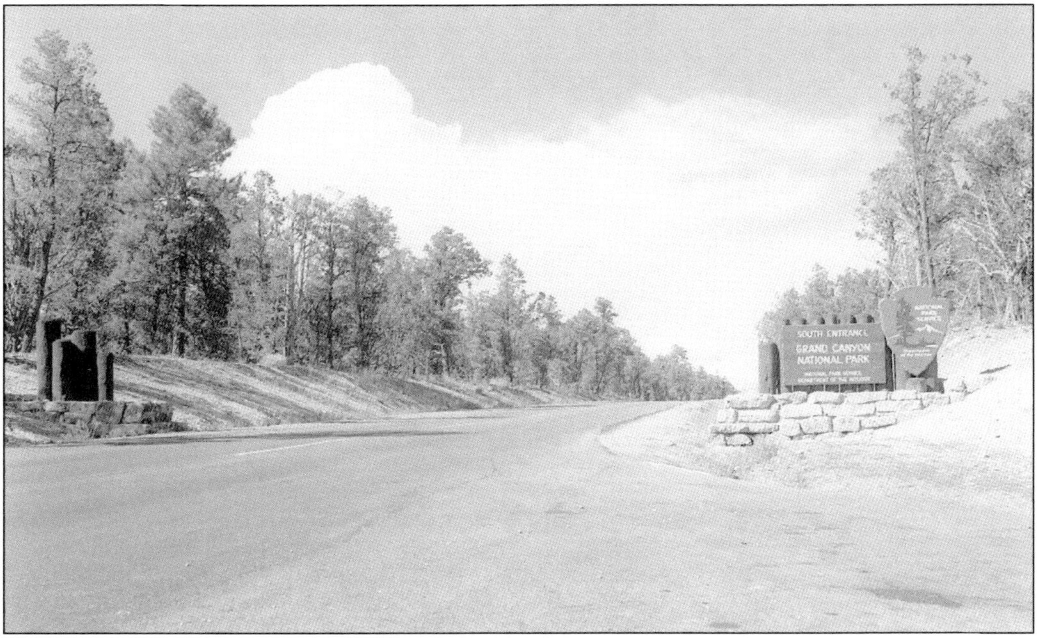

This 1958 photograph shows the new south entrance sign to Grand Canyon National Park from a wider perspective. The entrance to the park serves as a delineation letting visitors know where the national park begins and the Tusayan District ends. Those who live in the Tusayan area, however, rarely notice a separation. (Photograph by R. S. Leding; courtesy of the National Park Service.)

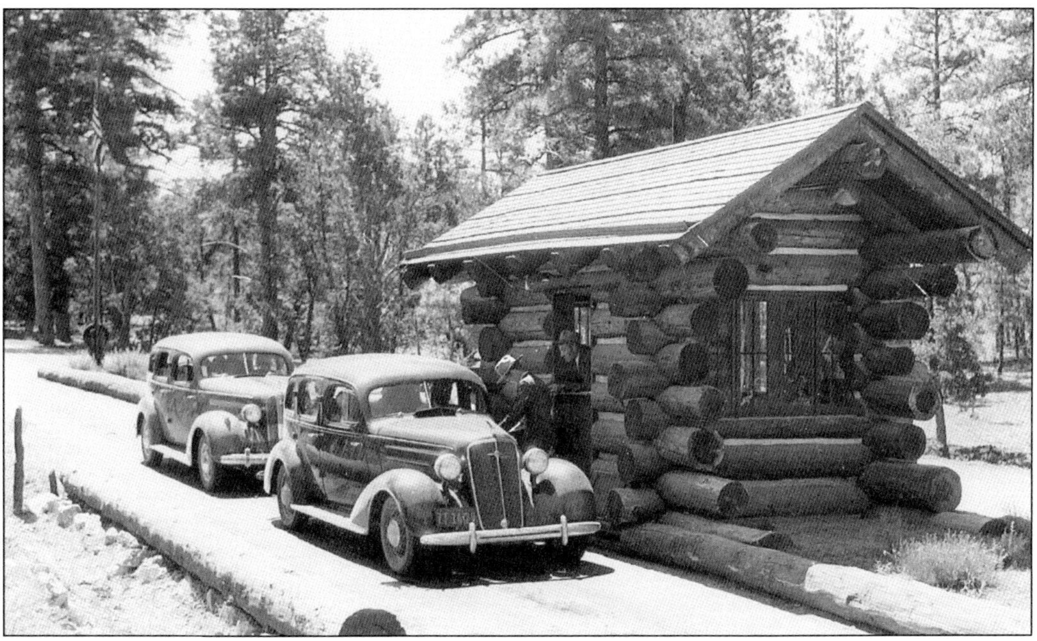

The south entrance checking station can be seen stopping visitors upon their entrance to the Grand Canyon National Park around 1935. The checking stations have been located at a number of different locations throughout the life of the national park. Once much closer to the South Rim, the entrance can now be found near the village of Tusayan. (Courtesy of the National Park Service.)

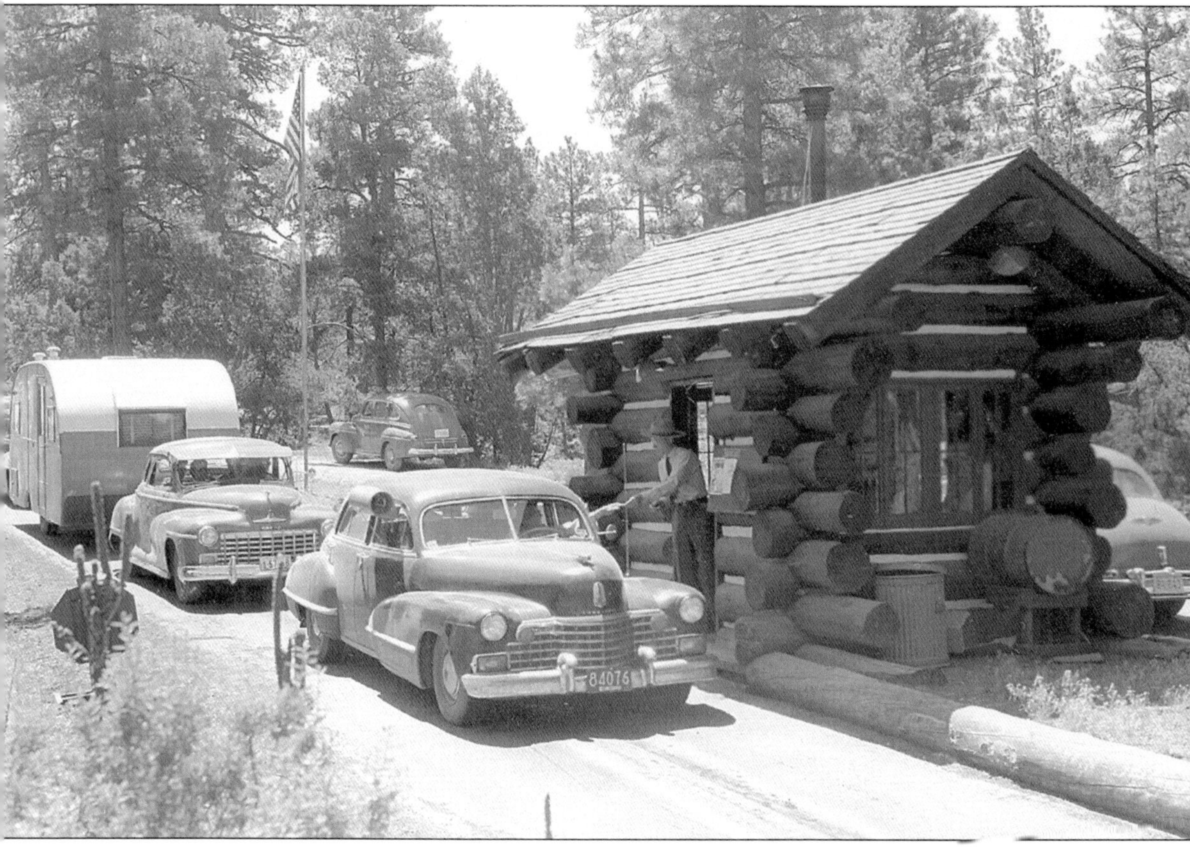

With the dawn of automobiles, vehicular traffic quickly surpassed the once common method of visiting the park via the railroad. Since the 1930s, vehicles became more and more visible in the park. In this 1948 photograph, ranger F. R. Brueck collects fees while a line of cars is backed up behind the south entrance station. (Courtesy of the National Park Service.)

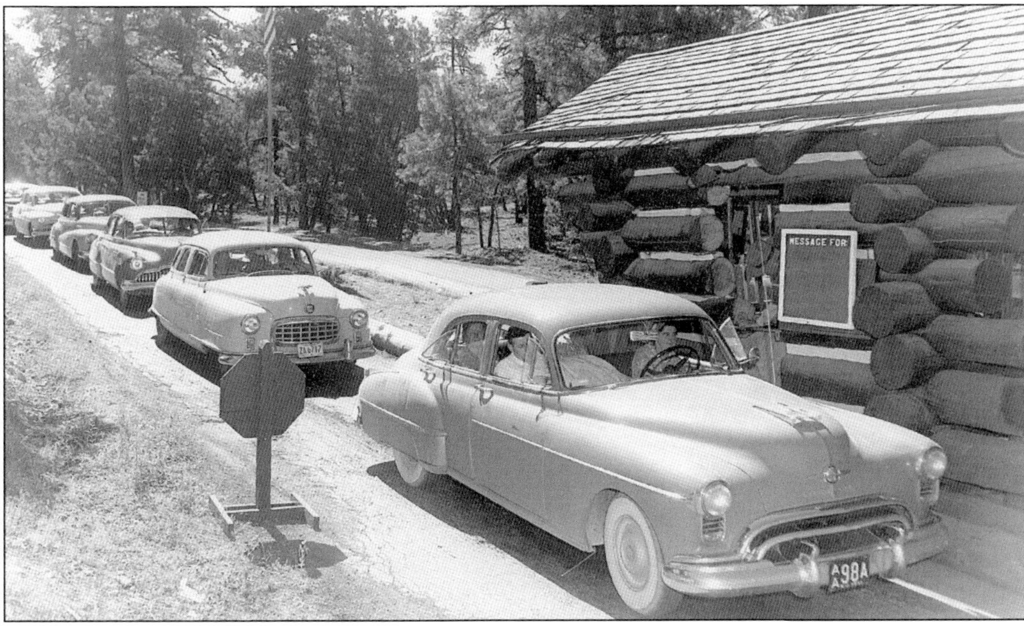

Automobile traffic continued to grow, as visitation to the national park also rose. One of the only declines in the park's visitation was during World War II, though the numbers soon began to rise again. Millions of visitors now travel to the South Rim area each year. This 1951 photograph shows a long procession of vehicles waiting to pay their entrance fees to the park. (Photograph by J. M. Eden; courtesy of the National Park Service.)

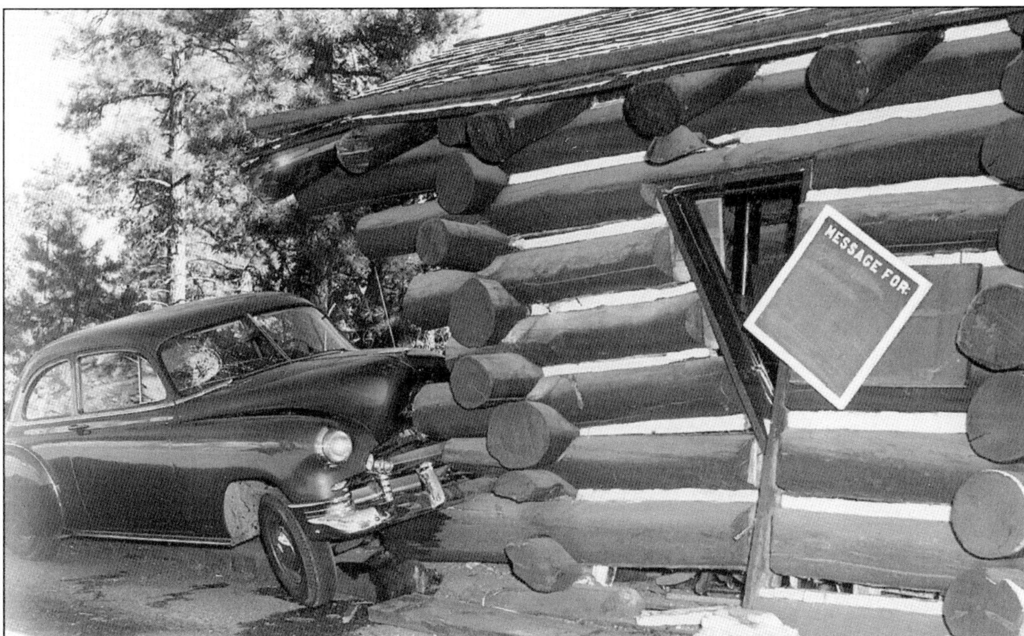

Accidents occasionally happen within the Grand Canyon and surrounding area. In this May 4, 1951, photograph, California resident Helen Hayes drove her car right into the south entrance station itself. This side view of the accident shows the damage to the log-built structure. (Photograph by J. M. Eden; courtesy of the National Park Service.)

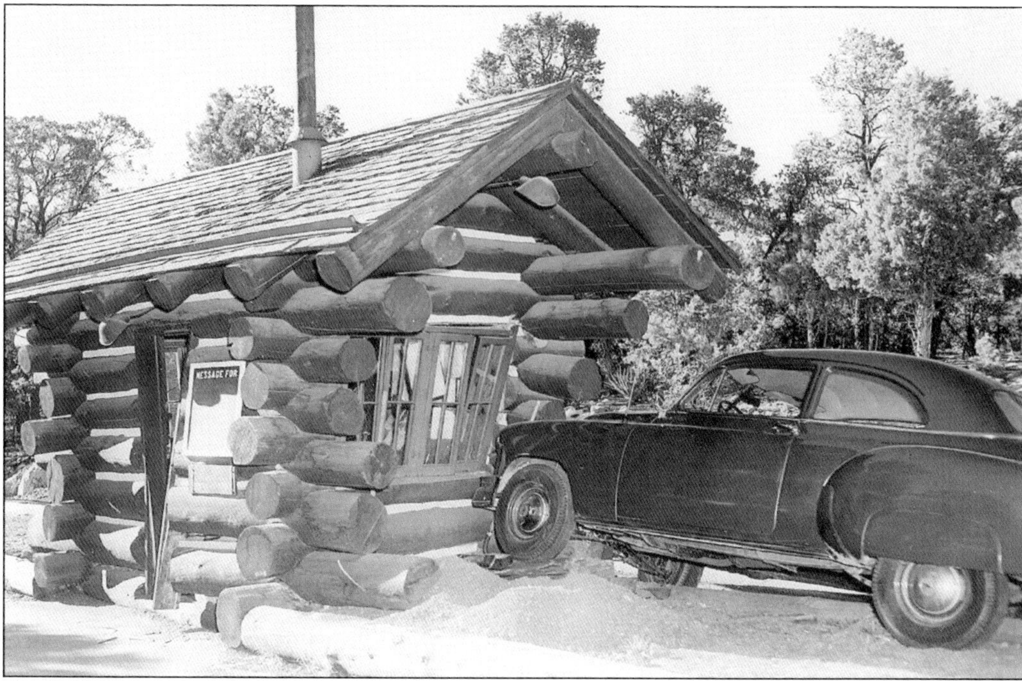

This view of the accident involving Helen Hayes of California shows her vehicle embedded in the park service structure. The mishap was considered one of the more severe accidents at south entrance to the Grand Canyon. (Courtesy of the National Park Service.)

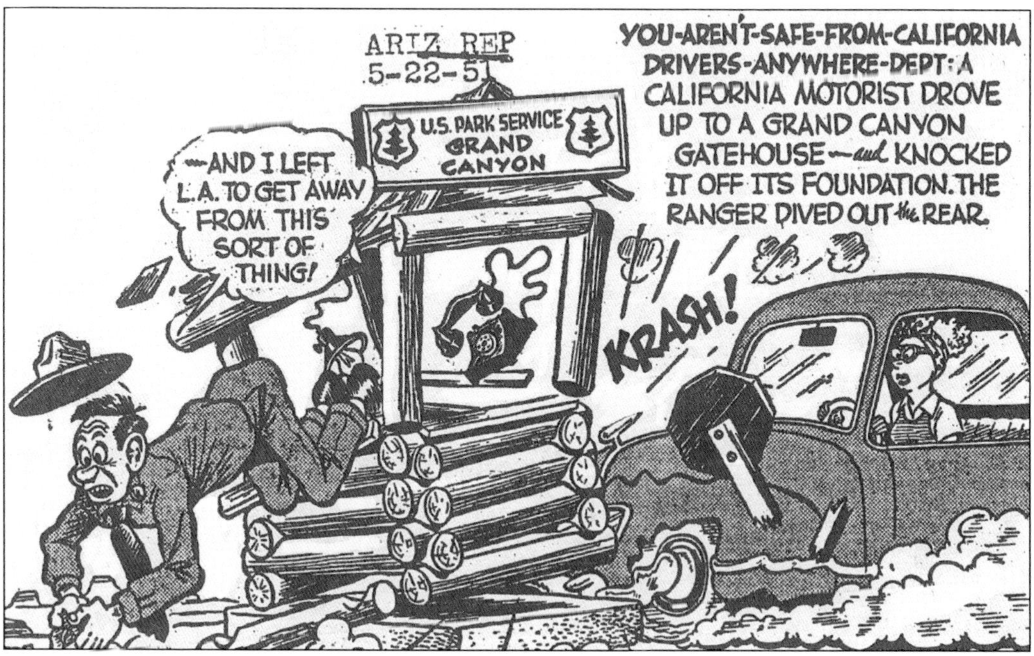

The May 1951 accident made a number of headlines around the state of Arizona at the time it occurred. Hayes's crash even became the butt of a number of jokes, including an editorial cartoon that appeared in the May 22, 1951, edition of the *Arizona Republic*, a statewide Arizona newspaper. (Courtesy of the National Park Service.)

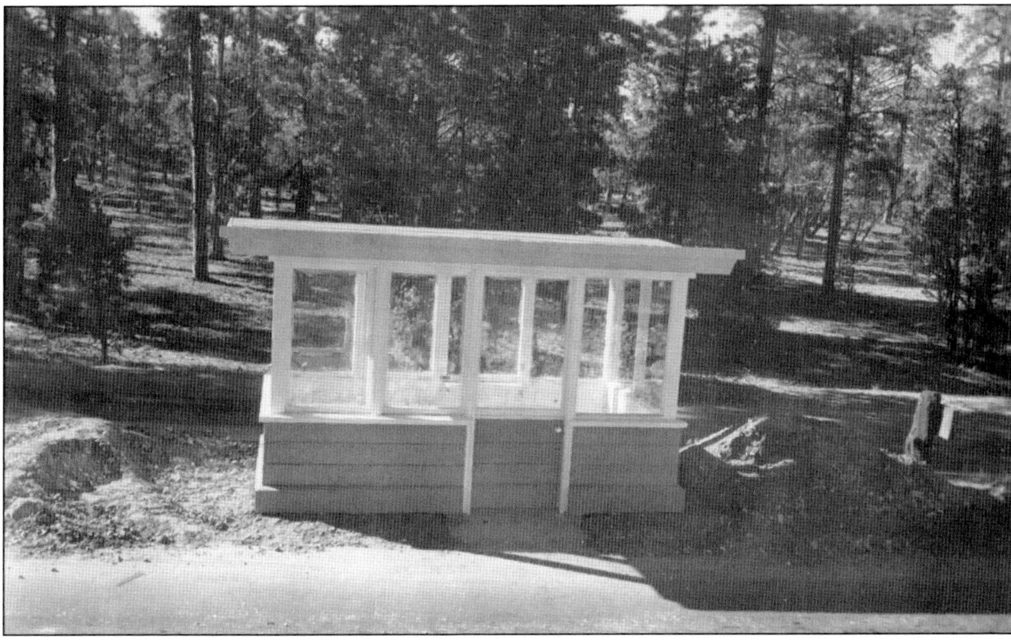

The incident involving Helen Hayes and the south entrance station to the Grand Canyon led to the construction of a new building later that same year. Called Building 235 by the National Park Service, a new south entrance station was unveiled in 1951, as visible in this photograph. (Photograph by J. M. Eden; courtesy of the National Park Service.)

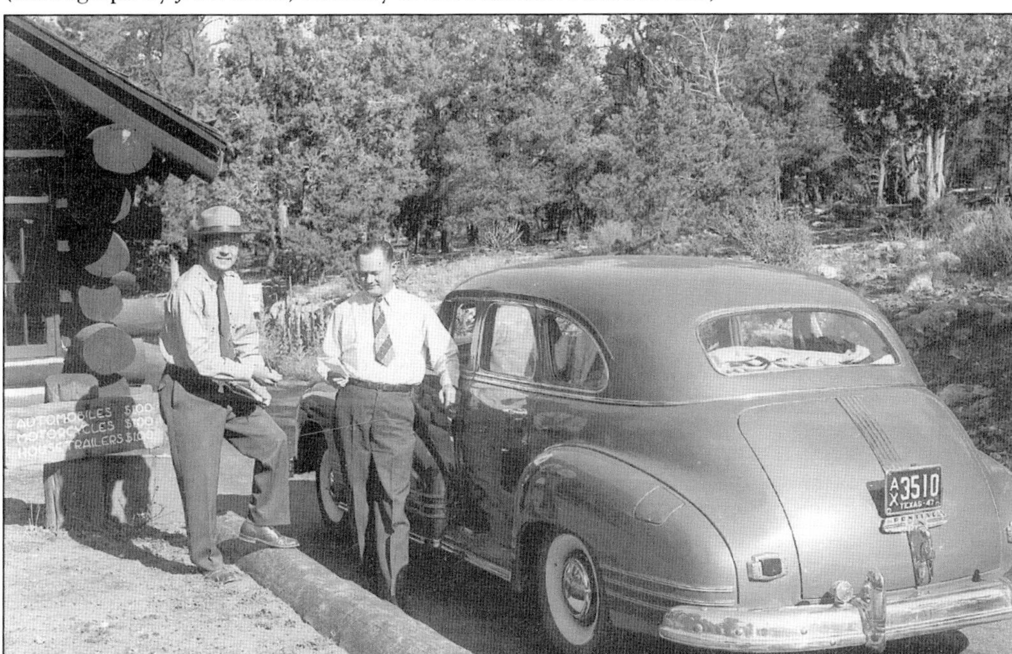

A milestone was celebrated on August 10th, 1947, when the Grand Canyon National Park celebrated the arrival of its 500,000th visitor. This photograph shows the man who held the title, V. A. Walston, as he poses for the camera with a national park ranger. (Photograph by J. M. Eden; courtesy of the National Park Service.)

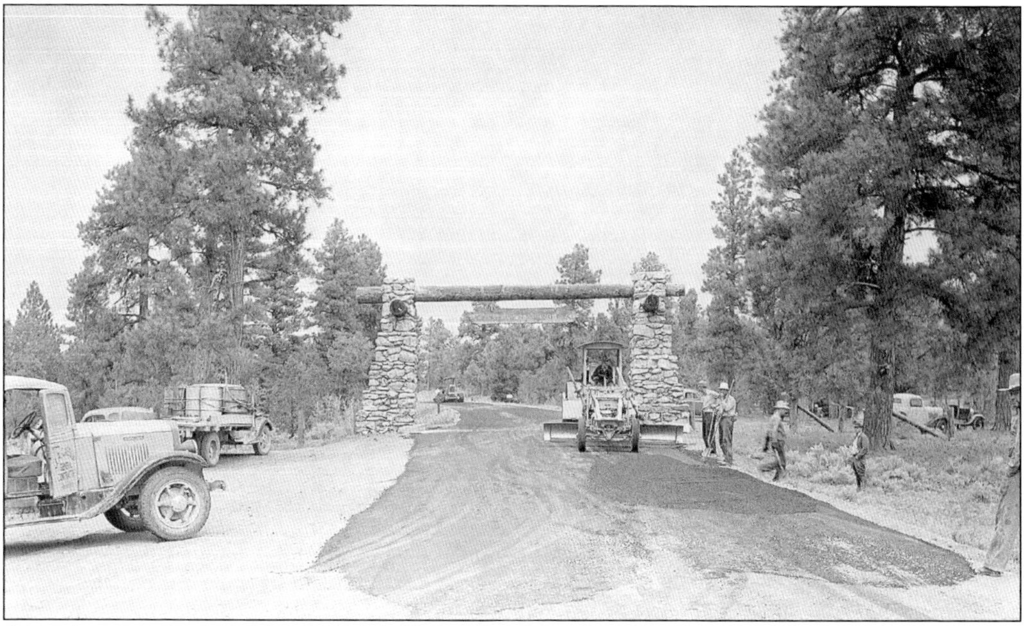

A road paving crew works at the south entrance gate to the Grand Canyon National Park in this May 1938, photograph. Crewmembers stand aside holding their shovels as a grader passes by. Another grader can be seen working the road on the opposite side of the sign. (Courtesy of the National Park Service.)

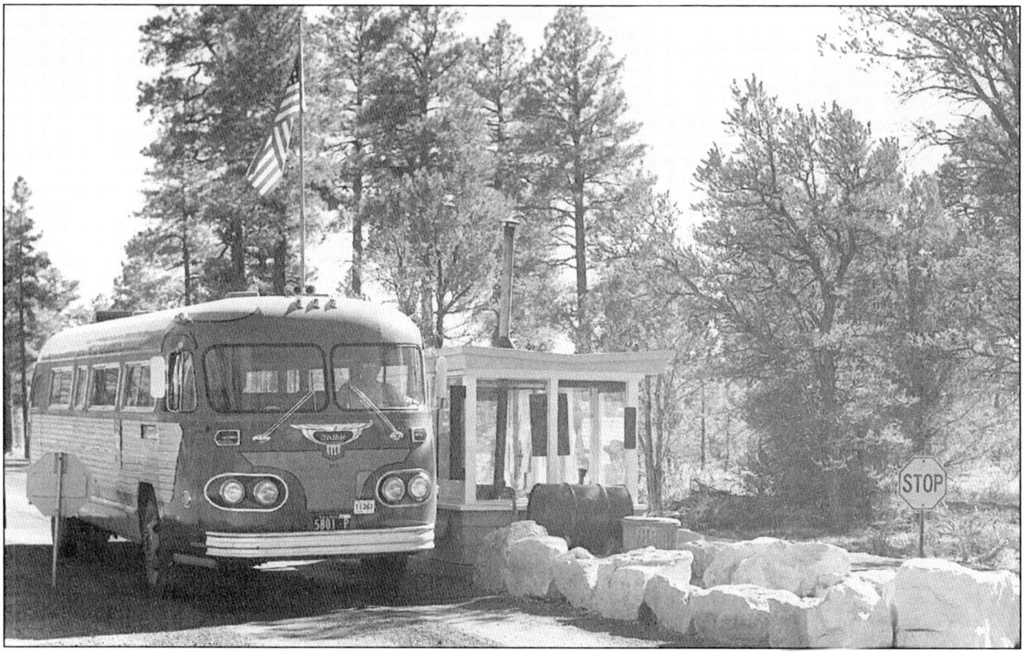

This photograph by R. S. Leding shows another view of the south entrance station to the national park as it appeared in April 1955. A Fred Harvey bus can be seen at the entrance. The Fred Harvey Company, and Harvey girls in particular, were once common sights at the Grand Canyon. Harvey girls were waitresses trained in hospitality and etiquette who worked for the Fred Harvey company. (Photograph by R. S. Leding; courtesy of the National Park Service.)

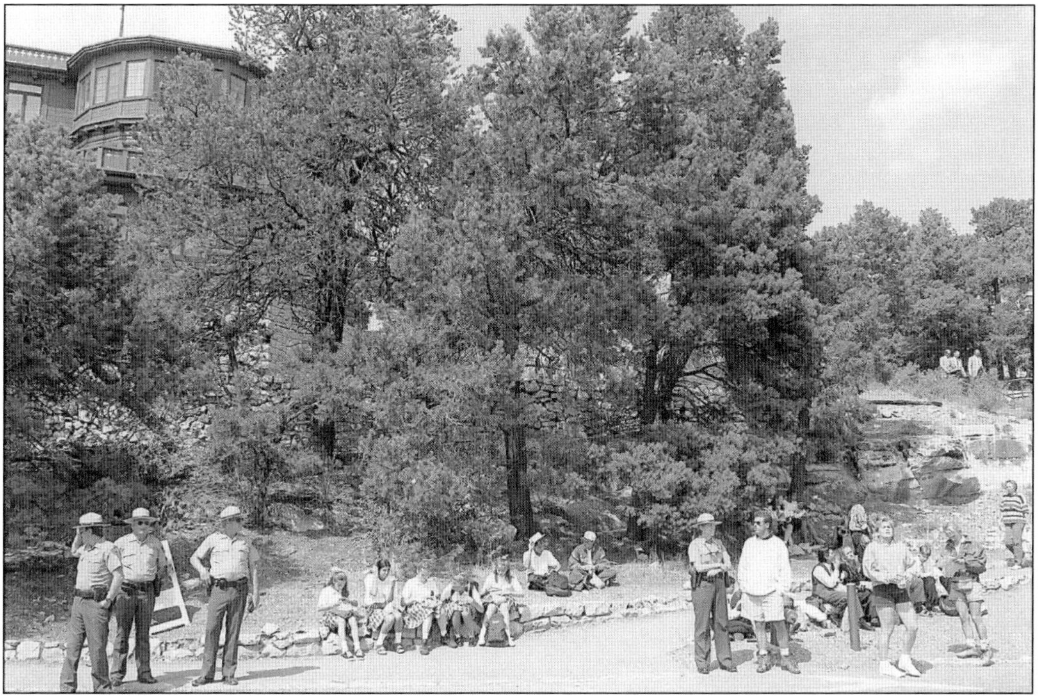

Personnel with the National Park Service and students with Grand Canyon School, the only school to be located within a national park, stand around the Grand Canyon Railway's South Rim Depot following a visit from Pres. Bill Clinton on September 18, 1996. (Photograph by Mike Quinn; courtesy of the National Park Service.)

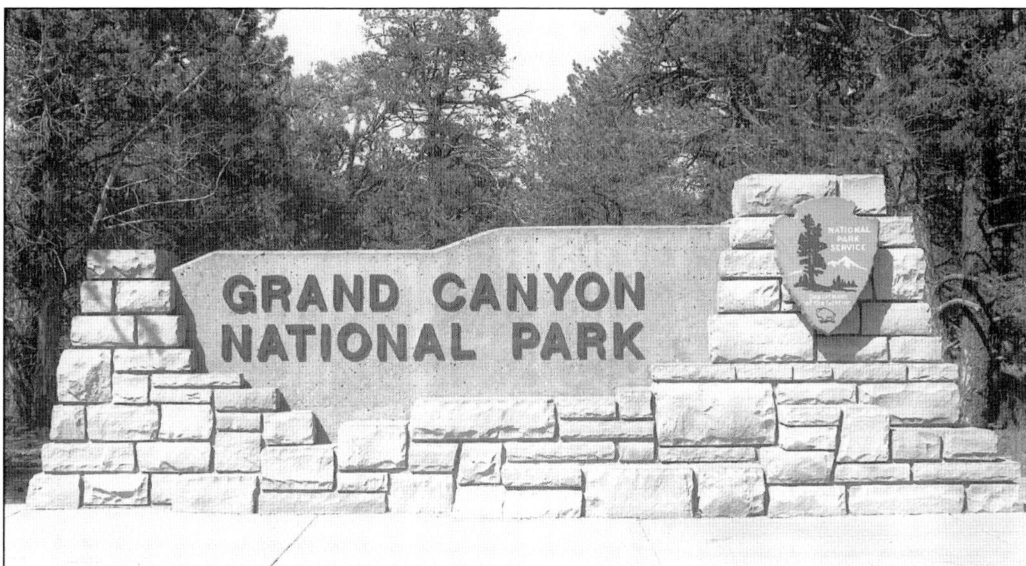

The south entrance sign, pictured in 1992, is made of stone and concrete. The sign, found near the current location of the south entry to the national park, is a popular stop for visitors passing through Tusayan toward the South Rim. At almost any time, photographers can be seen snapping pictures around the structure. (Photograph by Mike Quinn; courtesy of the National Park Service.)

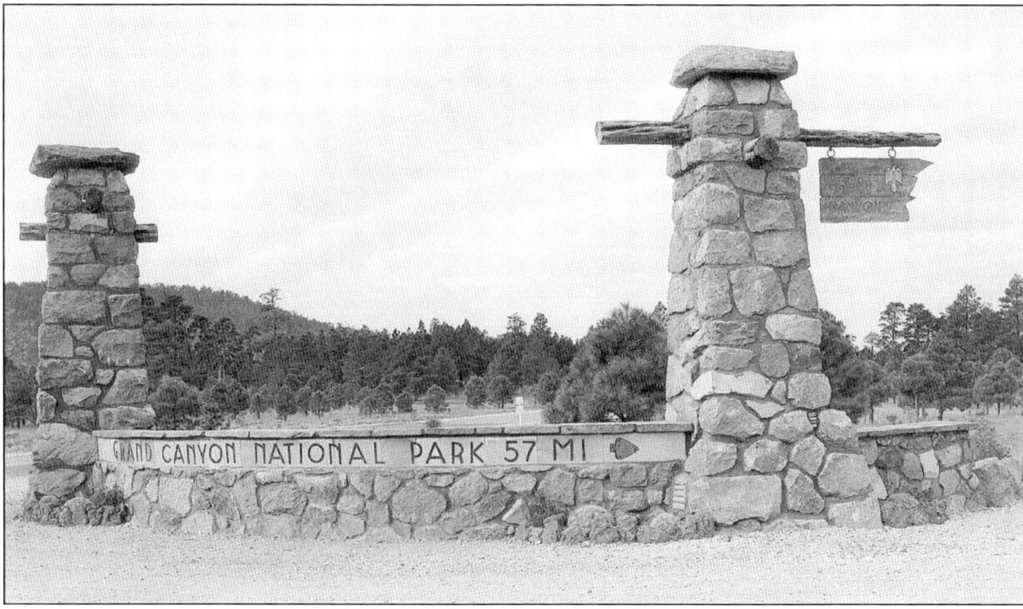

This sign shows how many miles travelers had left before reaching their destination on the Grand Canyon National Park's South Rim. The sign was once located near Williams on the route to the national park. Travelers would often stay in Williams for the night before making the last leg of their trip to the South Rim. (Courtesy Williams Public Library.)

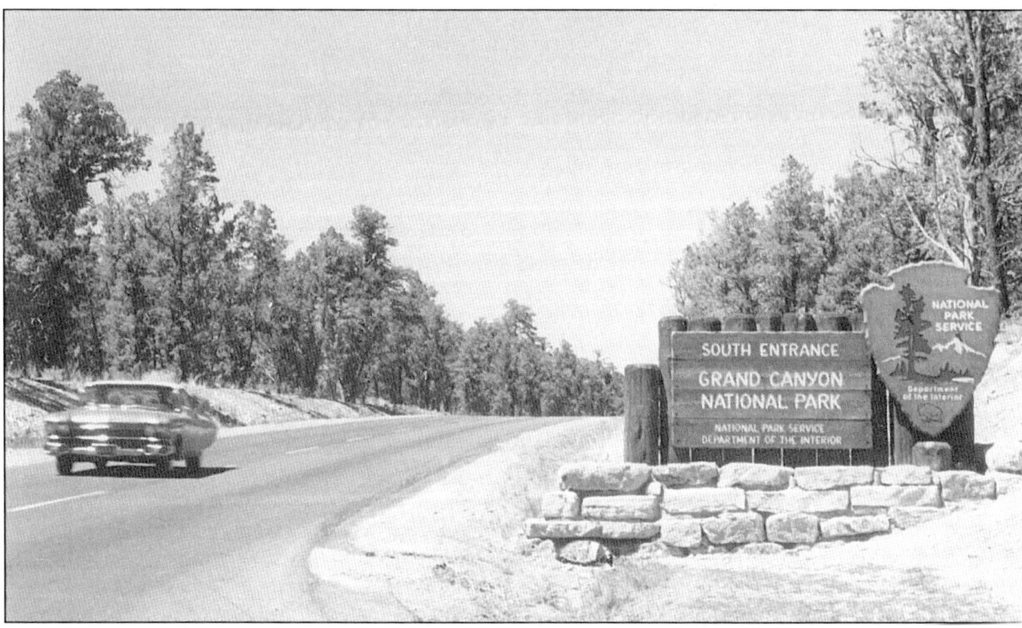

The newer sign replaced the older marker at the south entrance, which had been made using lumber, as pictured above in this 1959 photograph. Like the south entrance itself, the sign tells visitors today they are nearing the park. For residents, however, there is little difference between the village of Tusayan and the Grand Canyon. (Photograph by R. S. Leding; courtesy of the National Park Service.)

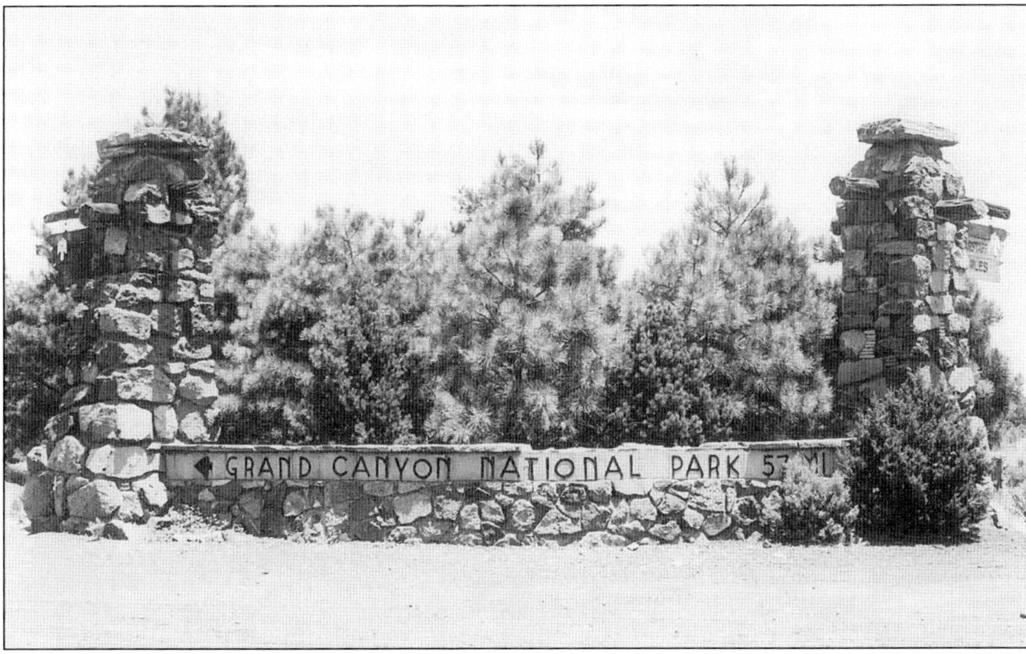

Pictured is another view of the sign to the Grand Canyon that greeted drivers as they made their way from Williams to the Grand Canyon. Today Williams is still known as one of the portal communities leading to the local natural wonder. It is known as the "Gateway to the Grand Canyon." (Courtesy of the National Park Service.)

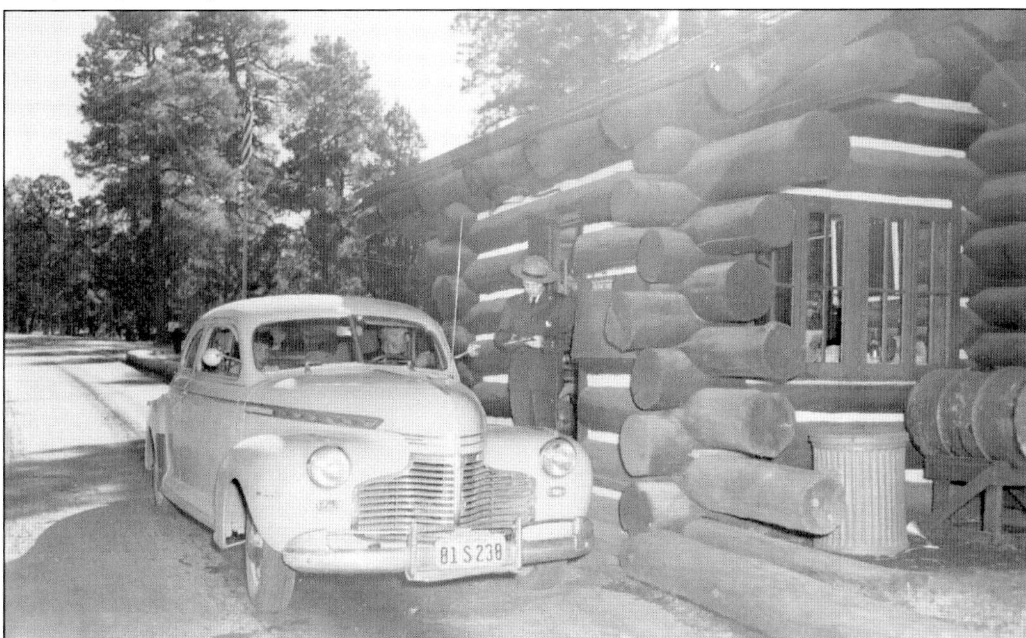

National Park Service ranger F. R. Brueck greets a vehicle at the South Rim entrance to the Grand Canyon in this 1949 photograph. While automobiles would grow smaller over the years, lines into the national park's south entrance near Tusayan would continue to grow larger. (Photograph by J. M. Eden; courtesy of the National Park Service.)

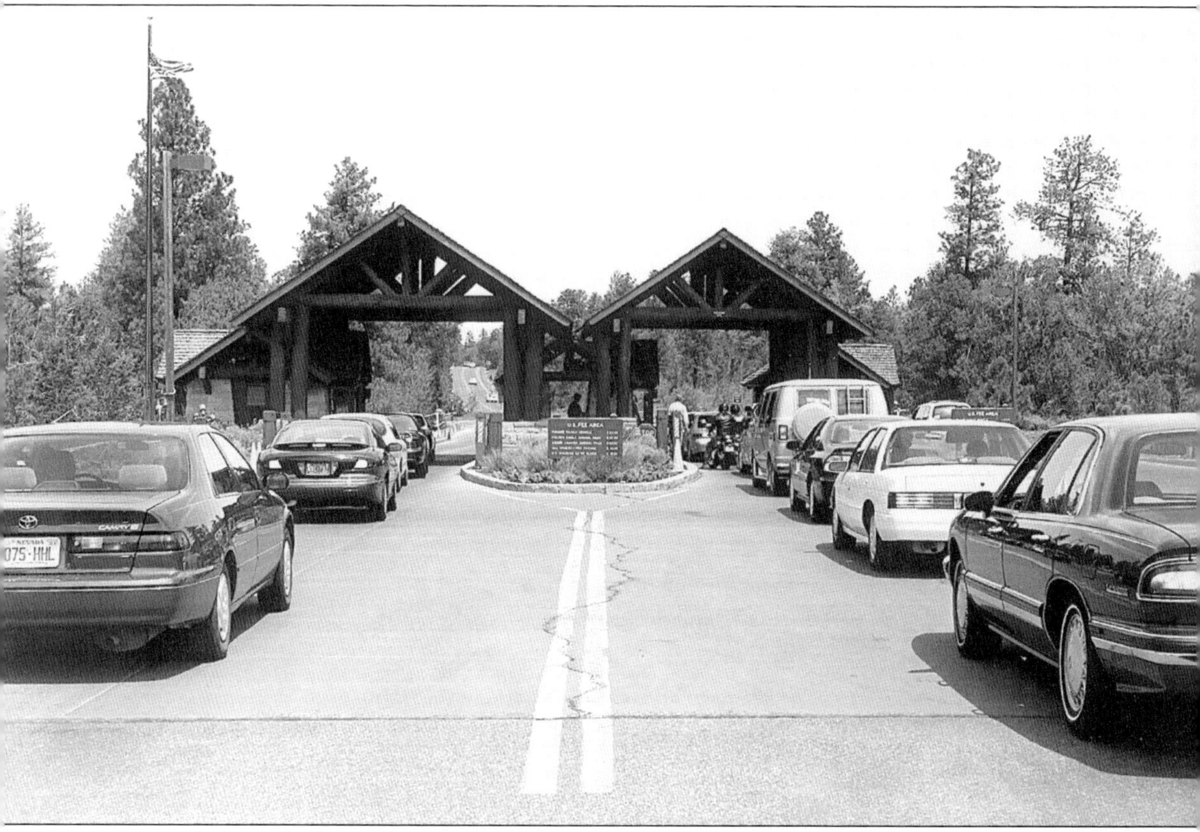

On peak days, the line of cars waiting to gain entry into Grand Canyon National Park can be quite long as millions of visitors pass through Tusayan, often stopping to enjoy the small village's amenities, on their way to the South Rim. Roughly five million visitors make the pilgrimage to the national park every year, as is evident by this 1997 photograph. (Photograph by Mike Quinn; courtesy of the National Park Service.)

Five

A Historical School

Serving students at the Grand Canyon, Tusayan, Valle and surrounding areas, the school at Grand Canyon has a long and unique history, predating the designation of the Grand Canyon as a national park. The first school began in 1911 under the tutelage of Grace Miller in a building located near Bright Angel Trail. The original school was known at the time as "Cameron's Green House," thanks to owners Ralph and Niles Cameron, who loaned the building out for use as a school.

Canyon pioneer William Wallace Bass is credited for supplying the lumber and manpower to construct a new school in the area, complete with a classroom and quarters for a teacher. Crews completed the structure by July 1913, and Minnie Webb from Payson, Arizona, became the first teacher at the new school. By the 1914–1915 school year, a total of 29 students were reported in attendance. One year later, county officials built the next school south of what was then known as the Fred Harvey Garage.

The school continued to grow in subsequent years. Just nine years after the first school opened in Cameron's Green House, organizers began a parent-teachers association at the school in order to provide playground equipment and community events. By the mid- to late 1920s, the school was enlarged to accommodate a growing student body.

A cooperative effort between then-senator Carl Hayden, the National Park Service, and other congressmen, helped build the current school. Crews finished work on the main structure in 1940, though work has continued on the school in the years since. The Grand Canyon School remains the only school in any national park throughout the country.

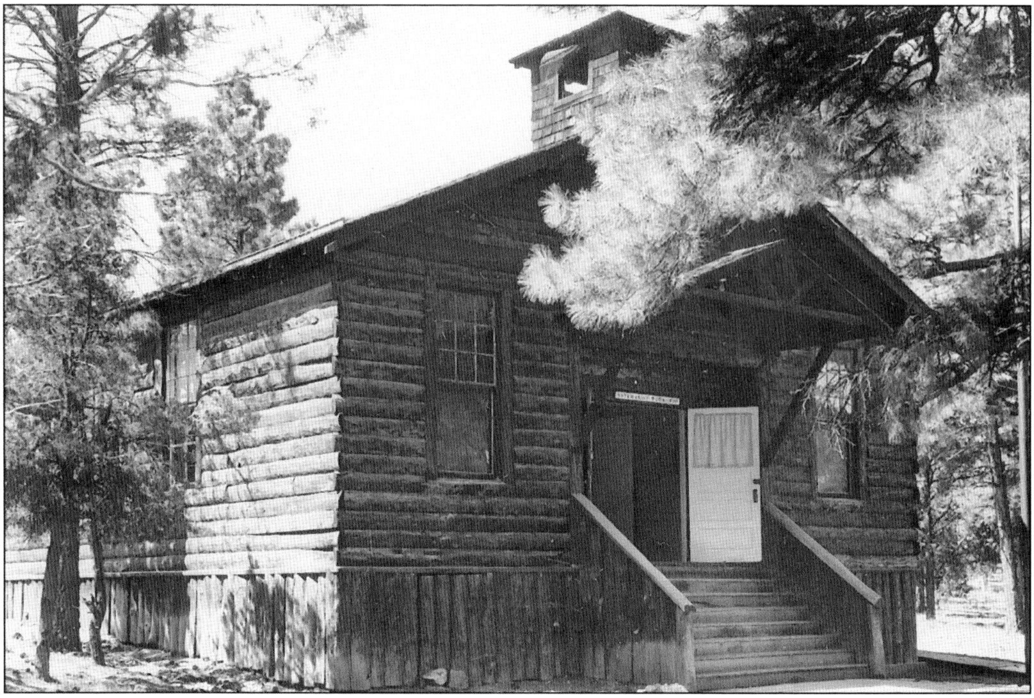

Pictured is a front view of the naturalist workshop as it appeared in the Grand Canyon's school building. The school's bell tower is visible at the top of the structures in this August 17, 1948, photograph. The building would later become home to the Grand Canyon Library. (Photograph by J. M. Eden; courtesy of the National Park Service.)

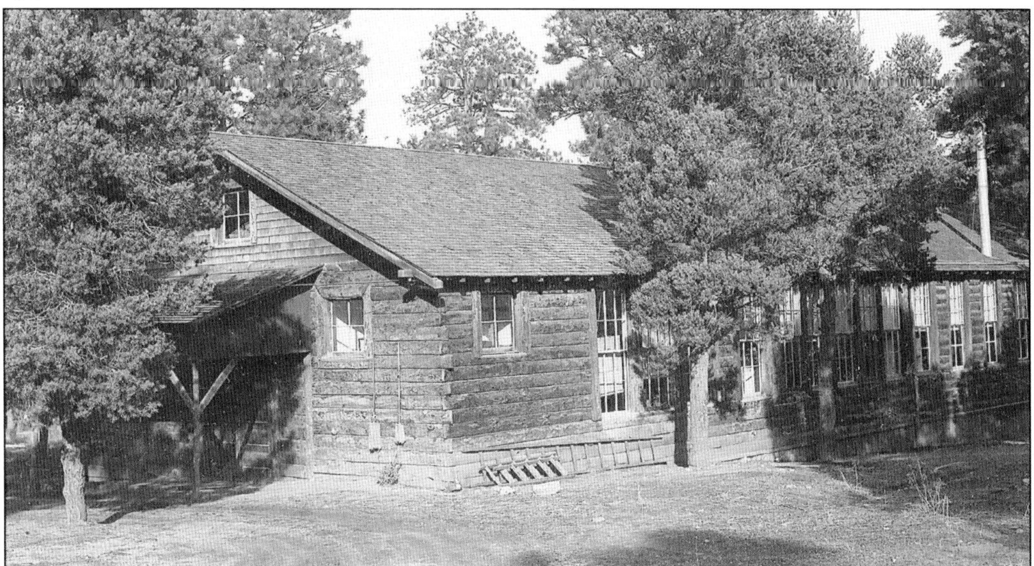

This photograph, taken around 1940, offers another view of the old schoolhouse at the Grand Canyon's South Rim. The building now houses the Grand Canyon Library. Like many of the buildings within the Grand Canyon National Park, the outside may look historical, but the interior offers a number of modern amenities. The library, for instance, offers DVD rentals and Internet usage for guests. (Courtesy of the National Park Service.)

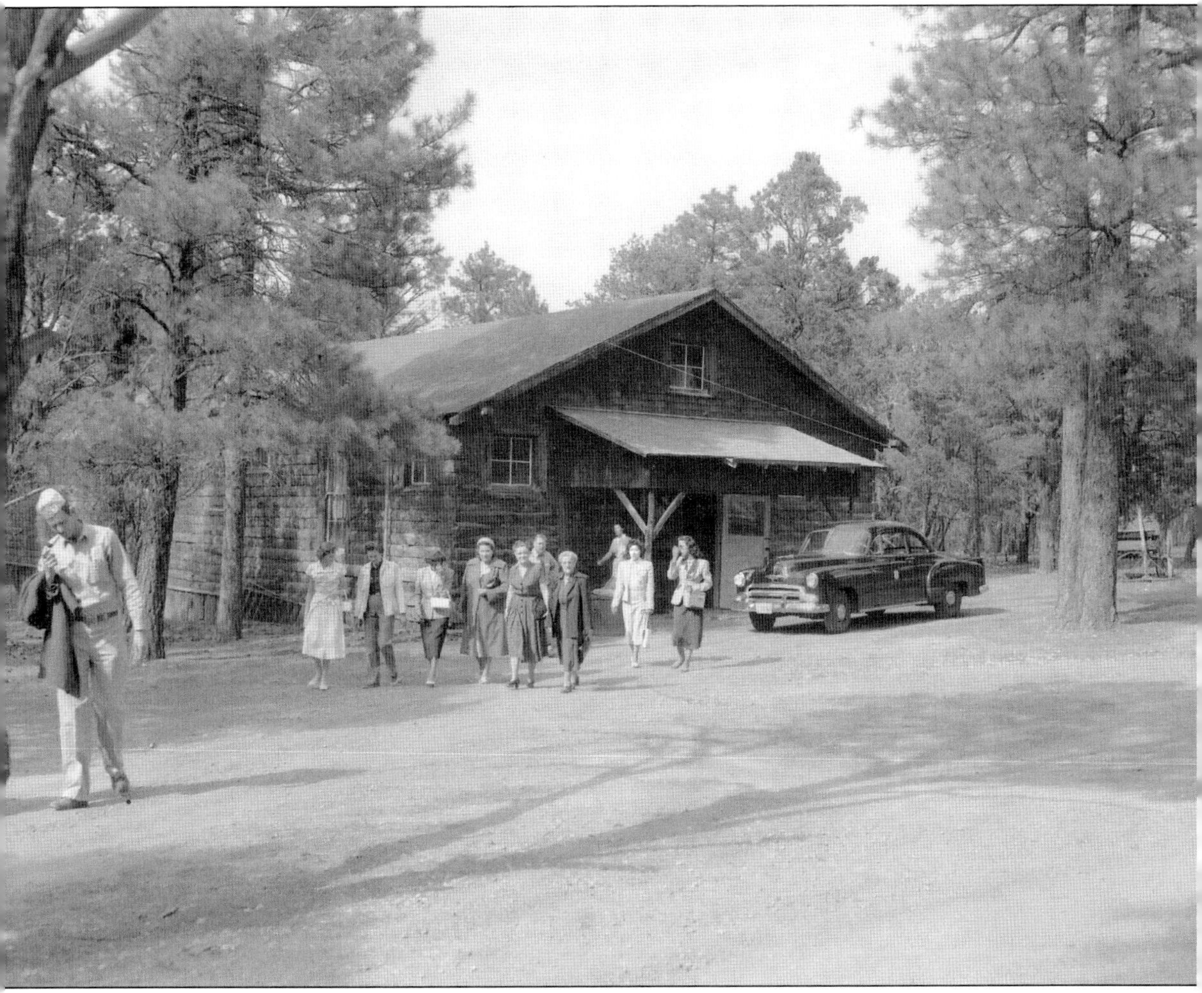

This May 10, 1951, photograph shows a group departing building number 208, also known as the naturalist workshop and former Grand Canyon School. The group is departing from the back of the structure in the photograph. Years later the area would be used as parking for visitors to the library. (Courtesy of the National Park Service.)

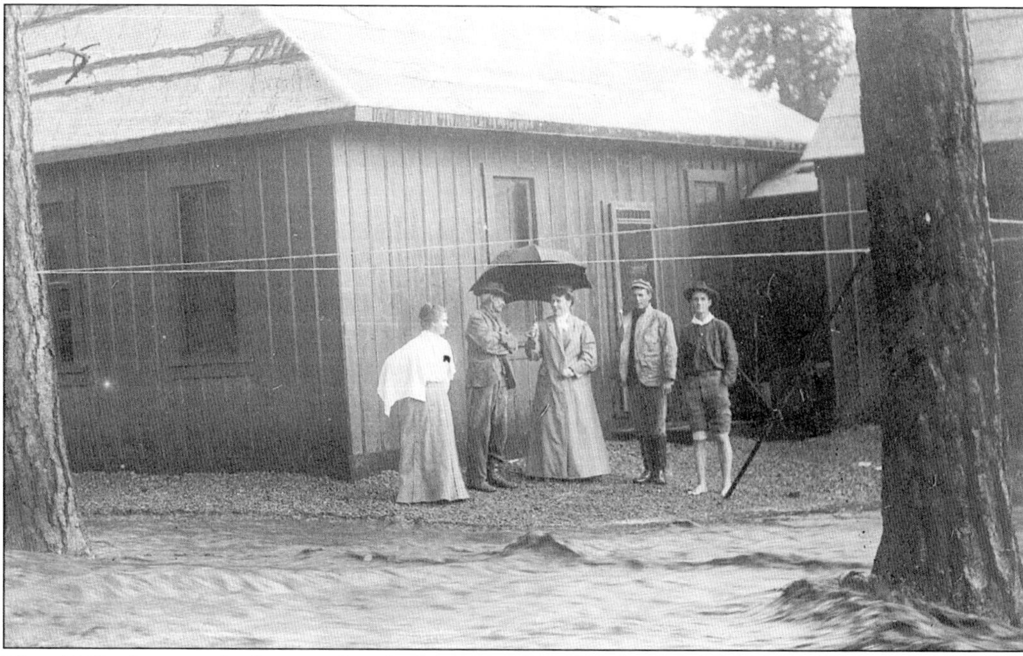

This 1907 photograph shows a flood of water rushing past the first Grand Canyon School. Five people stand at the edge of the water, caused by a flash flood. Monsoonal weather in northern Arizona can often create flooding in certain areas, though flash floods are not an annual occurrence. (Photograph by the Kolb brothers; courtesy of the National Park Service.)

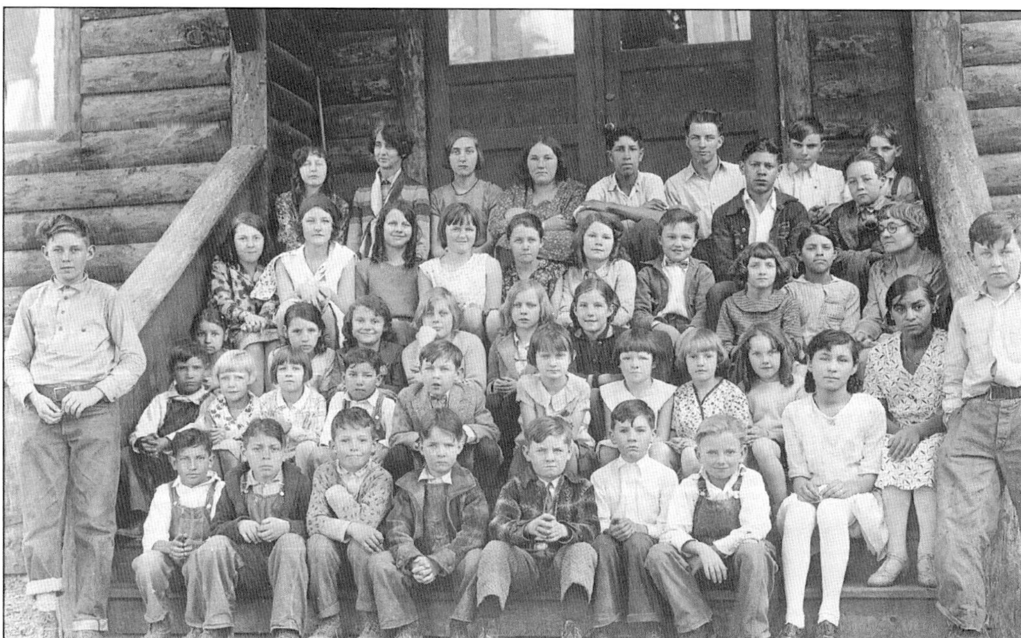

Children sit on the steps of the Grand Canyon School, located near the South Rim of the Grand Canyon, in this photograph taken on November 22, 1929. The Grand Canyon's school would become the first school in all of Arizona to be honored with a superior rating. (Courtesy of the National Park Service.)

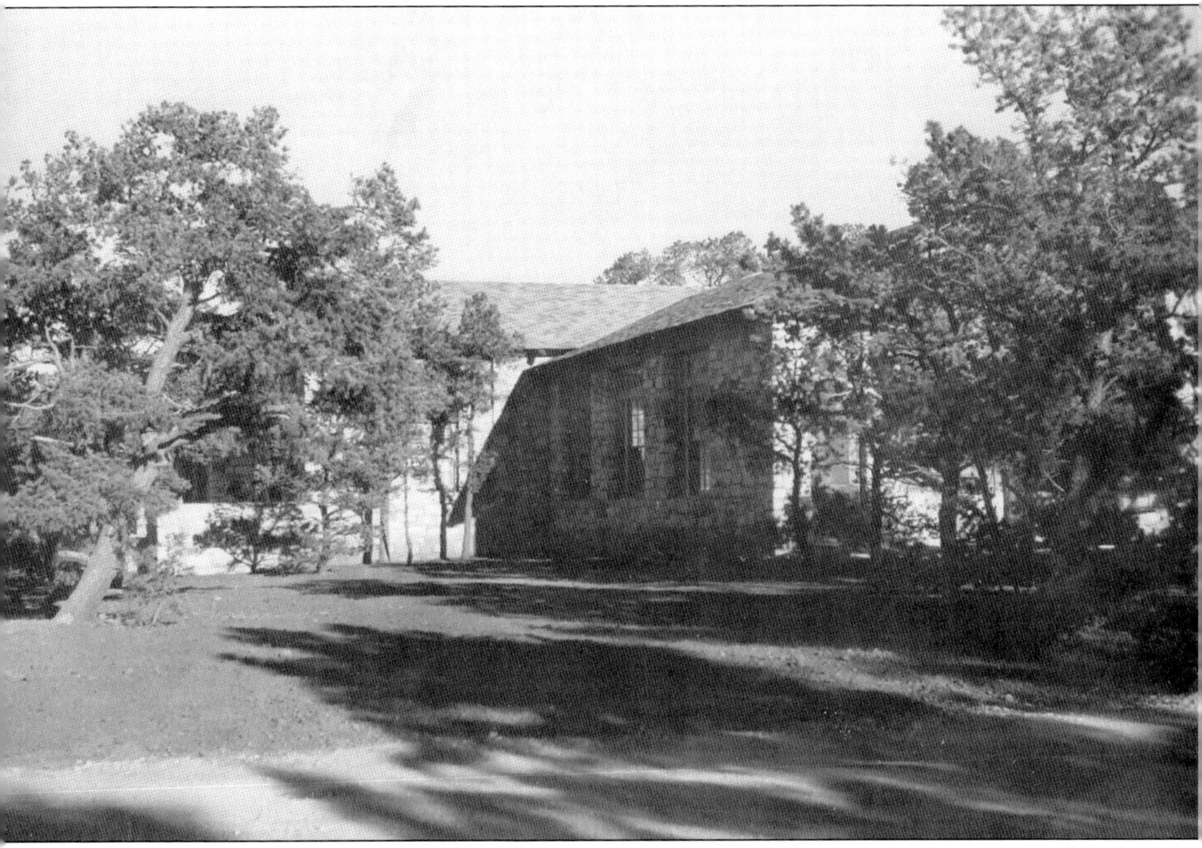

The newer school building was completed in the 1940s, though additional construction would continue in and around the educational structure. Enrollment at the school continued to rise following the opening of the area's first facility, offered by Ralph and Niles Cameron. There were 29 enrolled at the school in 1914. (Courtesy of the National Park Service.)

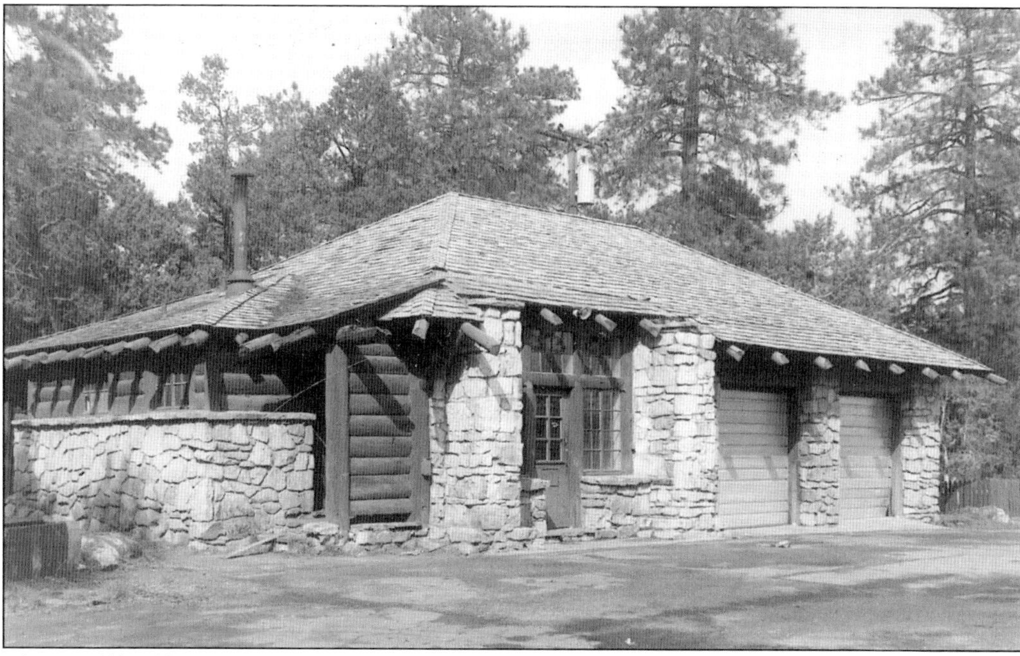

This small building at the Grand Canyon National Park is a well-known site for those who live in the Tusayan, Grand Canyon area. The 1938 structure is located on Center Road near the South Rim. It was once used as a filling station before becoming used as a garage for the Grand Canyon School. (Courtesy of the National Park Service.)

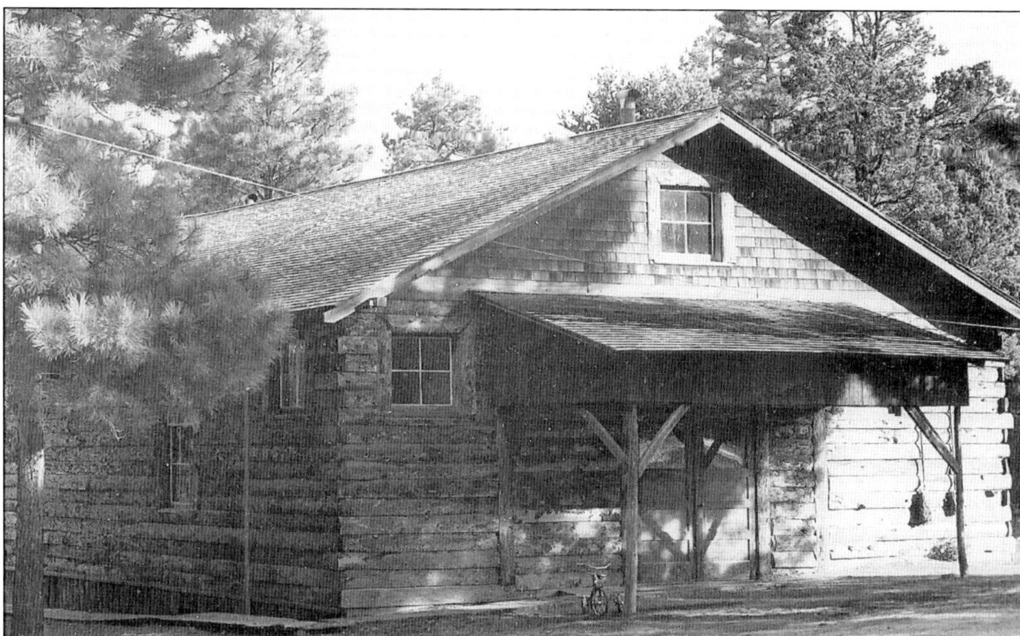

Here is another view of the Grand Canyon School's naturalist workshop, known as building number 208 to park service employees, as it appeared in 1945. The first permanent school can no longer be found in its original location. It was purchased by area resident Bert Lauzon in 1917 and moved to his homestead. (Courtesy of the National Park Service.)

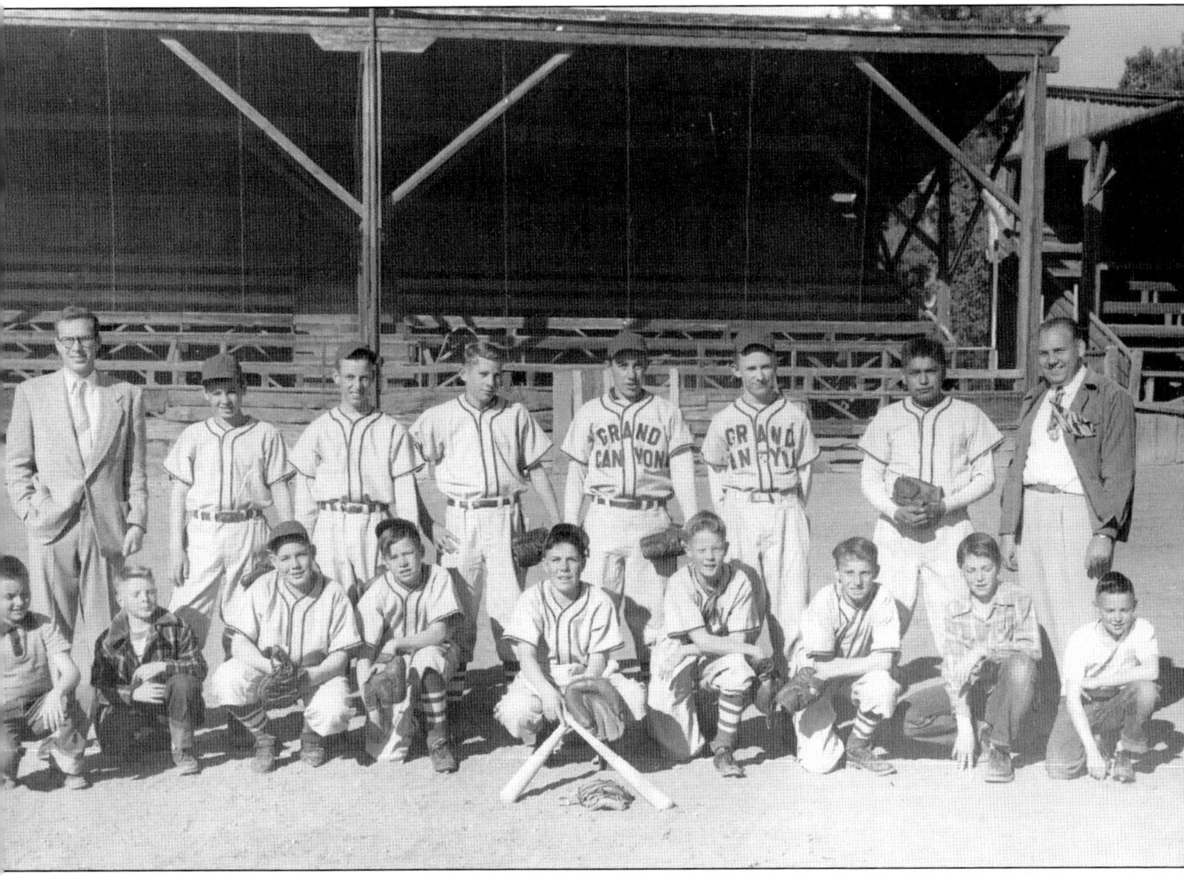

America's favorite pastime, baseball, was no stranger to residents of the Grand Canyon. A number of young baseball players and their coaching staff can be seen in this April 16, 1953, photograph. The 15 young players are posing near a collection of wooden bleachers. (Photograph by R. S. Leding; courtesy of the National Park Service.)

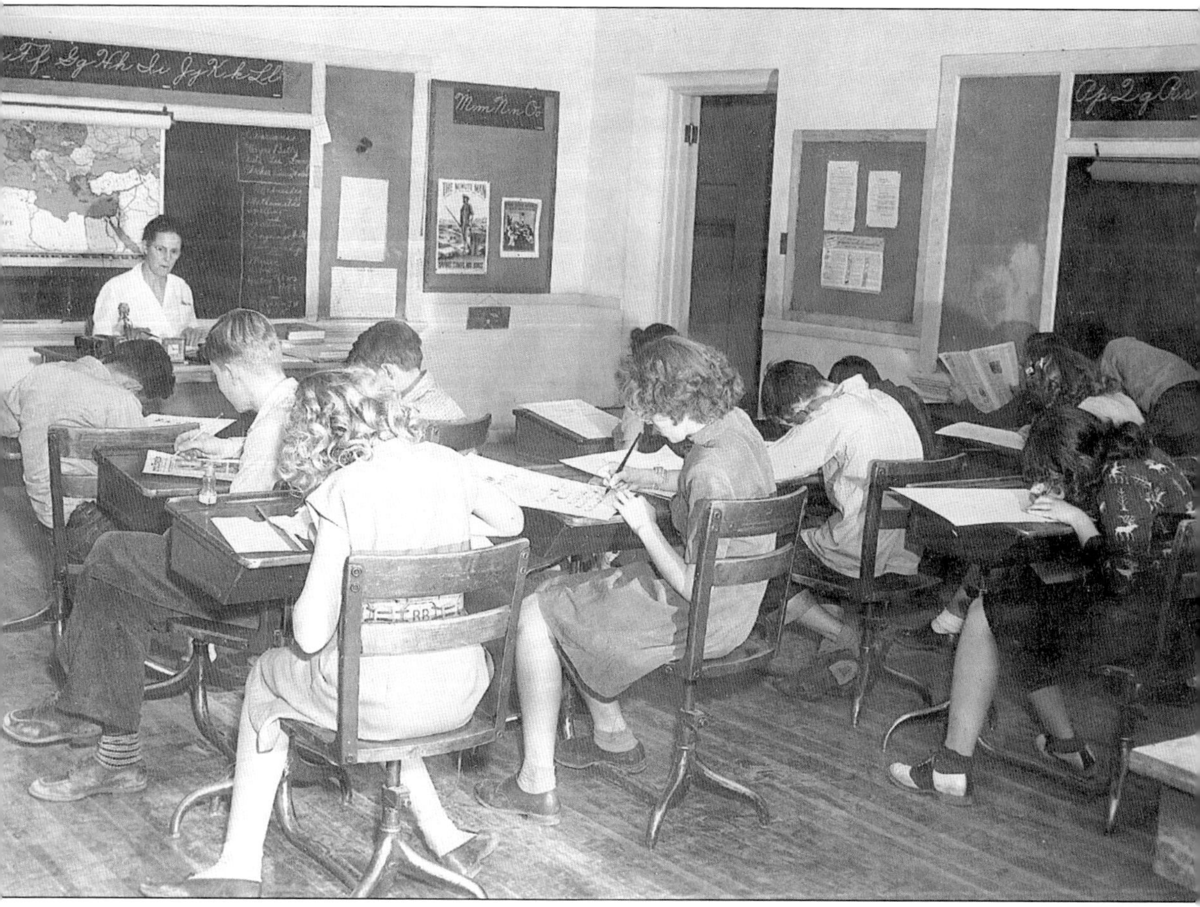

Students attend to their schoolwork in this 1960 photograph at Grand Canyon School. The first school within the Grand Canyon began on July 10, 1911. The first schoolteacher at the school was Grace Miller. She taught William Bass's four children, as well as others. (Courtesy of the National Park Service.)

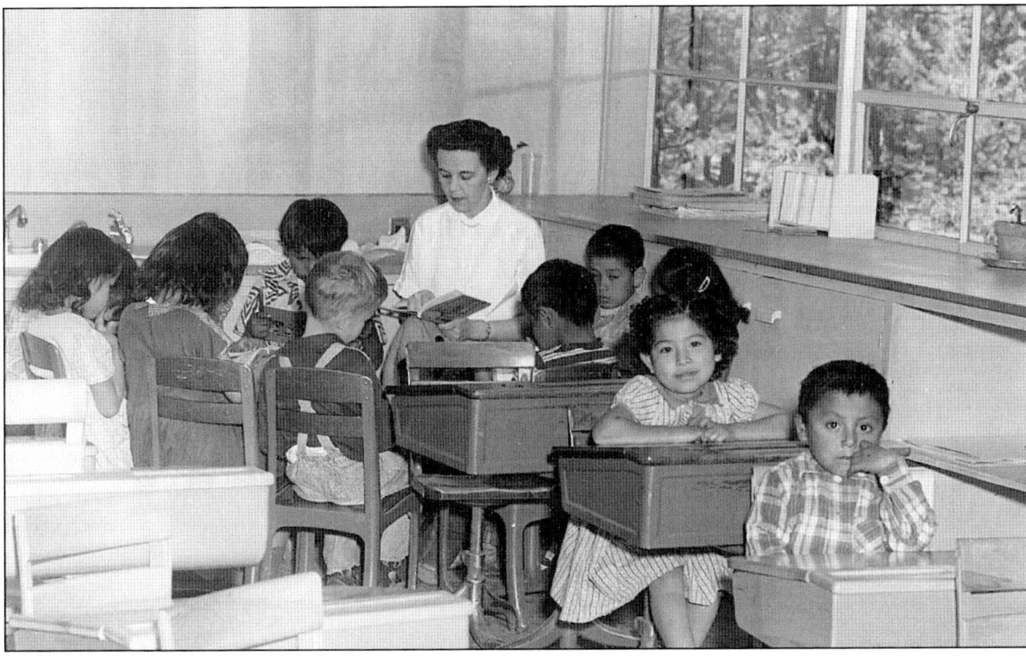

This February 1953 photograph shows Grand Canyon students hard at work in the first grade class. The students are seen in the school's newest addition to the Grand Canyon School at the time of the photograph. The first official school was completed on July 27, 1913. (Photograph by R. S. Leding; courtesy of the National Park Service.)

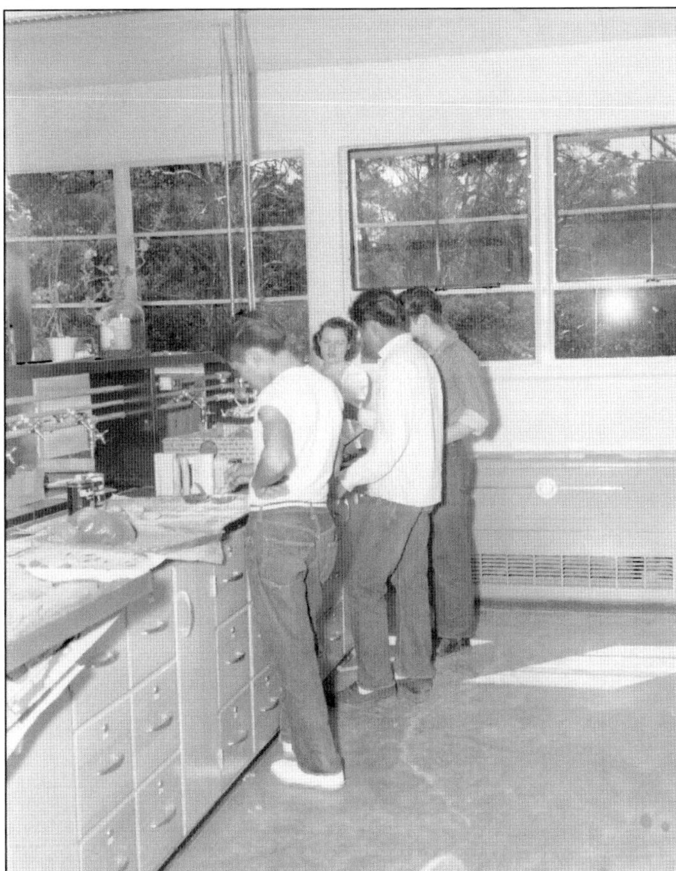

This 1959 photograph shows an interior view of the science classroom in the new Grand Canyon High School. Funding for the canyon's original school was provided by William W. Bass, who resided in the Grand Canyon area. He also provided labor for the project, according to historical records. (Photograph by R. S. Leding; courtesy of the National Park Service.)

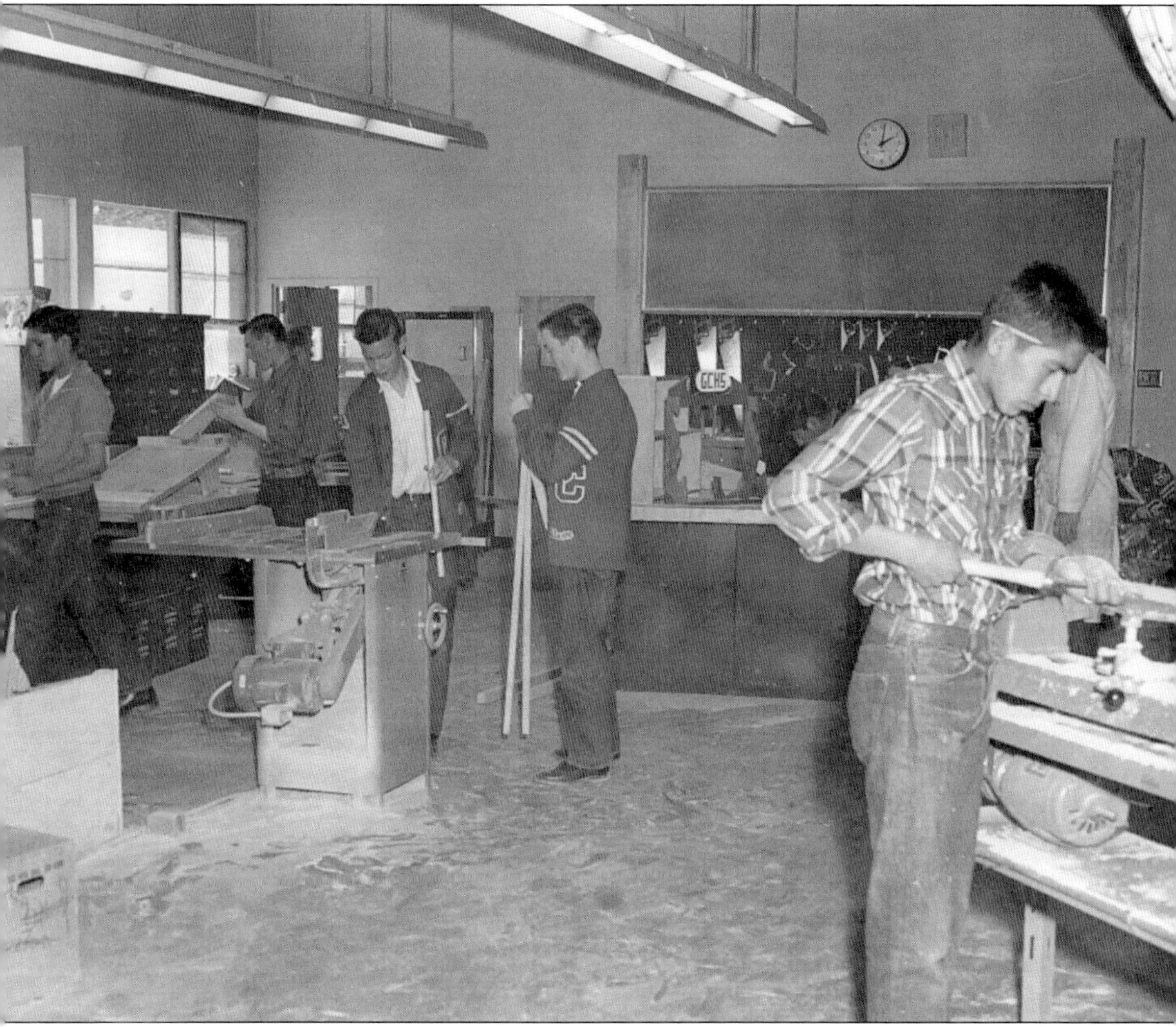

This 1959 photograph shows a number of students at work in Grand Canyon School's new shop. A parent-teacher organization was established at the Grand Canyon School in 1920 to help improve and develop the educational opportunities for students at the school. (Photograph by R. S. Leding; courtesy of the National Park Service.)

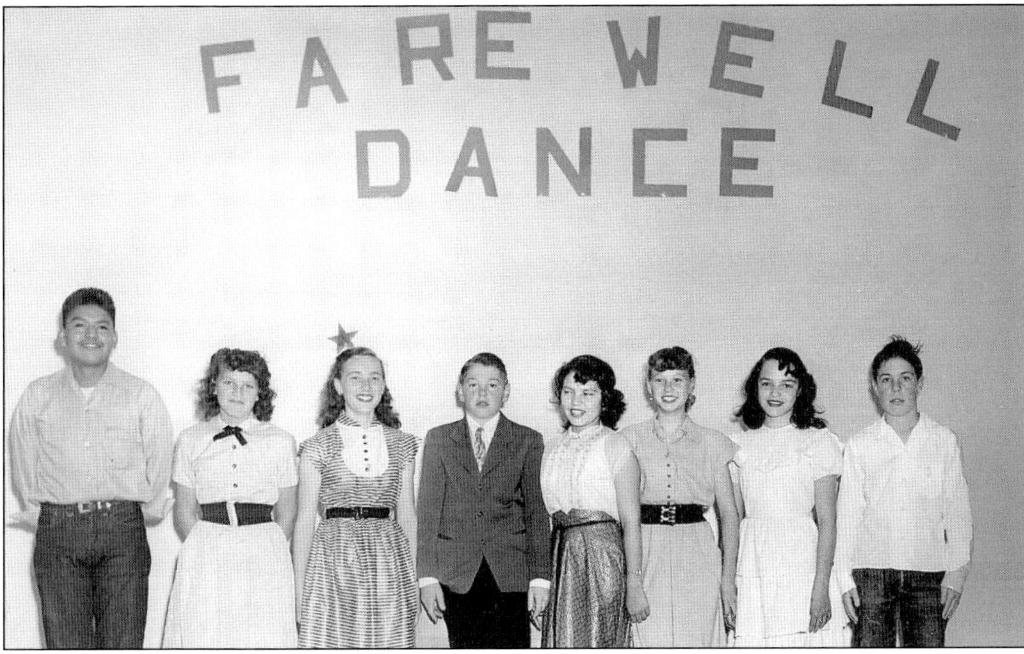

When it comes to the excitement of graduation and associated parties, young students at the Grand Canyon were no exception. In this May 28, 1953, photograph, a handful of eighth grade students show their enthusiasm during a party and dance, held as part of the graduation ceremonies. (Photograph by R. S. Leding; courtesy of the National Park Service.)

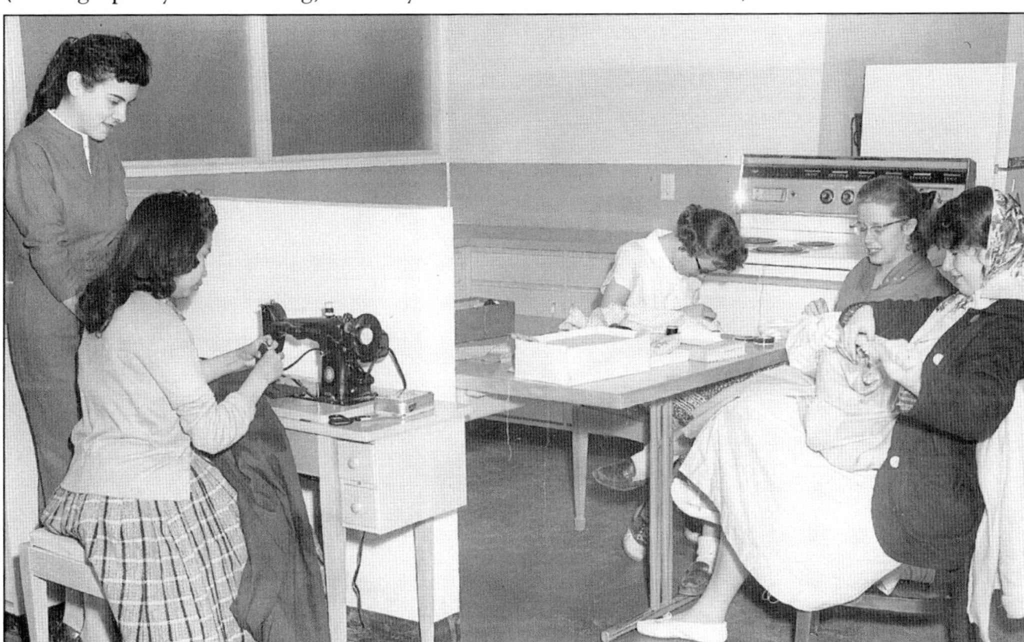

The Grand Canyon School's home economics classroom, part of the new Grand Canyon High School, provided a fresh educational atmosphere for pupils in this 1959 photograph. A number of groups, including park officials and congressmen, helped secure funds for the school over the years. (Photograph by R. S. Leding; courtesy of the National Park Service.)

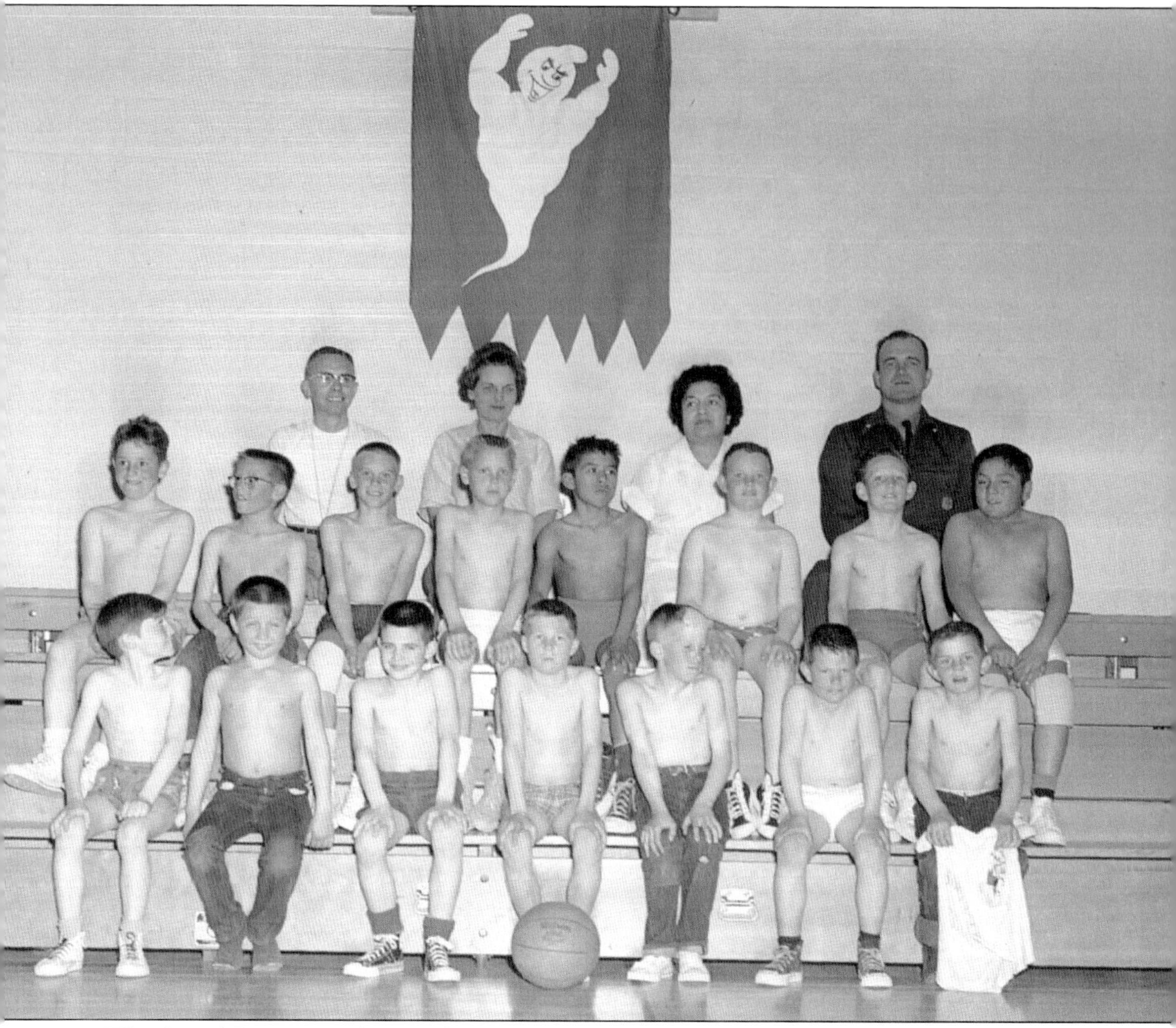

The Grand Canyon's Cub Scout basketball team, comprised of students from the Tusayan, Grand Canyon area, can be seen in this March 7, 1960, photograph. Others in the photograph include scoutmaster Robert Heyder, Mrs. John McLaughlin, and school counselors Elizabeth Arkie and Jack Settles. (Photograph by R. S. Leding; courtesy of the National Park Service.)

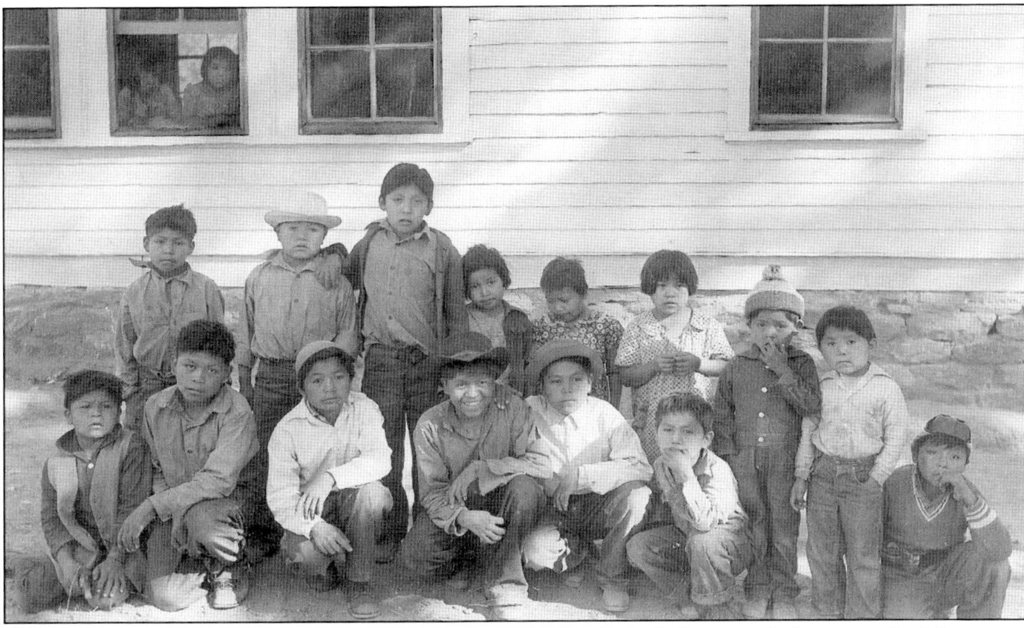

Another school in the area, this one located inside the Grand Canyon, belongs to the Havasupai tribe. A gathering of 15 students pose outside of the school in this November, 1938, photograph. The Havasupai Indian reservation was designated in 1882 for 593 acres. The designation confined the nomadic tribe within the Grand Canyon. That changed in 1975, however, when the U.S. government reallocated 185,000 acres to the Havasupai people. Besides homes located in the tribe's capital city of Supai, the city also offers a number of other amenities. Besides the school, a café, a general store, a tourist office, a post office, two churches, and more can be found within the Grand Canyon at Supai. (Courtesy of the National Park Service.)

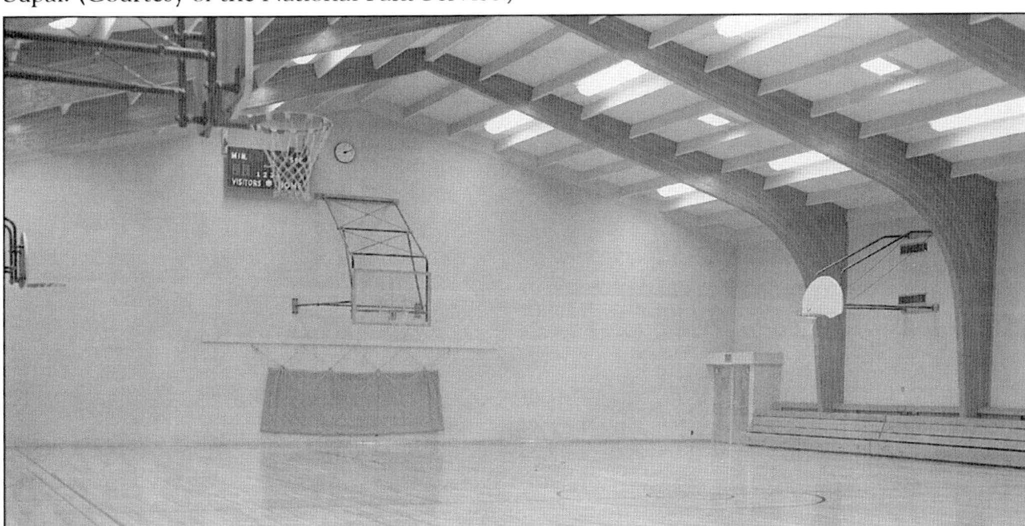

This June 1958 photograph shows the Grand Canyon High School's gymnasium following the completion of construction on the project. Portions of the gymnasium's roof were constructed by prefabricated lumber material. The official name for the Grand Canyon's sports team is the Grand Canyon Phantoms. The girls' team is called the Lady Phantoms. (Photograph by R. S. Leding; courtesy of the National Park Service.)

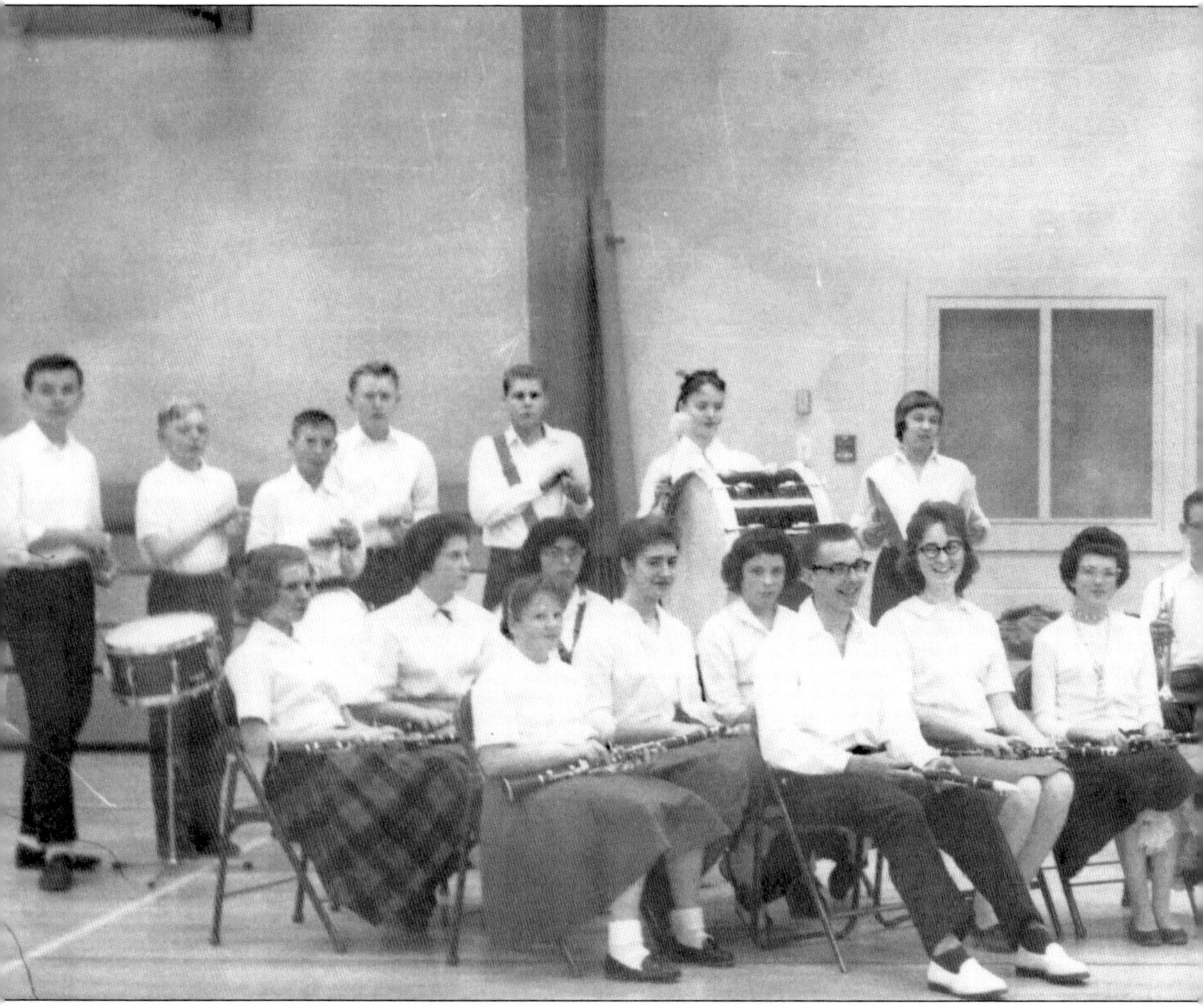

This 1959 photograph shows a number of Grand Canyon High School's band members during a recital. The school's band included nearly all of the school's students, as the band program was very active at that time. The program was made possible due to the efforts of teacher Ingrid Neilson.

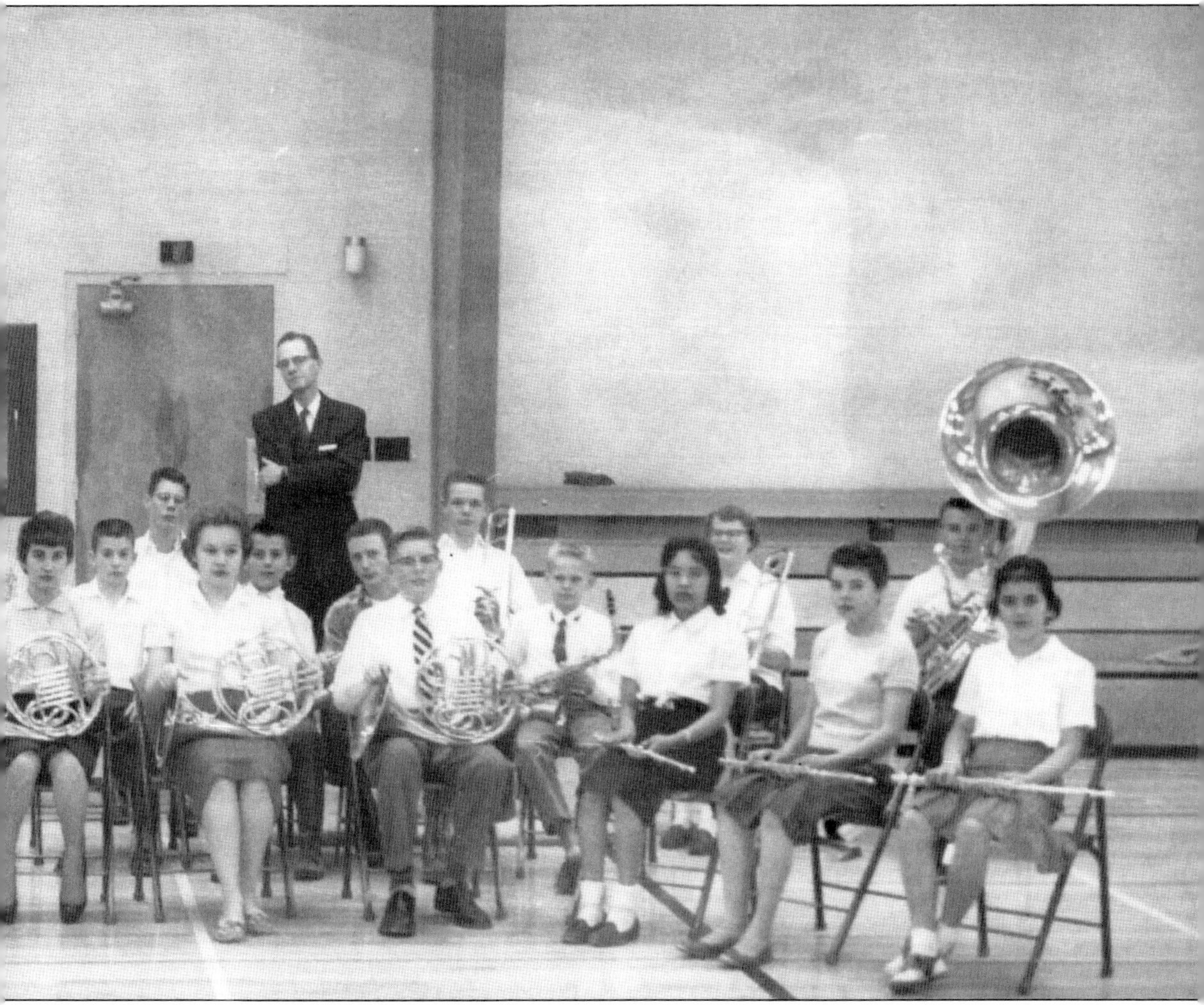

During the late 1950s and 1960s, teachers wore a number of hats at the small school. That period also saw the arrival of actors with the popular *Lassie* television program, who filmed a portion of the program at the South Rim. (Courtesy of Betty Bartlett.)

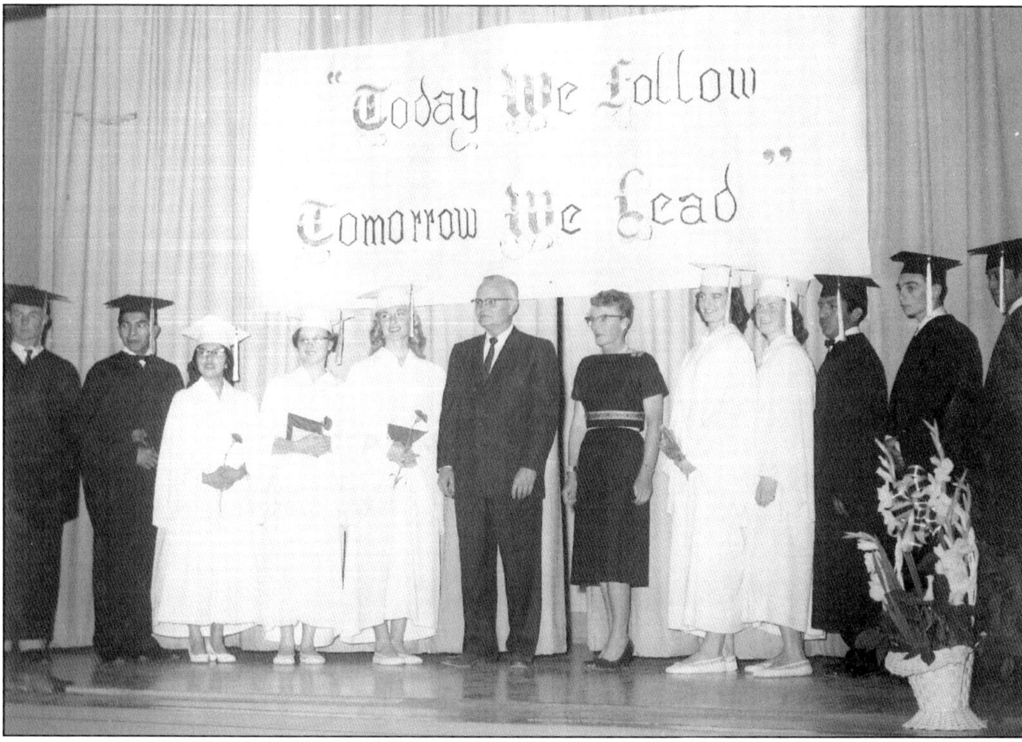

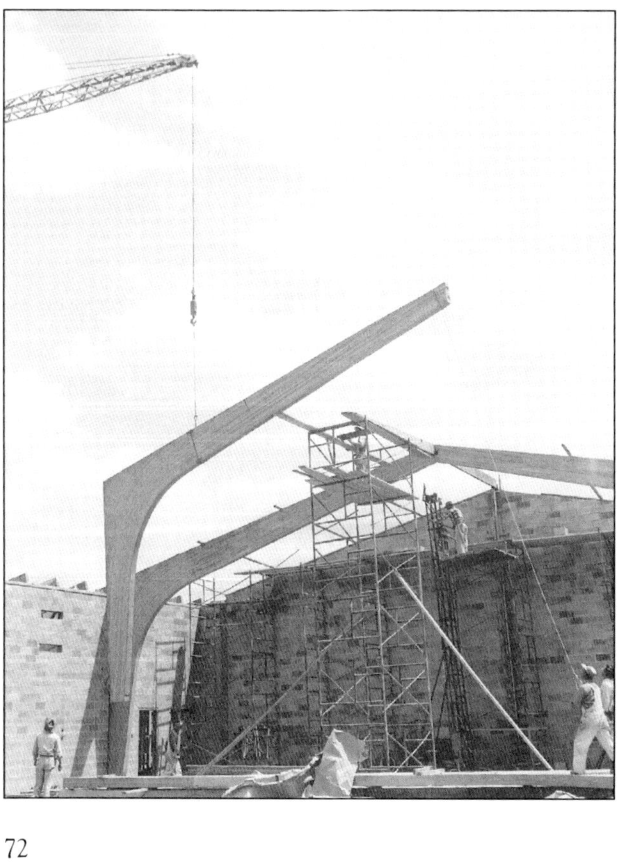

This photograph from Grand Canyon School shows all the happy seniors who made up the graduating class of 1958. School superintendent Carl Guthrie and Grand Canyon School Board member Peggy Verkamp performed the honors during the illustrious ceremony. A sign above the group reads, 'Today we follow, tomorrow we lead.' (Courtesy of Betty Bartlett.)

Construction on the Grand Canyon High School gymnasium continued through May 7, 1958. The arches in the gymnasium were constructed by layers of wood laminate. Each arch was fireproofed prior to being installed and was preassembled prior to being sent to construction crews at the school. (Photograph by R. S. Leding; courtesy of the National Park Service.)

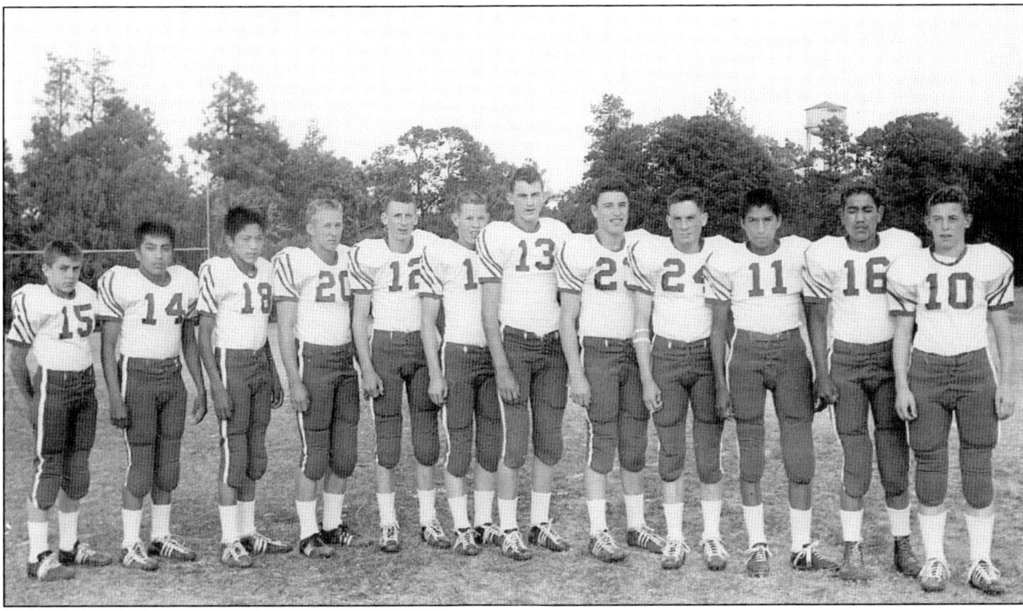

Players on the Grand Canyon High School Phantoms football team are pictured as they appeared on October 10 during the team's 1961 season. During the school's earlier years, the playground also served as a small athletic field. According to historical records, "over the fence is out" was the common rule for baseball games. (Courtesy of the National Park Service.)

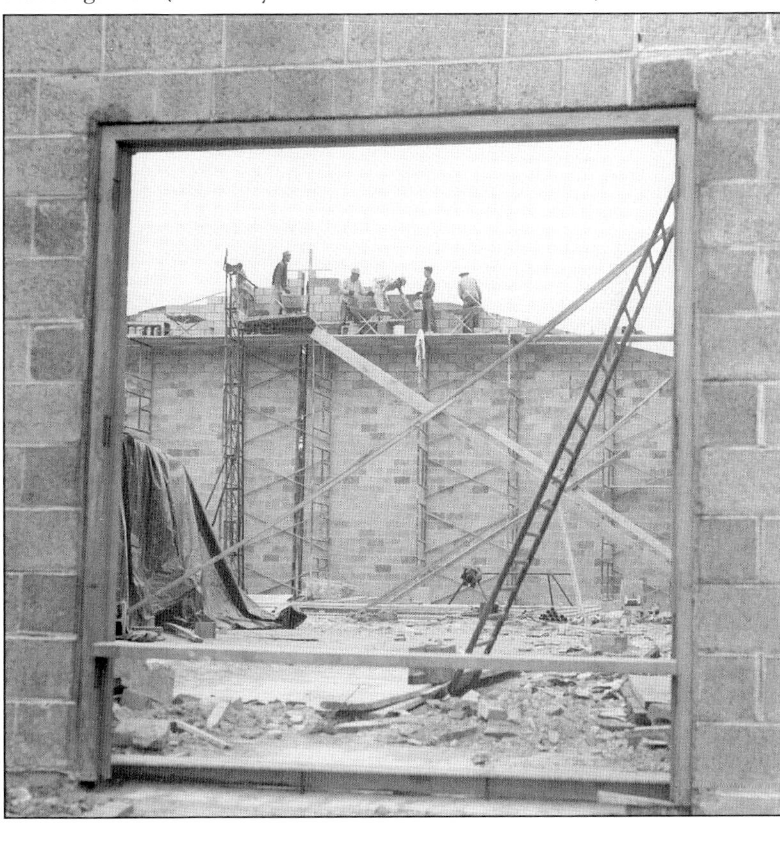

Workmen can be seen through the nearly completed front entryway to the Grand Canyon High School's new gymnasium in 1958. In this photograph, crews of construction workers install cinderblocks on the south wall of the high school gym. (Photograph by R. S. Leding; courtesy of the National Park Service.)

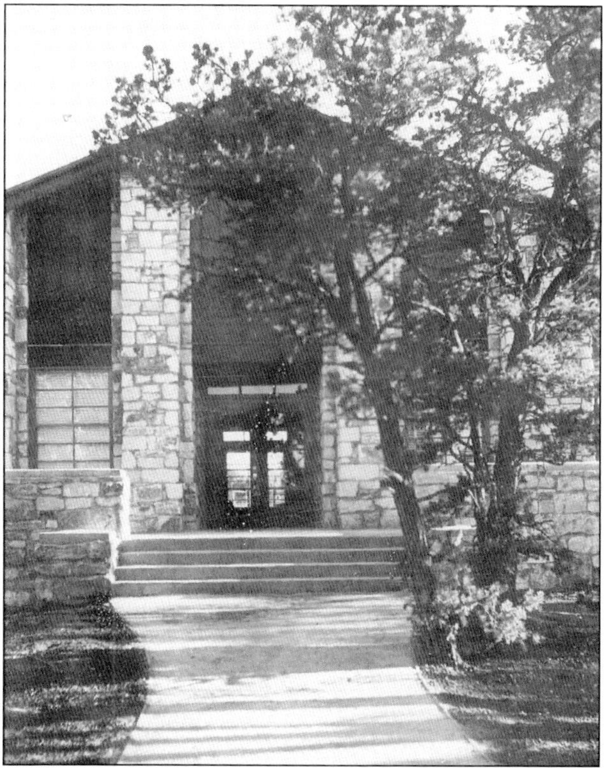

Here is the front entrance to the Grand Canyon School as it appears today. Known by National Park Service officials as building number 227, the school often plays host to more than just students, staff, and parents. Deer, elk, and other wildlife can often be seeing lounging on the school's wooded property. (Courtesy of the National Park Service.)

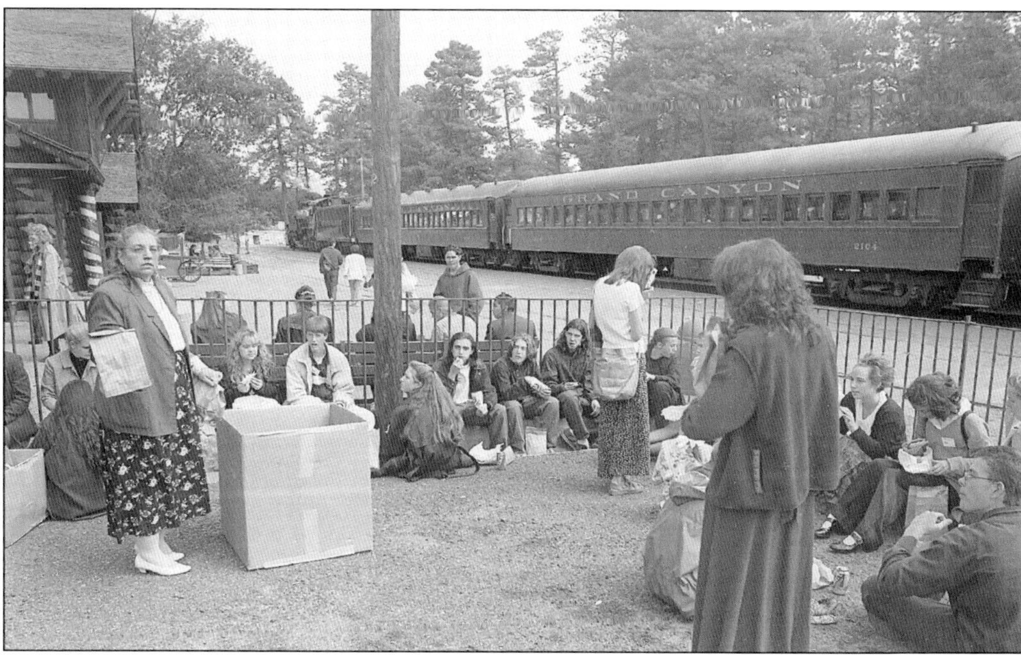

Northern Arizona students enjoy a sack lunch at the Grand Canyon Railway's South Rim depot following a speech by Pres. Bill Clinton on September 18, 1996. Schools from all over the state often visit the area to see the South Rim's Grand Canyon Village. (Photograph by Mike Quinn; courtesy of the National Park Service.)

Six

Grand Canyon Cemetery

As one of only a few national parks to have its own cemetery, the Grand Canyon Cemetery is home to some of the area's most notable and influential people. Buried within the property are the Kolb brothers, John Hance, and many other Grand Canyon notables. Famed geologist Edward McKee is also buried there, as are Fred Harvey girls and members of the Civilian Conservation Corps. While not established as a cemetery until 1924, a number of graves were recorded as early as 1919, with the death of John Hance. A number of early Grand Canyon area pioneers were also buried at the site, which is also known as the Grand Canyon Pioneer Cemetery.

Hance, who worked for the Hull brothers at their sheep ranch, was also quite well known in and around the South Rim area. Having tried his hand at mining in the area, Hance went on to become a sort of tourist attraction to those visiting the national park. Officials at the Fred Harvey Company hired the man, known for his tall tales, to entertain guests at the El Tovar. As a nod to his ability for storytelling, Hance's grave is a long one, indicating the man was as tall as his tales. Hance was also known as being a personal guide to Pres. Teddy Roosevelt.

Interest in Grand Canyon burials grew over the years, leading park officials no choice but to consolidate into one area. They officially established the Grand Canyon Cemetery in 1924. Rules for burial were also established. One of the biggest of which is that anyone who is buried at the Grand Canyon Cemetery has to have lived in the national park for three years. Those three years, however, do not have to be consecutive. There are currently around 250 people buried within the cemetery. On average, four people are buried there each year.

A memorial can also be found at the cemetery honoring those who lost their lives in a plane crash over the canyon in 1956. Over 128 died in the crash. Wreckage from the disaster can still be found in the area of the national park now known as Crash Canyon.

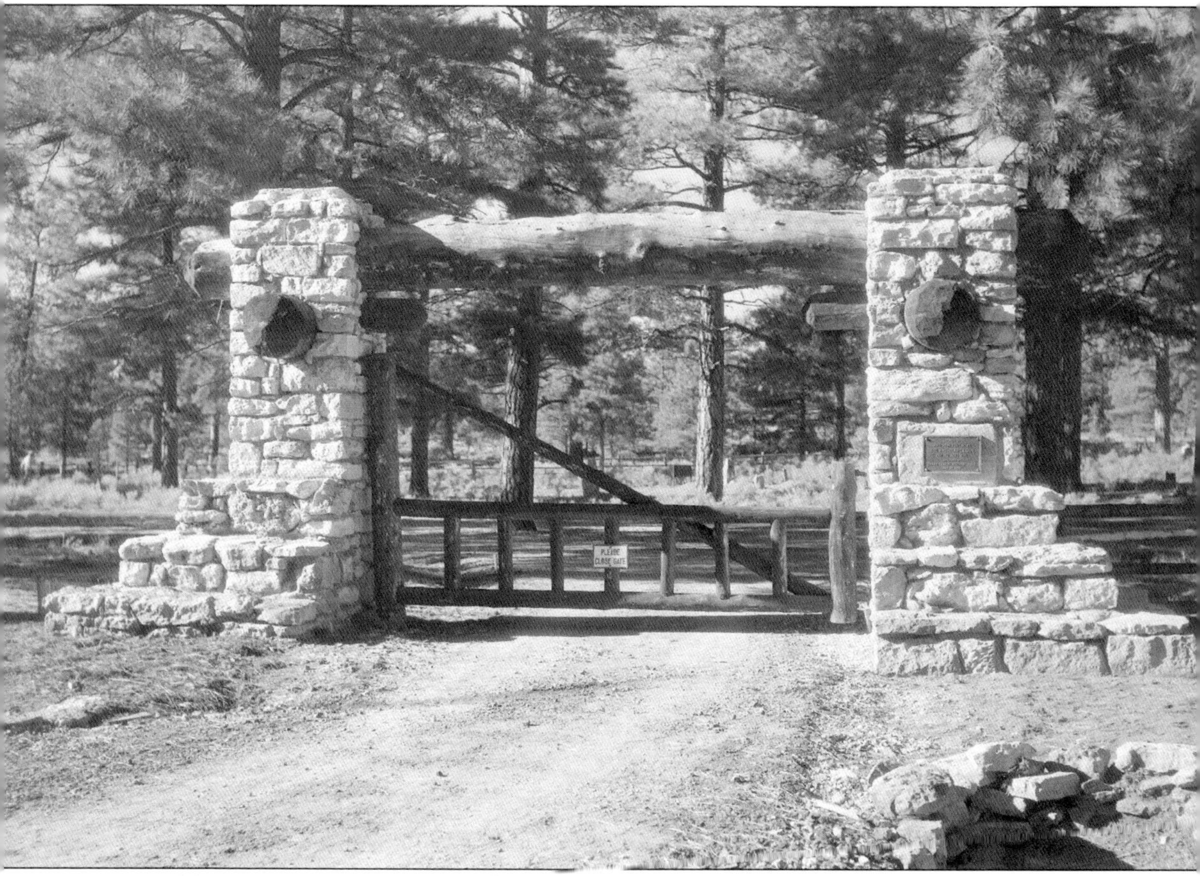

Part of the fence that surrounds the Grand Canyon Cemetery is visible in this December 22, 1936, photograph of the gated-arch entrance to the cemetery. A number of Grand Canyon notables can be found buried within the grounds. (Courtesy of the National Park Service.)

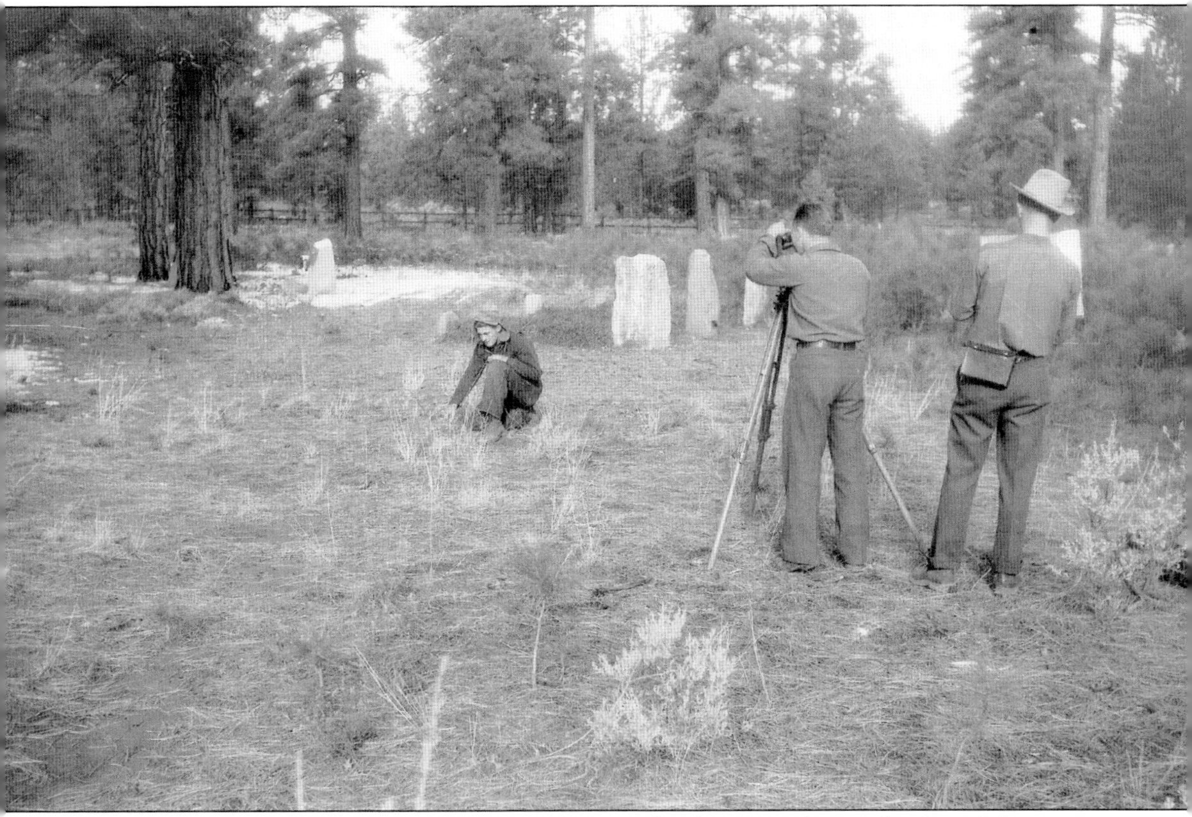

Crews with the Civilian Conservation Corps survey and stake grave plots at the Grand Canyon Cemetery on December 15, 1937. A number of people have expressed interest in being buried at the cemetery over the years, leading cemetery officials to develop rules for the site. (Courtesy of the National Park Service.)

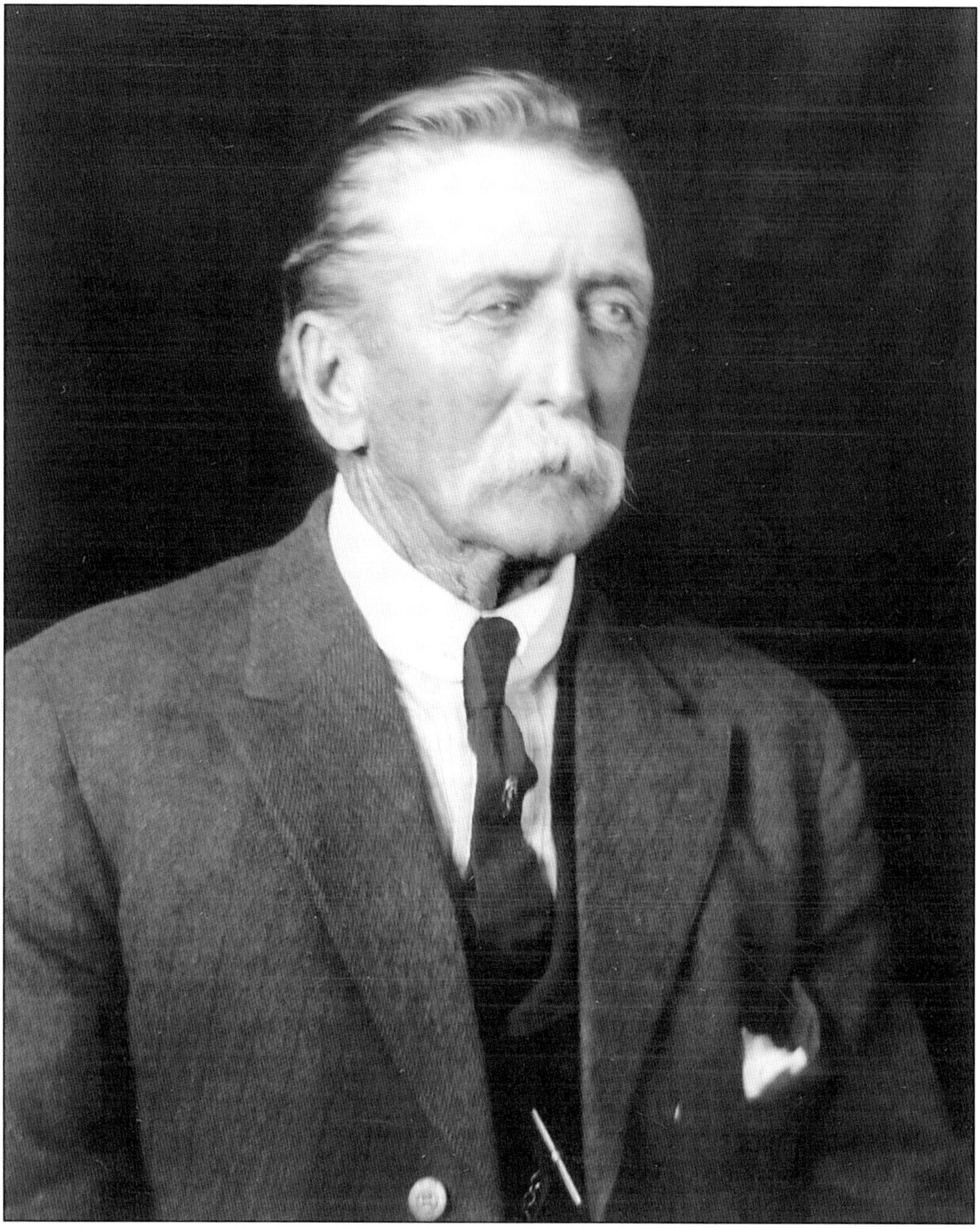

A well-known face at the Grand Canyon, John Hance is pictured here in 1918 at the age of 80. Besides being a ranch hand and miner, Hance also became known as a guide in the area. He was hired by the Fred Harvey Company to entertain guests visiting the Grand Canyon area. (Courtesy of the National Park Service.)

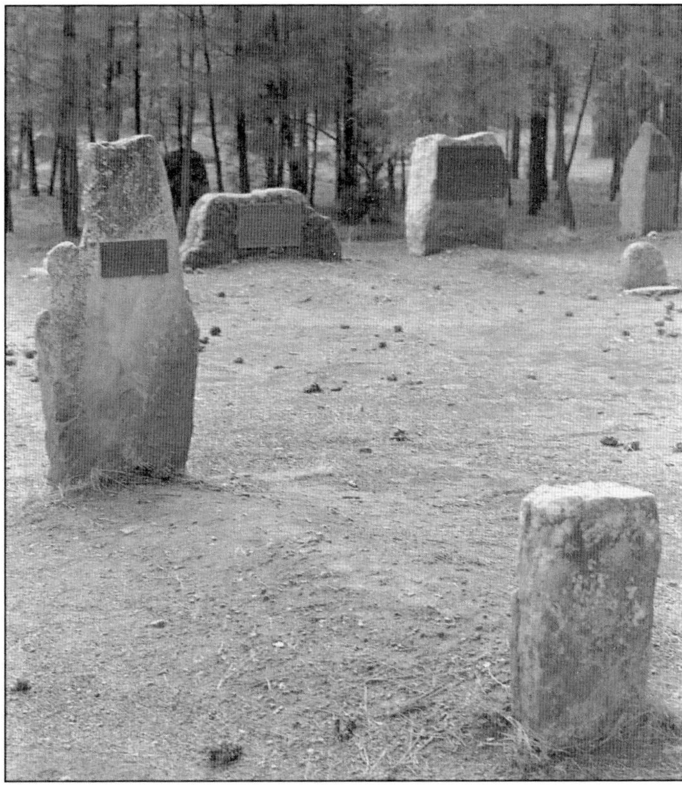

John Hance's striking tombstone, found at the Grand Canyon Pioneer Cemetery within the national park, illustrates the sense of humor that surrounded the man. His tombstone, and the shorter stone on the other end were designed as a nod to Hance's unerring knack for tall tales. (Courtesy of the National Park Service.)

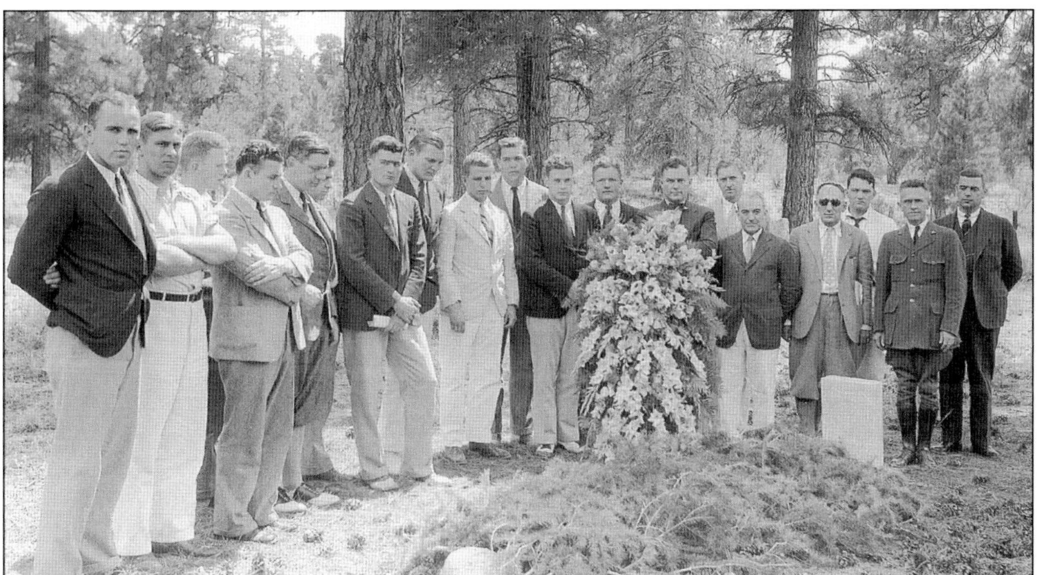

Members of the Yale, Harvard, and Princeton football teams visit the Grand Canyon Cemetery in this July 1932 photograph. The players stopped to pay tribute to Robert Bingham, who is buried at Grand Canyon. Bingham was a Grand Canyon Forest Reserve Ranger and a former player for the Yale football team. Those pictured were en route to the Los Angeles Olympic Games. (Courtesy of the National Park Service.)

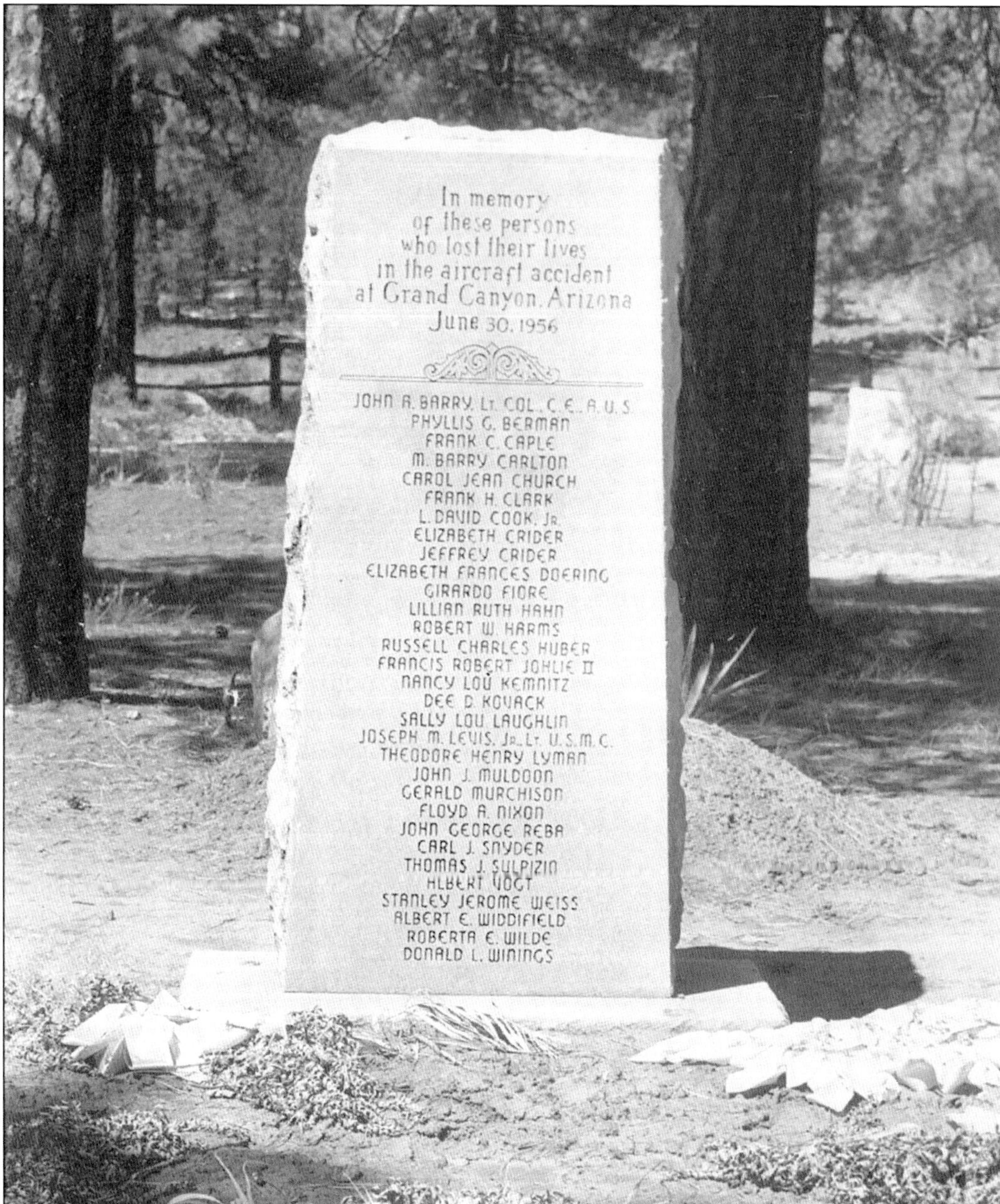

Pictured in this 1956 photograph is the United Airlines monument in the Grand Canyon Cemetery that commemorates those who lost their lives over the national park. Pieces of wreckage can still be found in portions of the Grand Canyon, particularly in an area that has come to be called "Crash Canyon" by those who hike inside the national park. (Photograph by R. S. Leding; Courtesy of the National Park Service.)

Seven

The Thurston Family Legacy

When it comes to modern-day Tusayan, there is nowhere better to begin than with R. P. "Bob" Thurston. His keen business sense is largely credited for developing the Tusayan visitors see today. The Thurston family had roots in the area dating back to the 1920s, but it wasn't until the 1940s that the family settled near the South Rim.

Known as a Williams rancher and businessman, R. P. Thurston was also involved in the northern Arizona community and served as a member of the Coconino County Board of Supervisors. He also served as mayor of Williams. He would often ranch his livestock in the Tusayan area. When the Ten-X Cattle Company opted to sell off portions of the Reed property, Thurston was one of the first in line. He bought roughly 160 acres of land. And when the state of Arizona decided to make much needed improvements to Highway 64 in 1951, Thurston took advantage of the construction project, designed to accommodate the high volume of car traffic at the national park. He offered the state of Arizona a right-of-way through his property, for a charge of $1. Within a couple of years, the new Highway 64 was completed. That new highway alignment changed the face of Tusayan from that day forward.

With the new highway now complete, the Thurston family soon began work on the Red Feather Lodge. Completed between 1963 and 1964, the lodge offered 40 rooms to weary canyon travelers. Thurston also built a service station on the opposite side of the highway, as well as a new Tusayan Bar. The service station was located near where the Trading Post is located today. The bar and restaurant was located where the McDonald's can be found today.

Thurston also helped develop the Grand Canyon Airport by allowing a portion of his land to be used for the airfield property. The new airport, built in the mid-1960s, soon led to a number of new ventures for Thurston, as a number of individuals leased or bought land from him in order to operate their own tourism business.

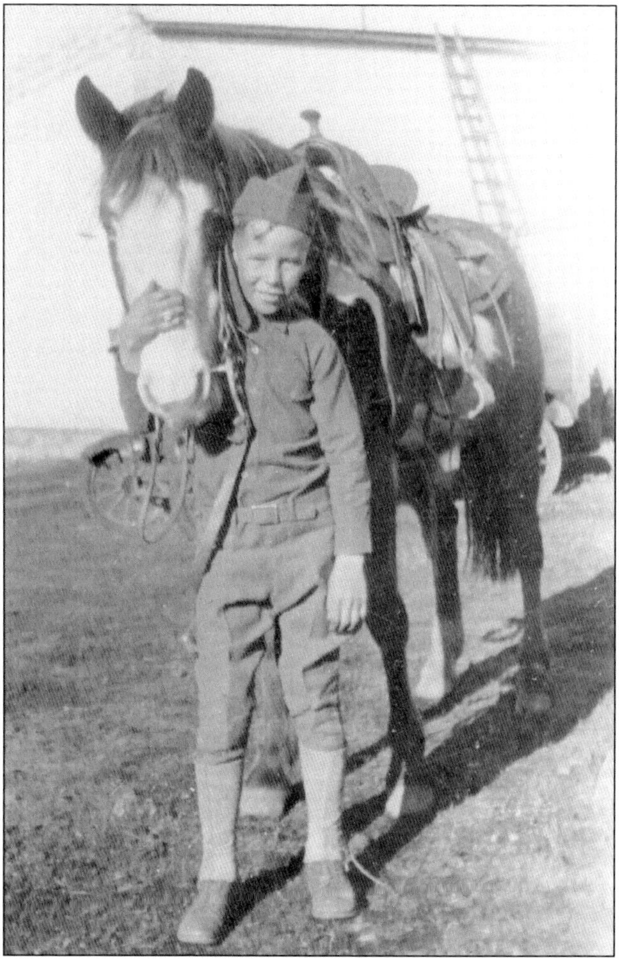

Leland (Bill) Thurston, R. P.'s son, is pictured here with his horse, Gingersnap. Thurston attended military school at a very young age. He is pictured in his uniform while home at the ranch. He attended high school in Williams, located a little over 50 miles from Tusayan. (Courtesy Clarinda Vail and the Thurston family.)

Horses and carriages were not uncommon in the early days of the Grand Canyon and the nearby village of Tusayan. This horse and carriage operated from the Grandview Hotel. Travelers were carried to their destinations via carriages. In the 1920s, when this photograph was taken, R. P. Thurston already had roots in the area, though it would be another 15 years before the family settled there. (Courtesy of Clarinda Vail and the Thurston family.)

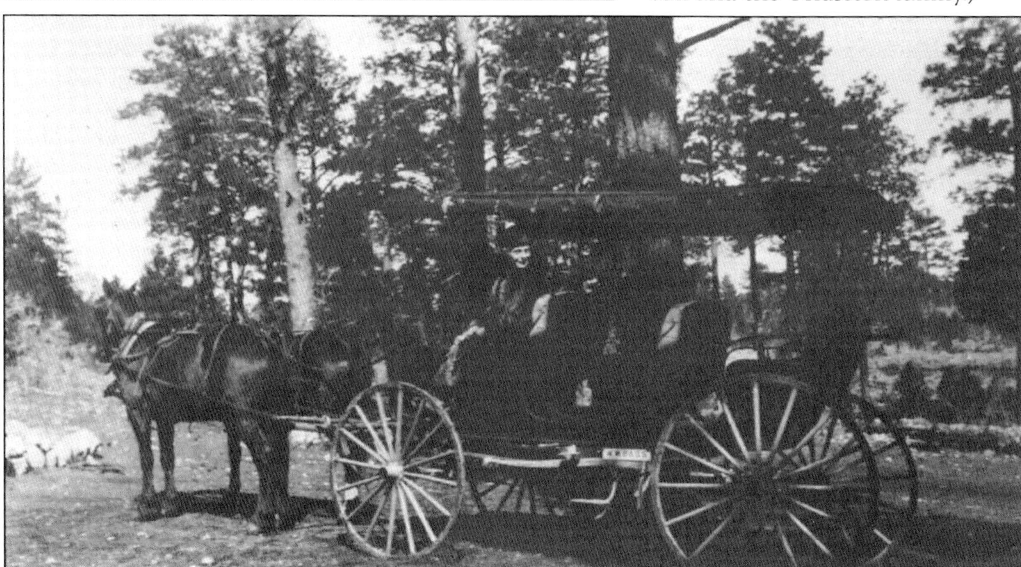

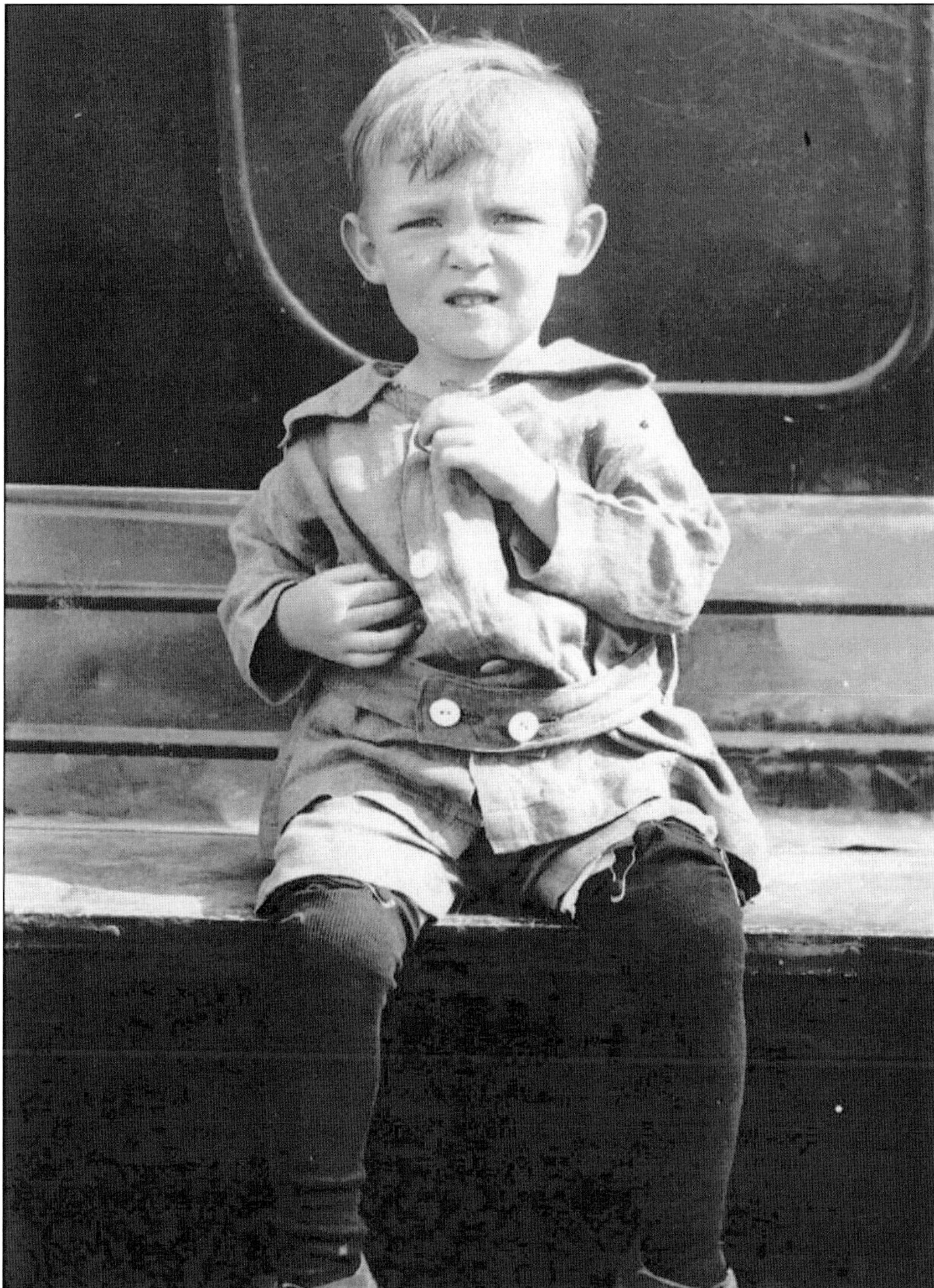

Bill Thurston can be seen here in his childhood years as he reclines on a wooden bench. The son of R. P. Thurston, Bill was born Leland Thurston in 1918. He passed away in 1988. Like his father, Bill also competed in various trick horse riding events. (Courtesy of Clarinda Vail and the Thurston family.)

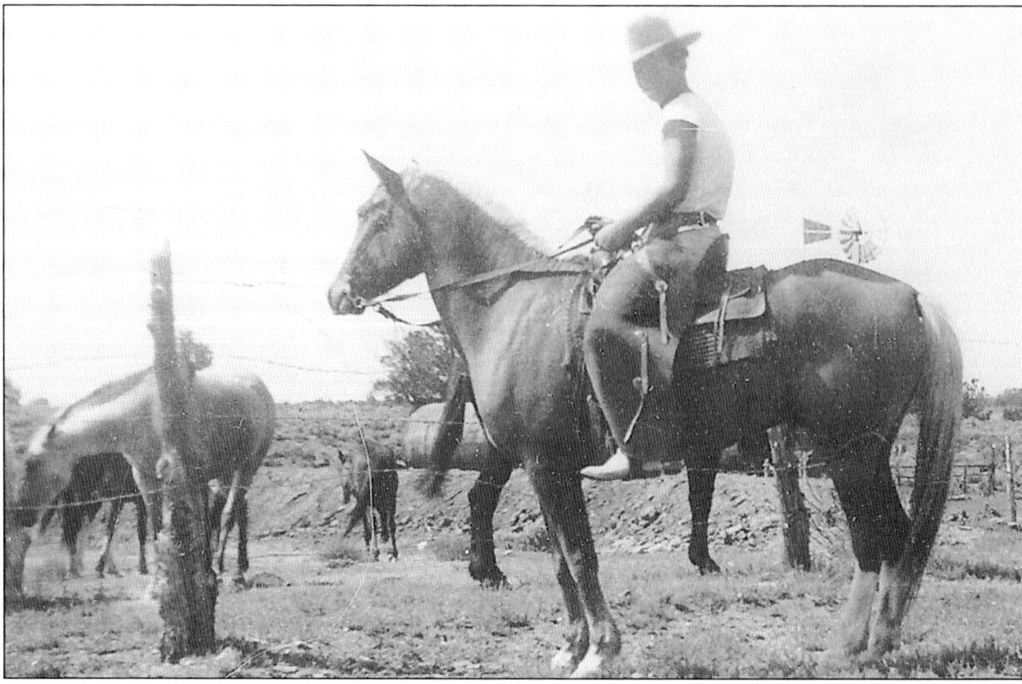

Pictured is Bill Thurston mounted on a horse at the Thurston family's Globe Ranch around the 1950s. The ranch, located near the Havasupai reservation, is identified on most maps as the Upper Wagner Ranch. R. P. Thurston originally owned the ranch, though it was later sold. The Thurston family eventually purchased the ranch back, however. (Courtesy of Clarinda Vail and the Thurston family.)

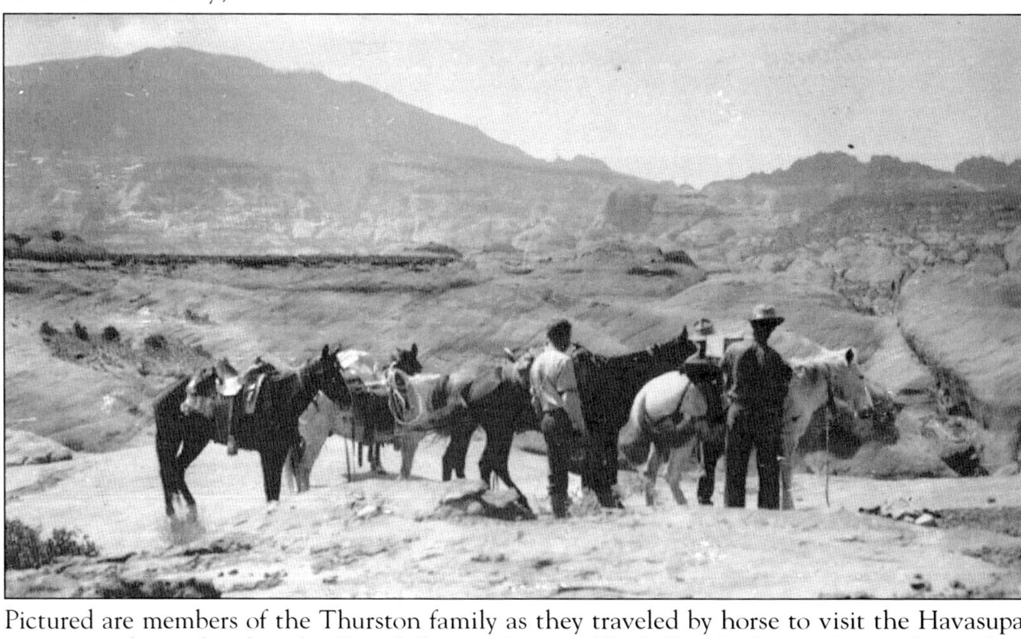

Pictured are members of the Thurston family as they traveled by horse to visit the Havasupai reservation located within the Grand Canyon National Park. Besides being close with members of the tribe, the Thurston family also owned a ranch near the reservation. (Courtesy of Clarinda Vail and the Thurston family.)

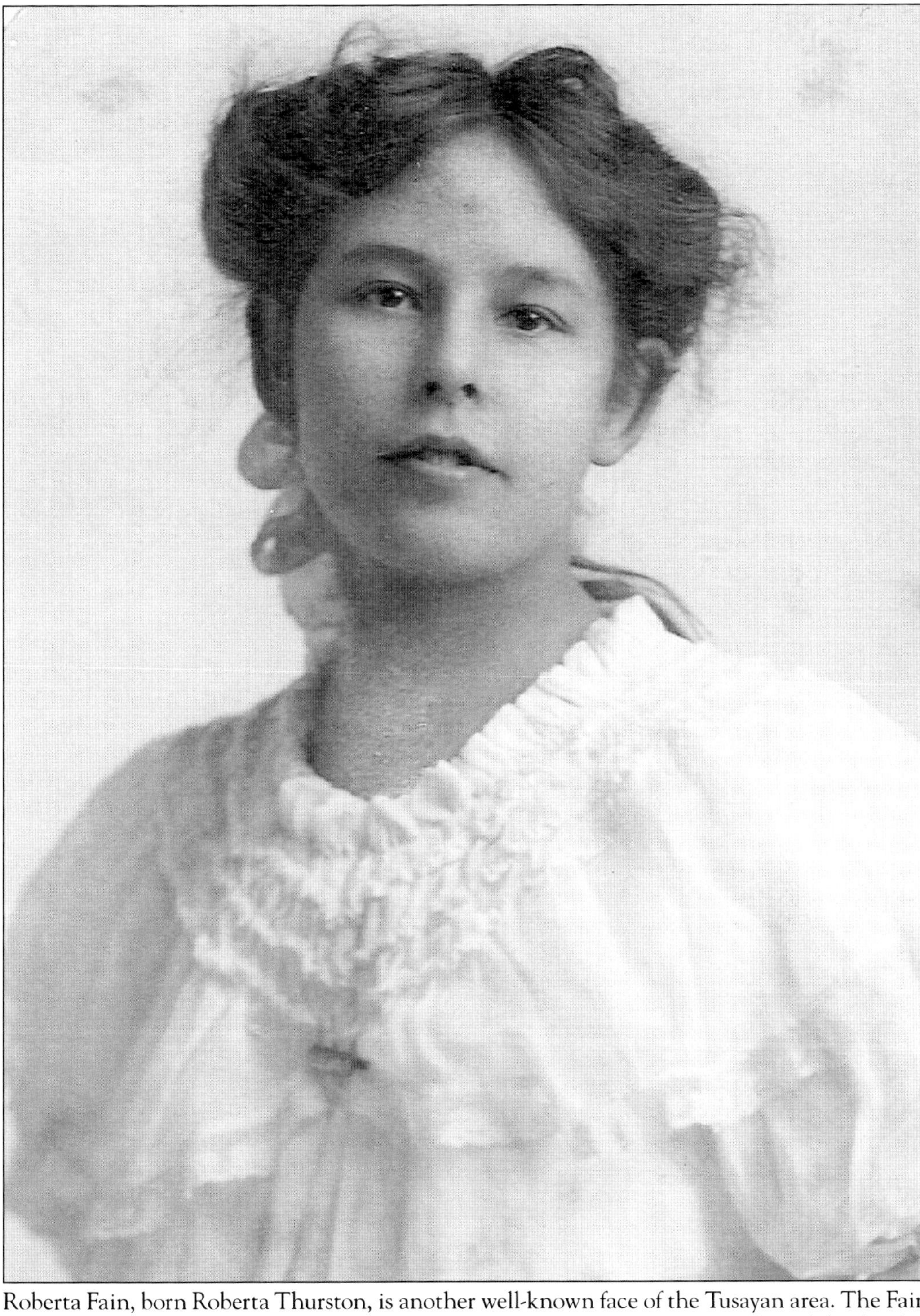

Roberta Fain, born Roberta Thurston, is another well-known face of the Tusayan area. The Fain family continues to play a part in the history of Tusayan to this day. A number of the family's descendants currently live in the Williams area, roughly 50 miles south of the Grand Canyon National Park. (Courtesy of Clarinda Vail and the Thurston family.)

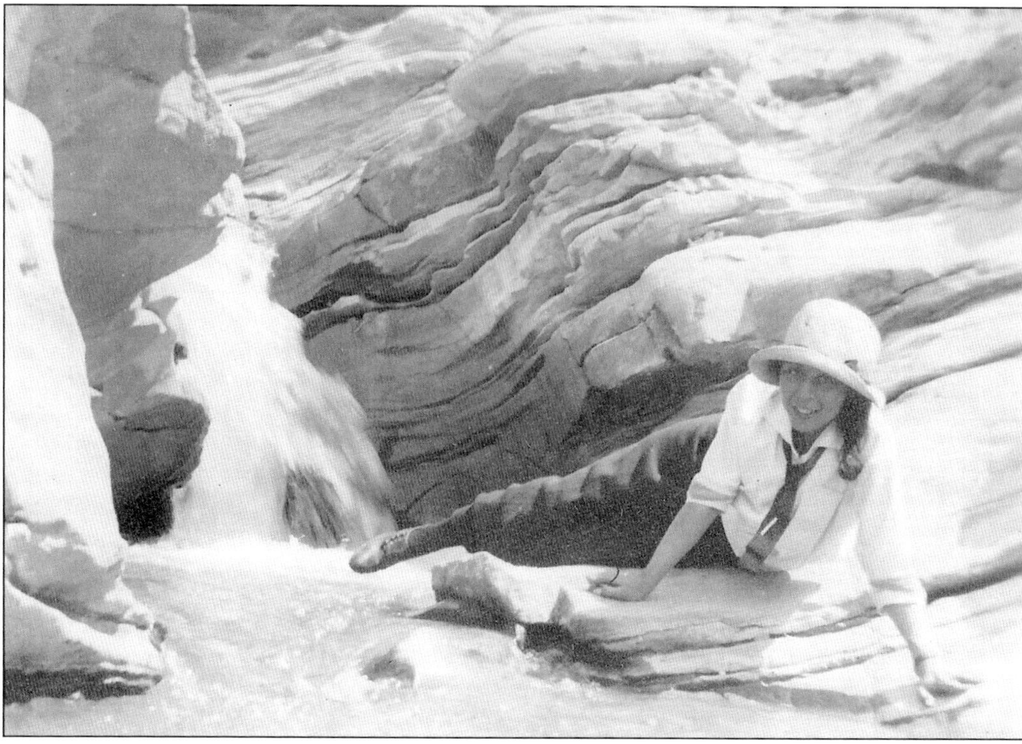

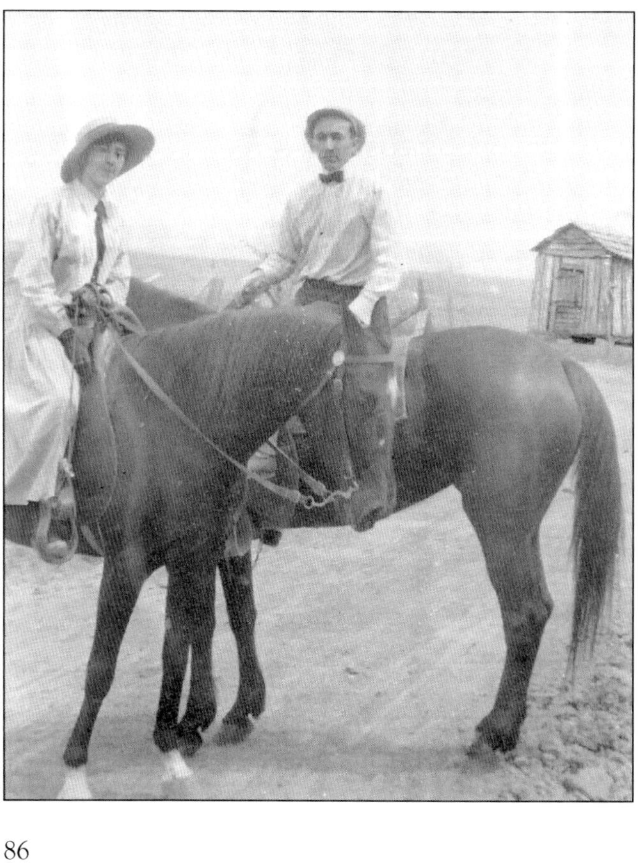

Bess Thurston, pictured near a waterfall somewhere at the South Rim, would often travel around Grand Canyon from horseback. She would often write to horseman associations in an effort to promote horseback travel to the Havasupai reservation and other points in the Grand Canyon National Park. (Courtesy of Clarinda Vail and the Thurston family.)

Two dapper riders pose for the camera in this photograph. Bess Thurston was fond of equestrian expeditions around the village of Tusayan and throughout the South Rim area, and she would often organize expeditions by horseback with friends and members of equestrian clubs. (Courtesy of Clarinda Vail and the Thurston family.)

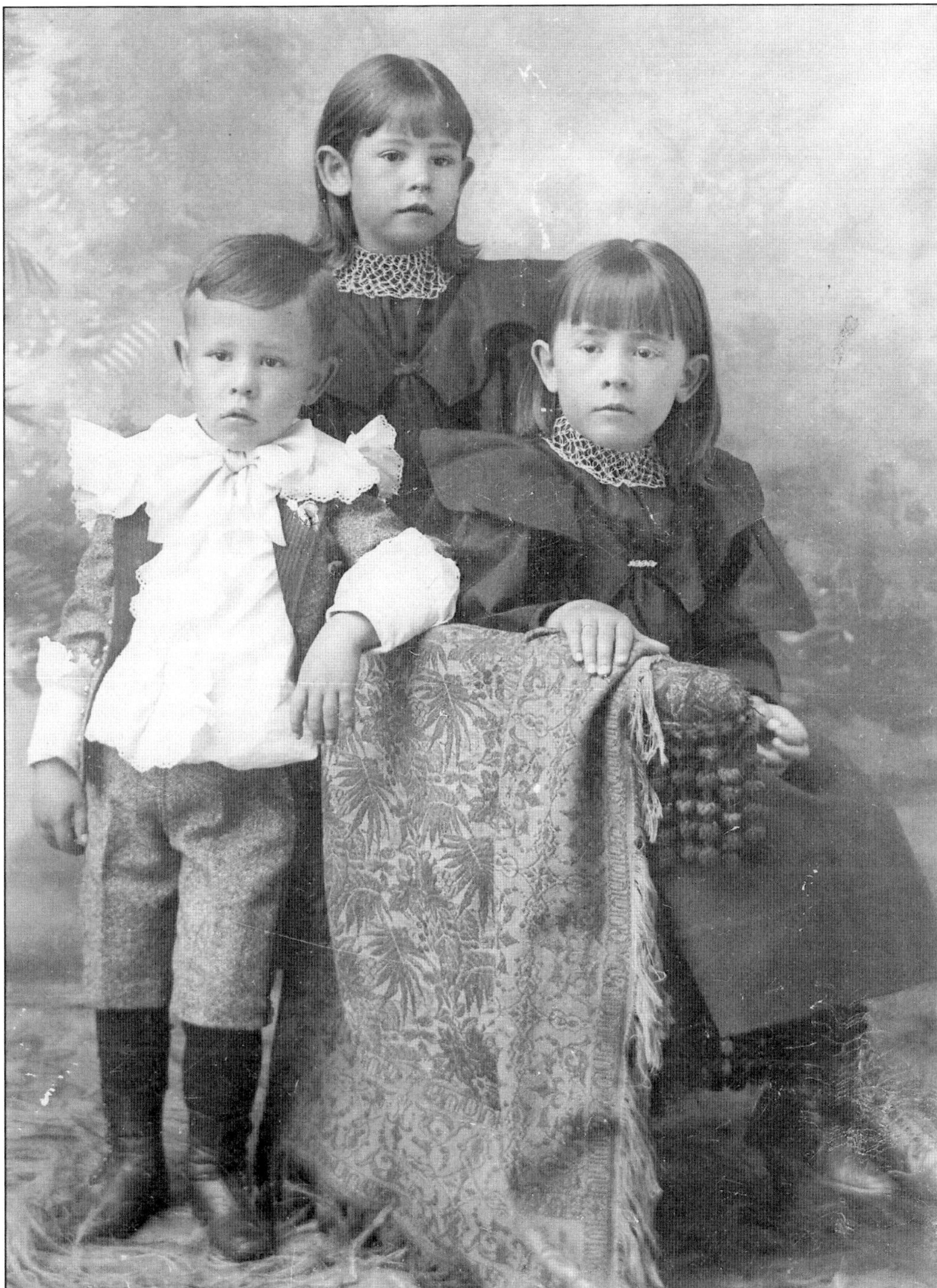

Three young members of the Fain family can be seen in this photograph taken around 1900. Members of the Fain family included Rise, Ted, Pamela, Bo, and Louis. The family, descended from Roberta Fain (Thurston), would often visit Bess Thurston at their Globe Ranch. (Courtesy of Clarinda Vail and the Thurston family.)

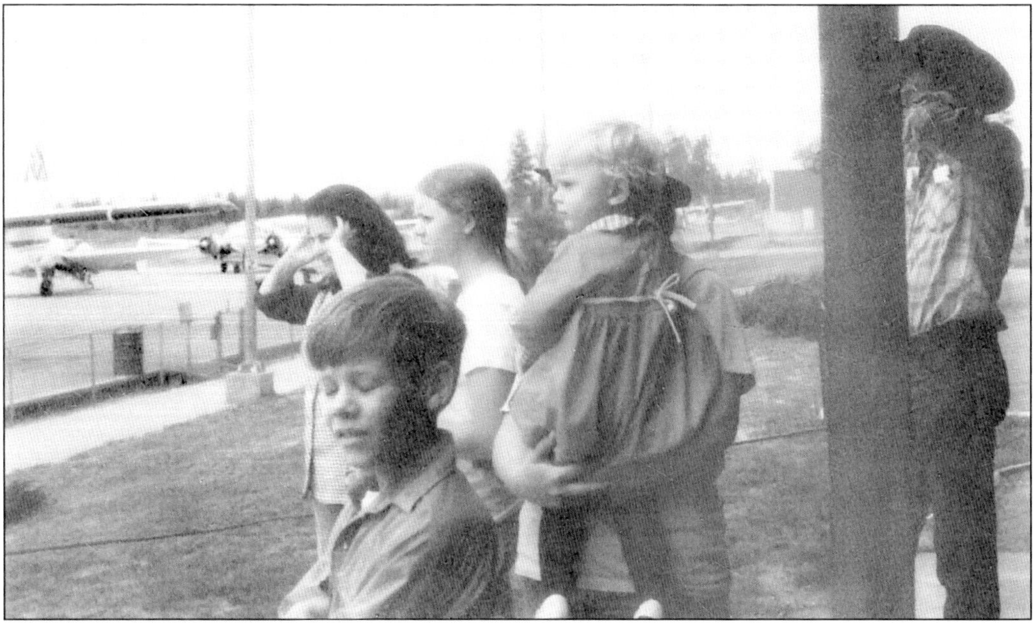

The Thurston family is pictured in the early 1970s while they watch a jet plane land at the Grand Canyon Airport. John Thurston is pictured in the front, while Clarinda Thurston (Vail) can be seen as she is held in the arms of a family member. The family would often visit the airport to watch interesting planes land. (Courtesy of Clarinda Vail and the Thurston family.)

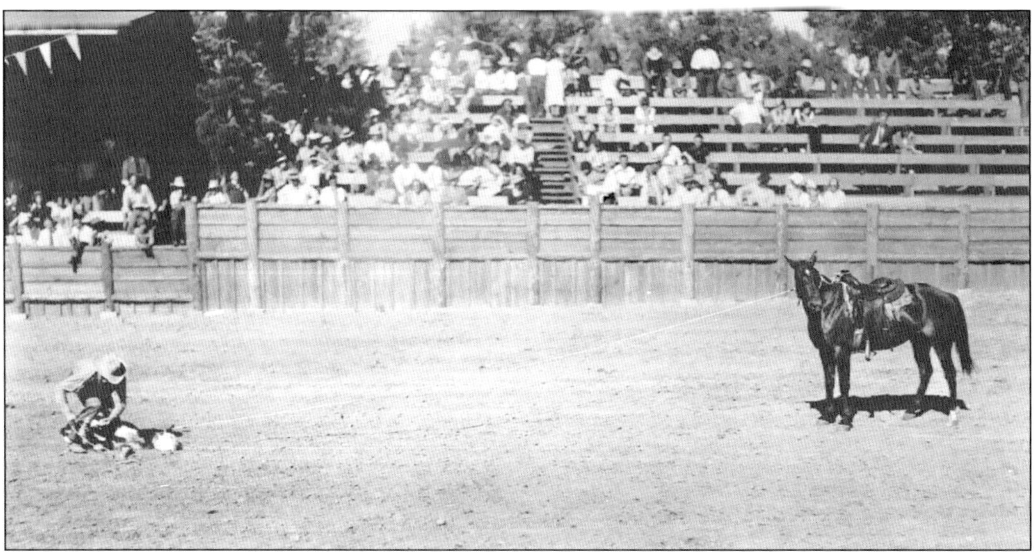

R. P. Thurston is pictured as he participates in a rodeo in northern Arizona before a crowd of fans. Thurston competed in team roping with his friend and attorney, Vern Gasser of Phoenix. The two competed together well into their senior years. (Courtesy of Clarinda Vail and the Thurston family.)

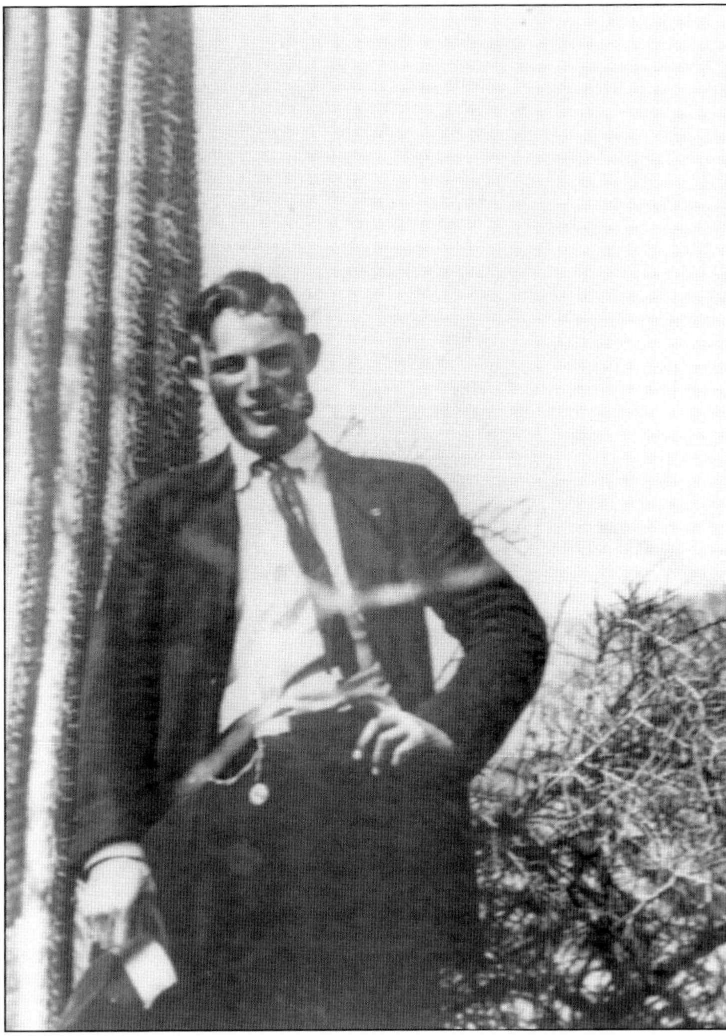

R. P. Thurston can be seen in this photograph as he relaxes in a leisurely fashion against a cactus. Thurston once owned land in what is now known as Laughlin in Nevada. He sold the land in the area for $1 an acre, according to family members, before making his move to northern Arizona. (Courtesy of Clarinda Vail and the Thurston family.)

This photograph shows the first gas station under construction in the Tusayan village area. The building was torn down in the 1970s. In 1972, when another service station was built across the street, the building was used as a repair shop for the many water trucks in the vicinity. (Courtesy Clarinda Vail and the Thurston family.)

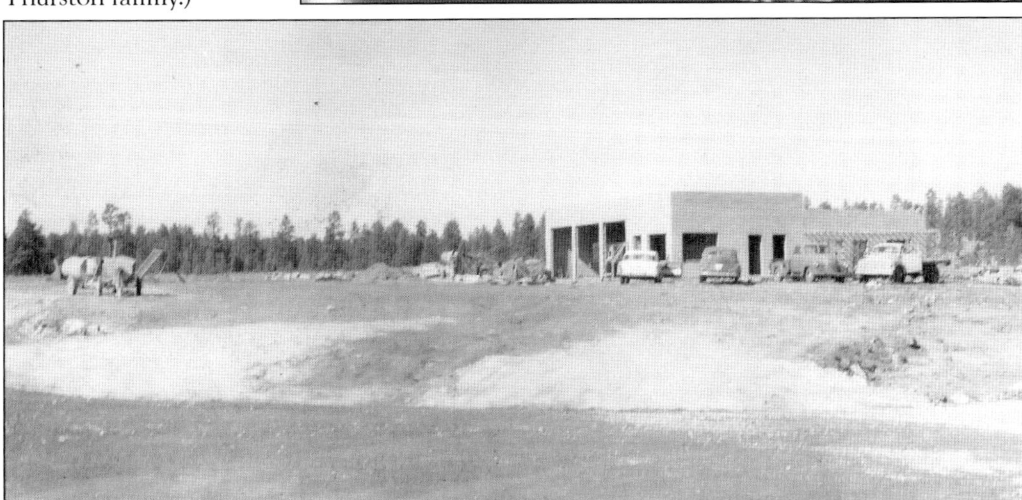

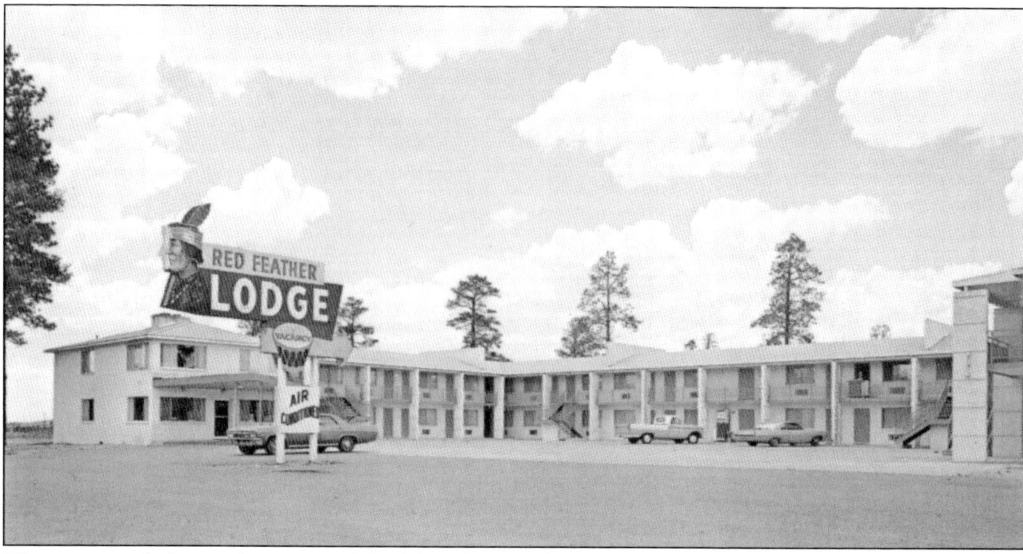

This postcard shows the original Red Feather Lodge in the late 1960s prior to renovations on the establishment. The lodge currently boasts over 200 rooms, an outdoor swimming pool, an onsite restaurant, and historical photographs from the Thurston family collection on the walls. (Courtesy of Clarinda Vail and the Thurston family.)

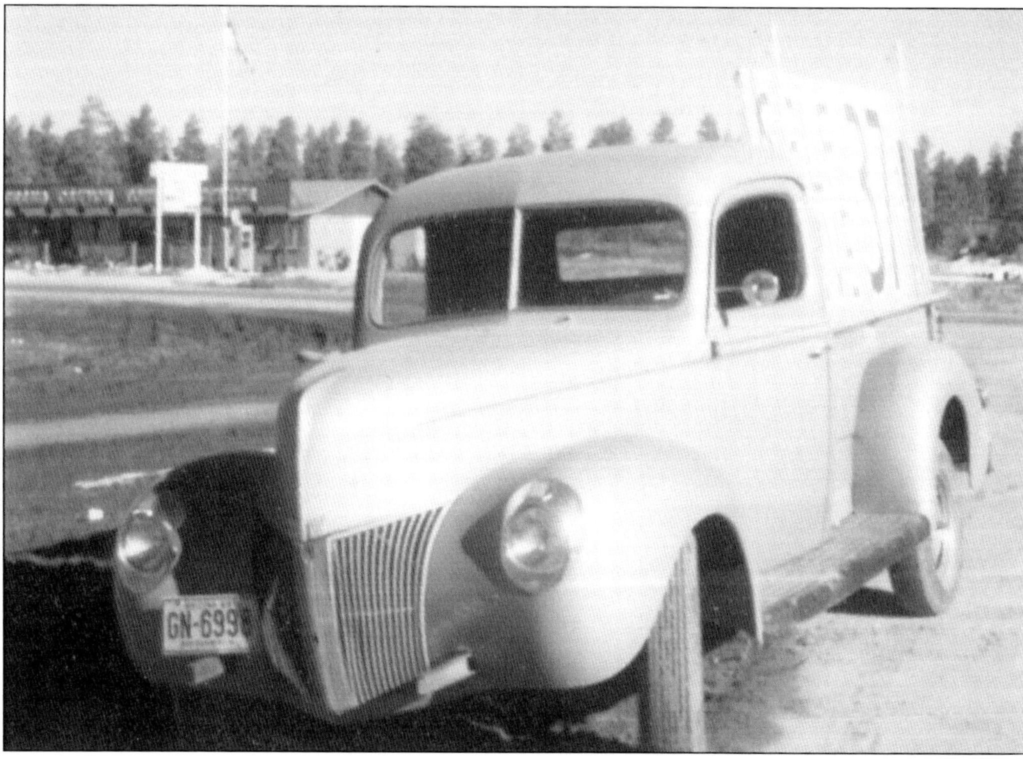

This photograph of a 1940 Ford truck illustrates the price of gas in the early part of the 1970s. At 37¢ a gallon, gas was far cheaper back then. A gallon of milk cost $1.15, though the average household income was only a little over $8,000 a year. (Courtesy of Clarinda Vail and the Thurston family.)

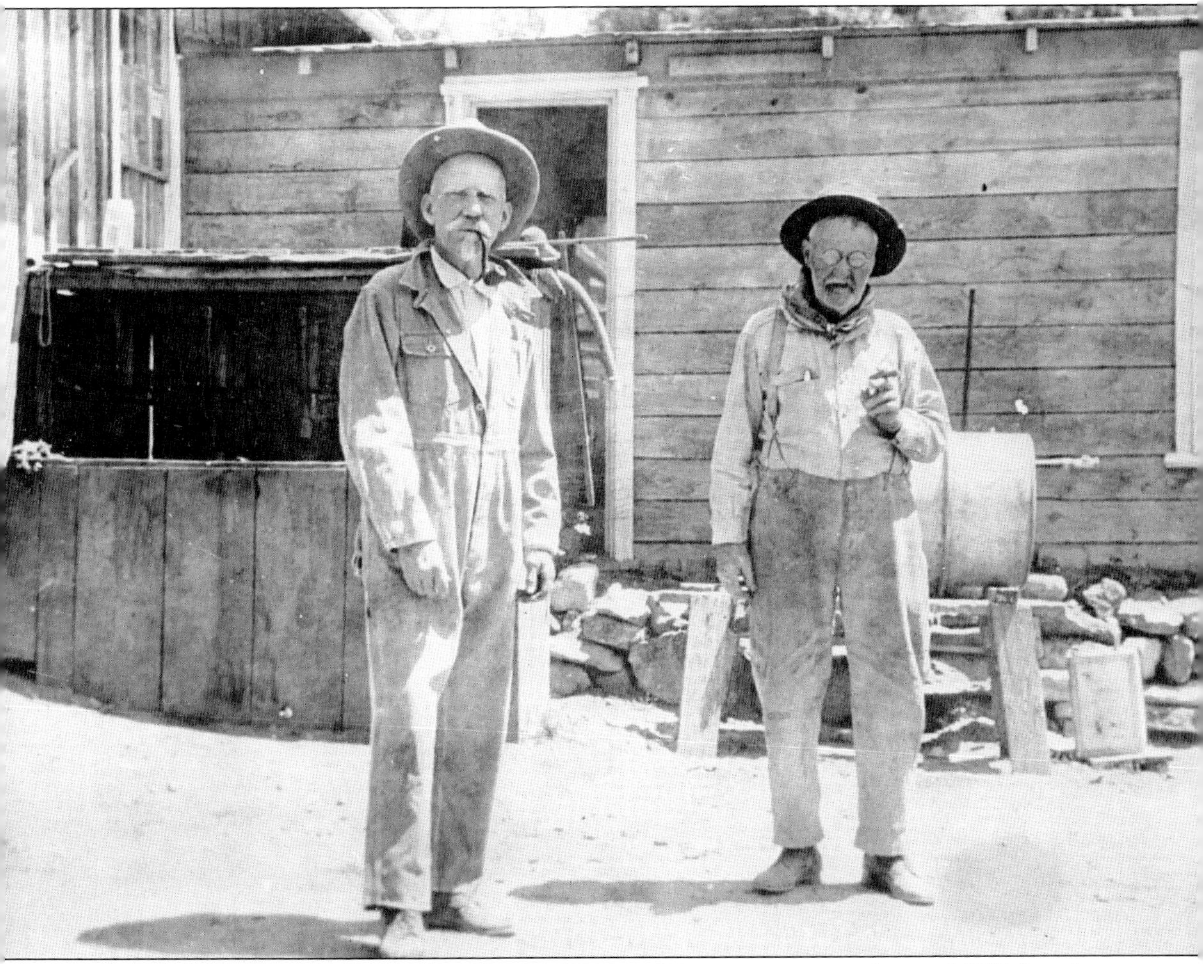

Pictured is the entrance to the Rowe Well Auto Court and Store as it appeared around 1931. Locals Ed Hamilton, Rowe Well operator, and miner Bill Donelson were well known in the Tusayan area. A portion of Tusayan village was used to house miners who worked nearby. (Photograph by Metzger; courtesy of the National Park Service.)

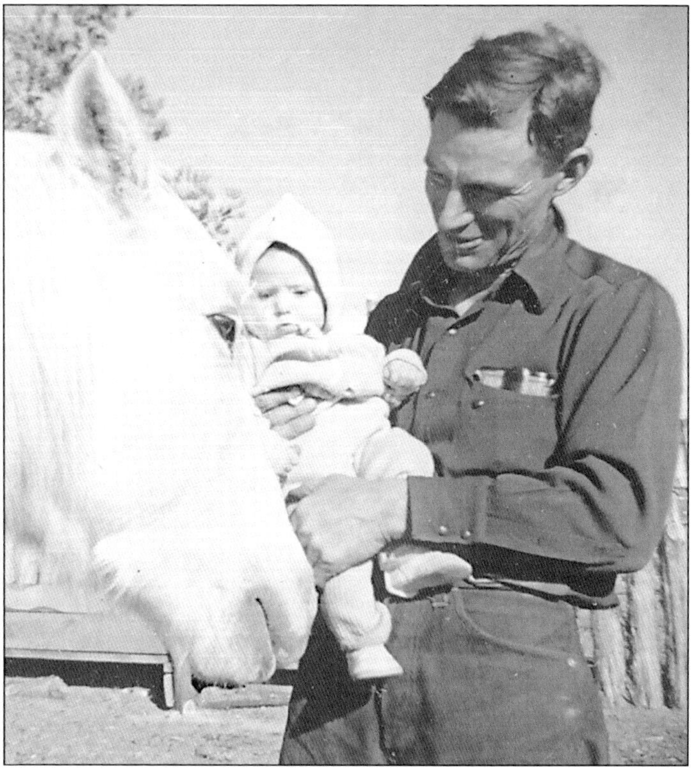

R. P. "Bob" Thurston can be seen in this 1969 photograph as he introduces his son Chris Thurston to a palomino horse named Pally. While everyone befriended the local Tusayan horse, it was most fond of Bess Thurston. The family owned at least two stables in the area. (Courtesy of Clarinda Vail and the Thurston family.)

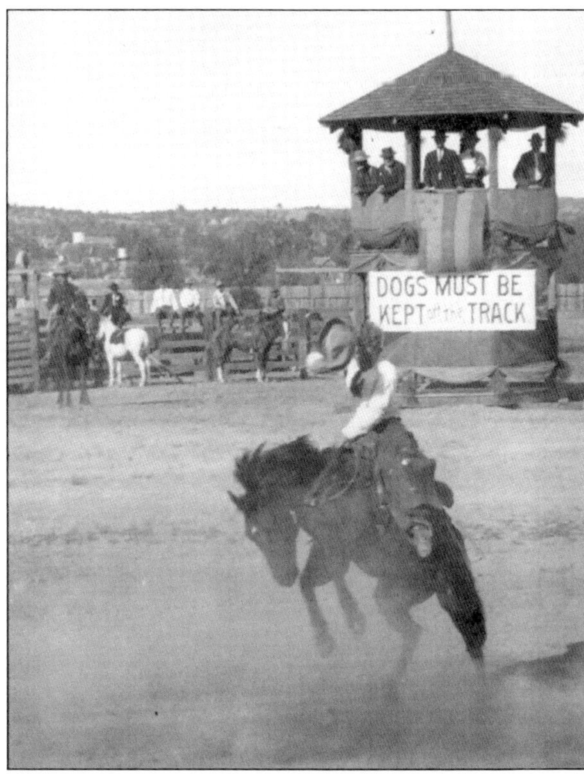

R. P. Thurston participates in a rodeo as a number of rodeo fans look on. Originally from Georgia, Thurston found life in the southwest to his liking. He participated in rodeos in nearby Williams and Prescott, as well as other locations. Thurston owned a ranch, as well as his other lodgings in the Tusayan community. (Courtesy of Clarinda Vail and the Thurston family.)

The Thurston family has had a long history with the Havasupai reservation. In this photograph from the Thurston collection, a helicopter delivers material to the tribe at the bottom of Grand Canyon. R. P. Thurston often hired members of the tribe to work for him. (Courtesy of Clarinda Vail and the Thurston family.)

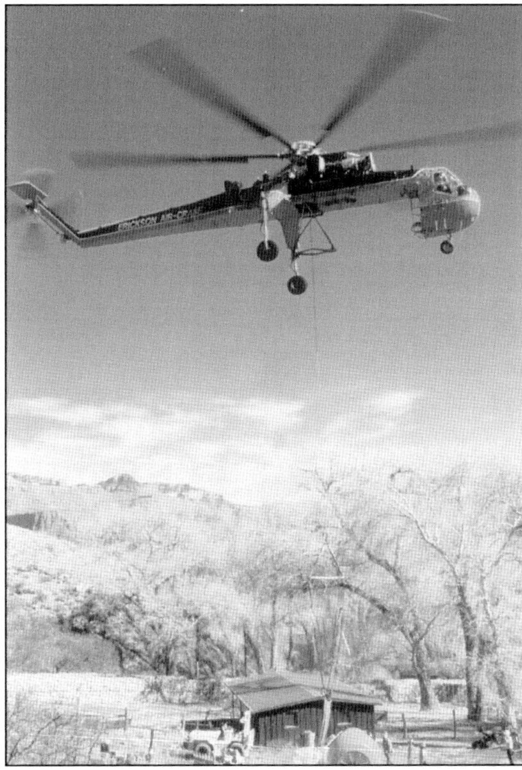

Bill Thurston can be seen in this 1976 photograph as he oversees construction work on the family's home in Tusayan. The home is still owned by members of the Thurston family to this day, though work continued on the property in subsequent years. (Courtesy of Clarinda Vail and the Thurston family.)

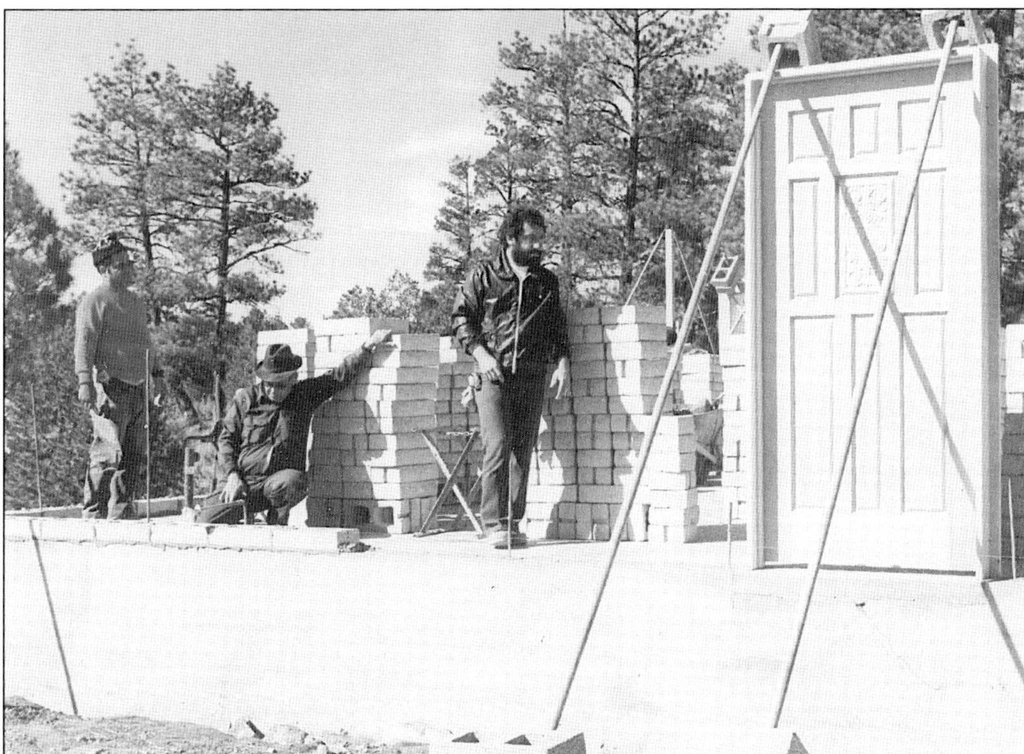

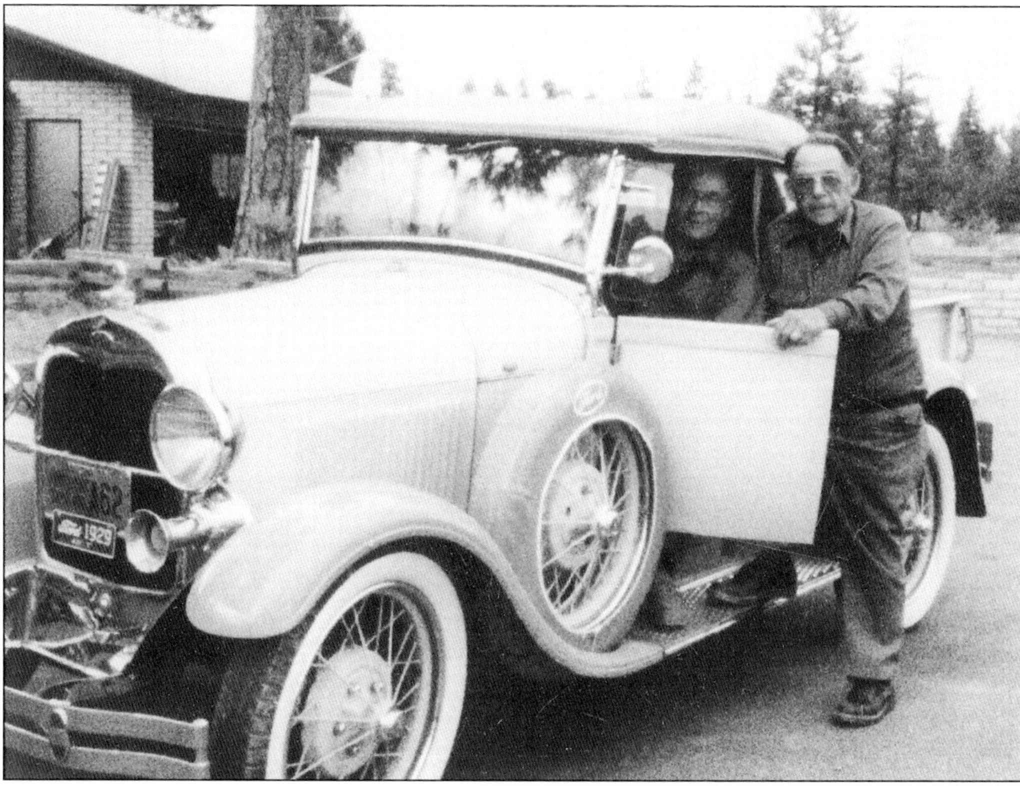

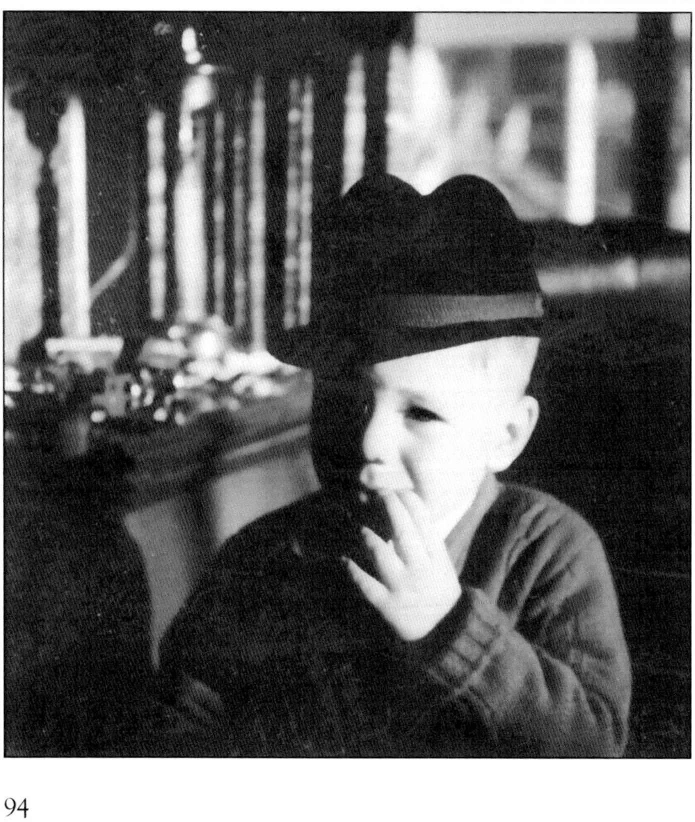

Bill Thurston stands next to one of his favorite vehicles, a 1929 Model A, parked outside of his home in Tusayan. The Ford Model A is often referred to as the successor to Henry Ford's Model T. Another nickname for the popular 1929 vehicle was "Baby Lincoln." (Courtesy of Clarinda Vail and the Thurston family.)

Pictured is three-year-old John Thurston, dapper in his hat in the original lobby of the Red Feather Lodge. The former lobby now serves as private offices for the hotel. John Thurston still lives in Tusayan village, as do other members of the Thurston family. (Courtesy of Clarinda Vail and the Thurston family.)

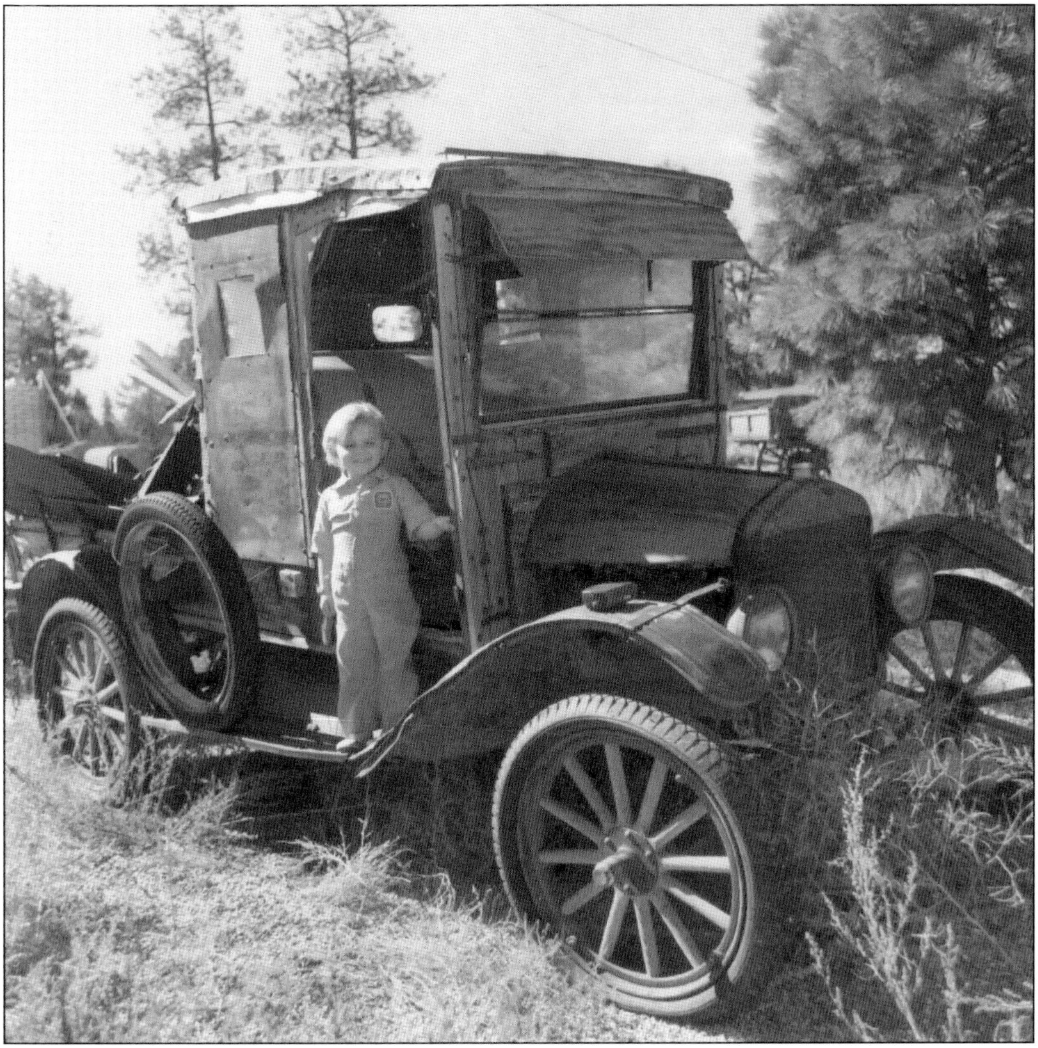

Clarinda Thurston (who would later become Clarinda Vail) can be seen in this mid-1970s photograph on her parents' property in Tusayan. She is pictured standing on an old Ford owned by the family. Vail still holds the title to the antique vehicle. (Courtesy of Clarinda Vail and the Thurston family.)

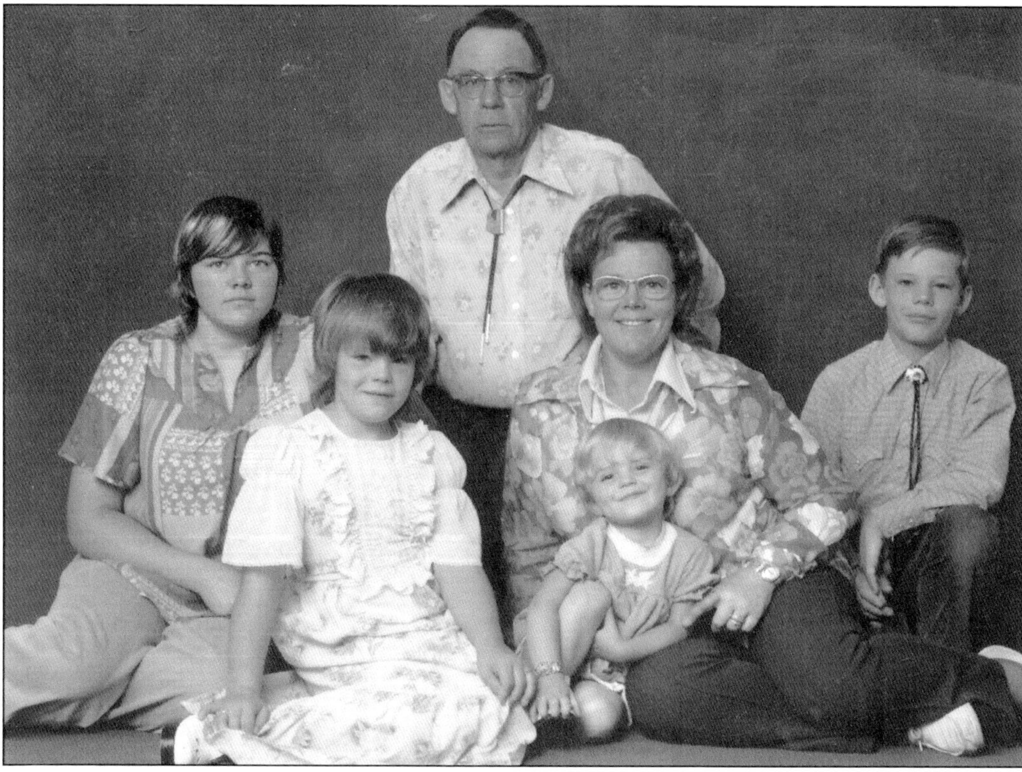

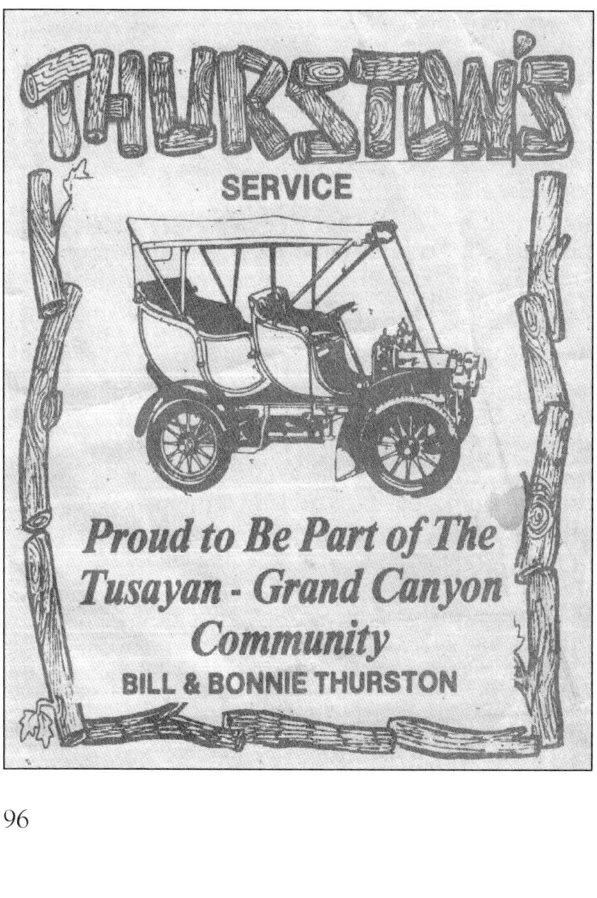

Members of the Thurston family can be seen in this 1975 photograph. Pictured are Bill, Tammy, Bess, Bonnie, John and Clarinda as they pose for the camera. Bill and Bonnie Thurston were 21 years apart in age. Bill Thurston was in his fifties when his daughter, Clarinda, was born. (Courtesy of Clarinda Vail and the Thurston family.)

An old *Grand Canyon News* advertisement offered the Thurston family's services to travelers and locals in the Tusayan area. Thurston's Services was the name of the family's gas station, which was run by Bill and Bonnie Thurston. (Courtesy of Clarinda Vail and the Thurston family.)

Eight

Grand Canyon's American Legion Post

While John Ivens Post No. 42 once operated in the Tusayan area, the organization's beginnings lay much closer to the Grand Canyon. Now based roughly 55 miles from the national park in Williams, Arizona, the American Legion Post has a long history of community service both in Tusayan and in the National Park, and included student scholarships, community improvements and much more.

John Ivens himself was drawn to the natural beauty of the area in 1911. After working on a farm in his home state of Wisconsin, Ivens was employed by the Fred Harvey Company upon his arrival to the Grand Canyon, though he soon left for other endeavors. He returned in 1916, finding employment with the famed Kolb brothers. Ivens remained at the canyon until 1917, when he enlisted in the army. His experiences at Grand Canyon obviously impressed him, however, as Ivens named Emery C. Kolb as his nearest relative, though his father remained alive and well in Wisconsin.

Unfortunately Ivens would soon become the first World War I casualty from the Grand Canyon area of Arizona. The young Pvt. 1st Class suffered a German mustard gas attack in 1918 while stationed in Coullmelle, France. The American Legion John Ivens Post No. 42 formed shortly thereafter in 1923. Emery C. Kolb became one of the founding members of the post.

Legion members held their initial meetings at the Grand Canyon's historical community building and would remain near the edge of the South Rim for a number of years. By 1953, however, the legion moved to new quarters in Tusayan. They took over the home of Tusayan founder George Reed and, with a few additions, christened their new location as the "Legion Hut." Members of the post, including longtime member Buford Belgard, helped secure the 2 acres of land, as well as the hut itself, with the help of Jack Verkamp of Grand Canyon. Belgard, who originally operated a laundry business at the canyon, would go on to become one of the legion's most prominent members and remained involved in the post until his death in 2009.

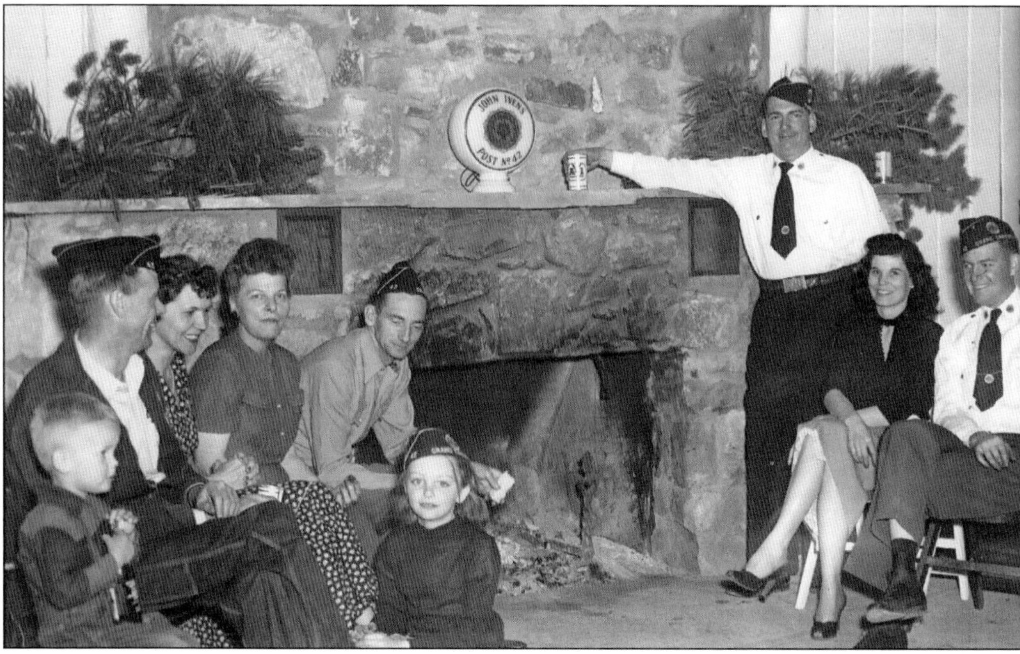

Pictured are Donnie Scheier, Lawrence Scheier, Jo Scheier, Bessie Reed, J. J. Reed, Eleanor Frank, Buford Belgard, Comdr. Ernie Greening, and Nora Greening at the dedication of the Tusayan American Legion Hut in 1953. The post was originally housed within the national park, but was eventually moved to the village of Tusayan. (Courtesy of American Legion Post No. 42.)

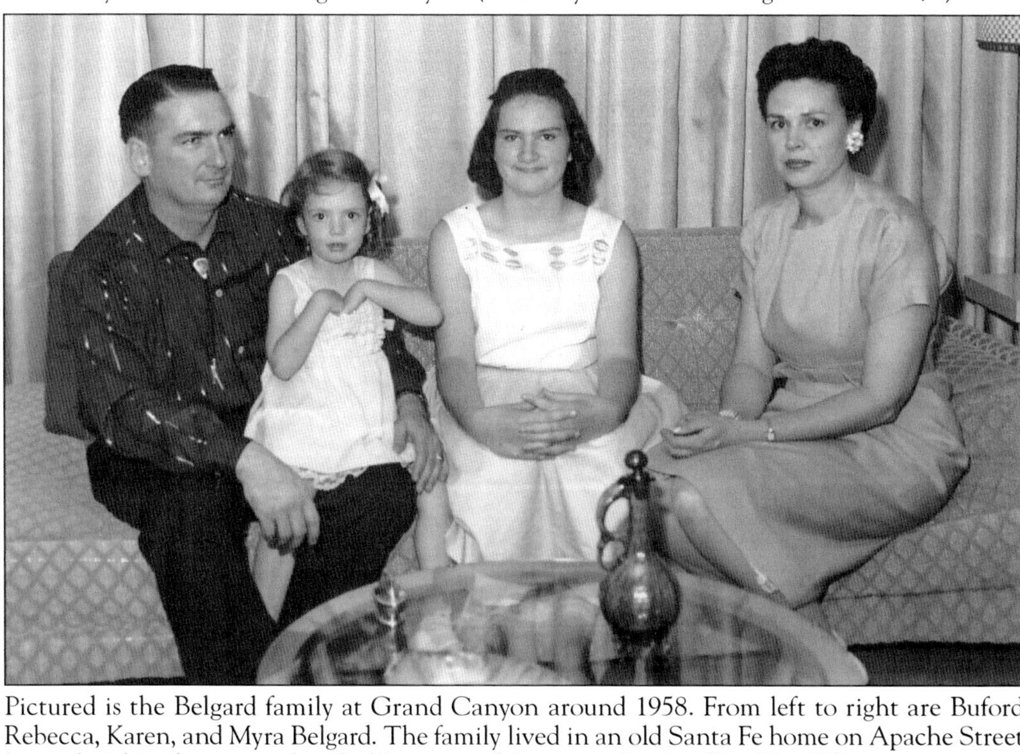

Pictured is the Belgard family at Grand Canyon around 1958. From left to right are Buford, Rebecca, Karen, and Myra Belgard. The family lived in an old Santa Fe home on Apache Street, located within the national park. (Courtesy of American Legion Post No. 42.)

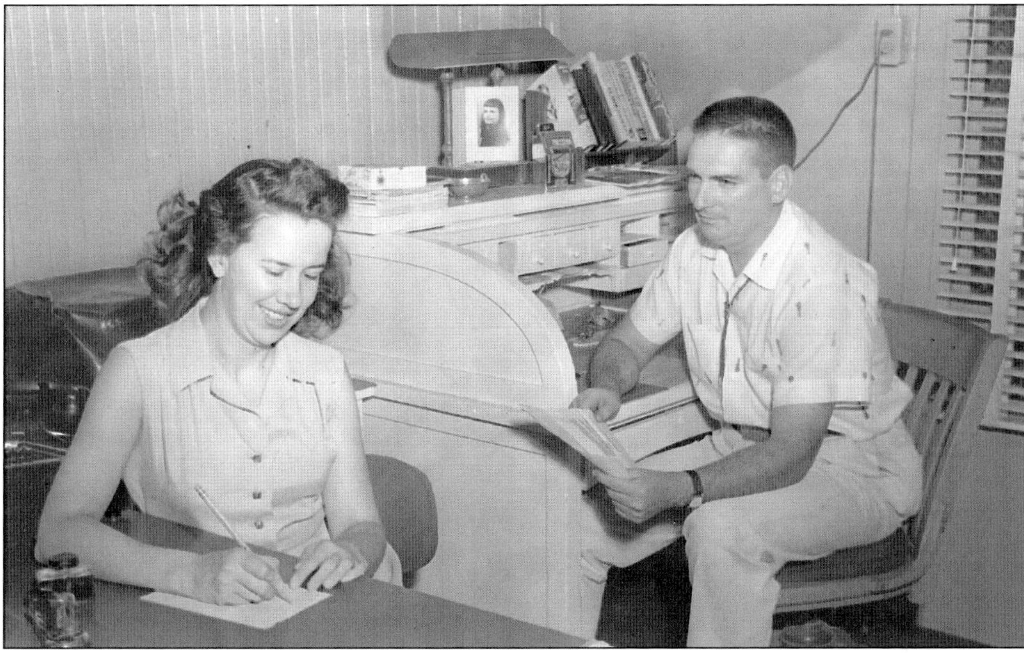

Buford Belgard dictates a letter to Mary Hoover around 1950. The two worked together for the Fred Harvey Company and would continue to work together for the American Legion's Grand Canyon Post. The photographer who took the picture was telling a number of jokes to the two, leading to their amused looks in the photograph. (Courtesy of American Legion Post No. 42.)

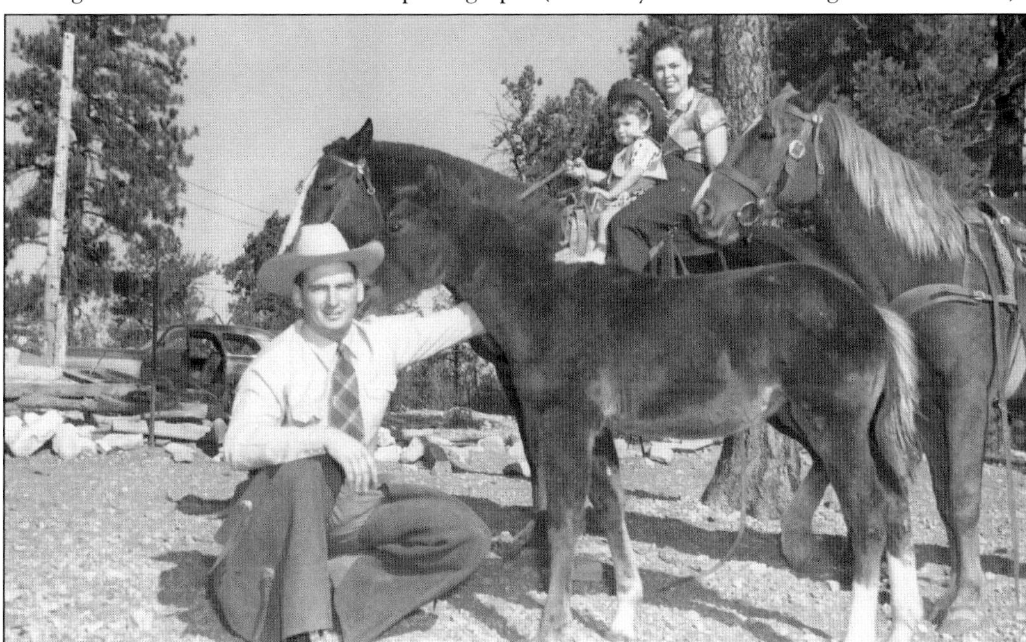

Buford and Myra Belgard, along with their daughter Karen, sit atop horses near Rowe Well around 1950. The family kept their two horses, along with a pet burro, in the Tusayan area, which they visited frequently. The family eventually relocated to the Williams area. (Courtesy of American Legion Post No. 42.)

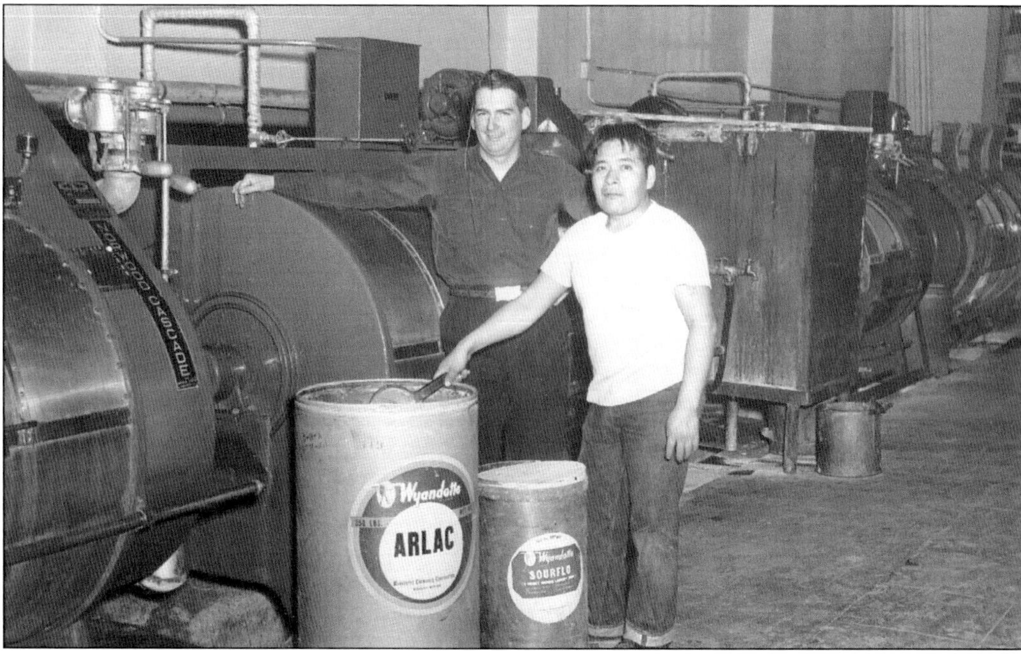

Pictured are Buford Belgard and Fred Harvey employee Ranspie Kyasyousie, a member of the Hopi tribe, as they pose for a promotional photograph in the 1950s. The promotional photograph was used in an advertisement for Arlac that ran in a laundry digest. Belgard managed the laundry and cleaning facilities for Fred Harvey at the canyon. (Courtesy of American Legion Post No. 42.)

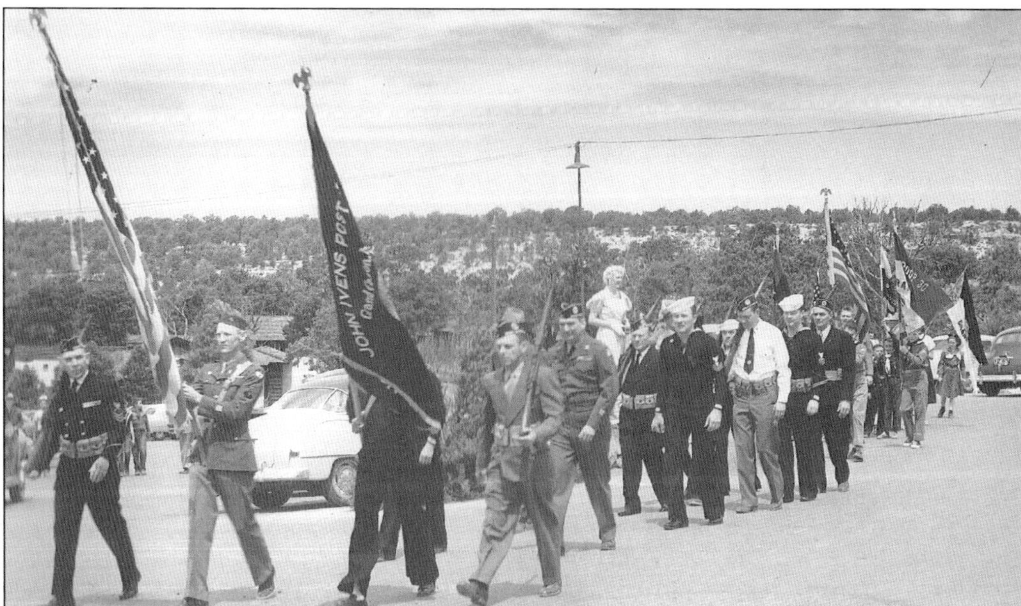

Members of the Grand Canyon American Legion Post are pictured on Memorial Day in 1959 as they walk near the South Rim. Color guard members in the photograph included Grant Wedoff and Donald Gillis. Color bearers included Oscar Willis, David Keevama, and Legion Comdr. Buford Belgard. The woman watching the procession is Christine Greening. (Courtesy of American Legion Post No. 42.)

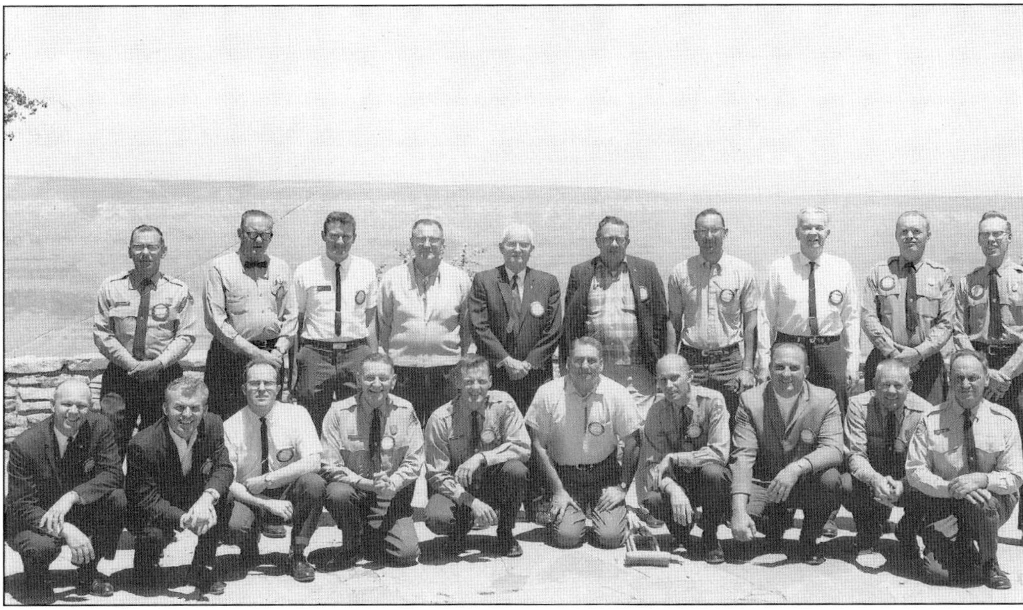

Members of the Grand Canyon's Rotary on the Rim Club pose at the South Rim. Buford Belgard served as president of the organization in the 1950s. Members of the club included national park superintendent Howard Strickland, Grand Canyon School principal Bob Pavlich, and Santa Fe special officers, who were the peacekeepers within the Grand Canyon National Park. (Courtesy of American Legion Post No. 42.)

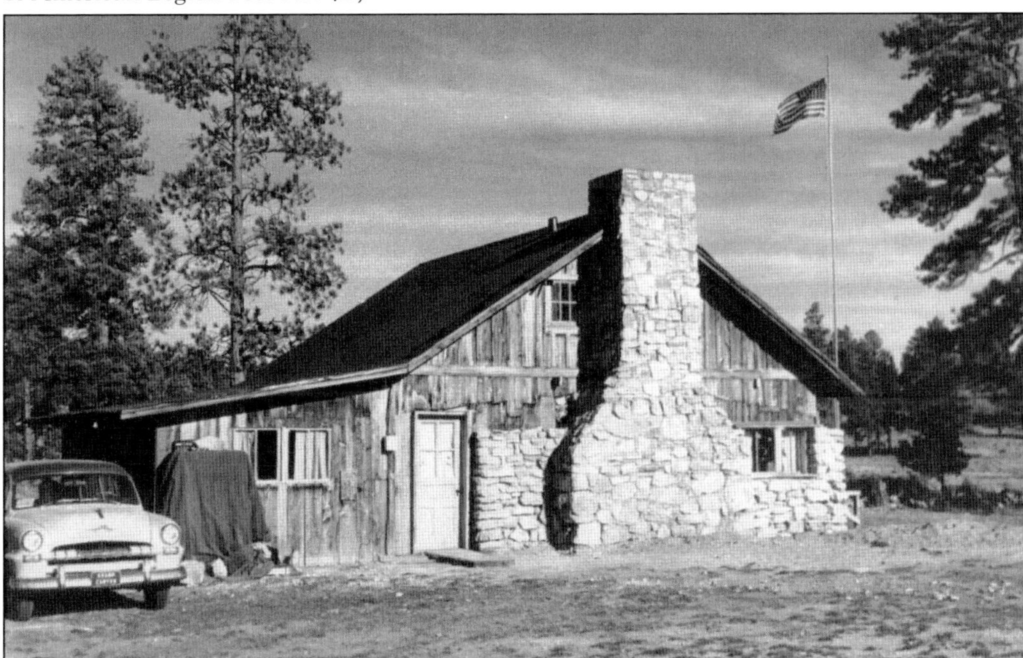

This photograph shows the old George Reed homestead cabin can after it was converted to the Legion Hut by members of the John Ivens American Legion Post No. 42. The fireplace was added on by legion members. The hut was dedicated by W. R. "Bill" Bourdon of Holbrook, who was national vice commander of the American Legion. (Courtesy of American Legion Post No. 42.)

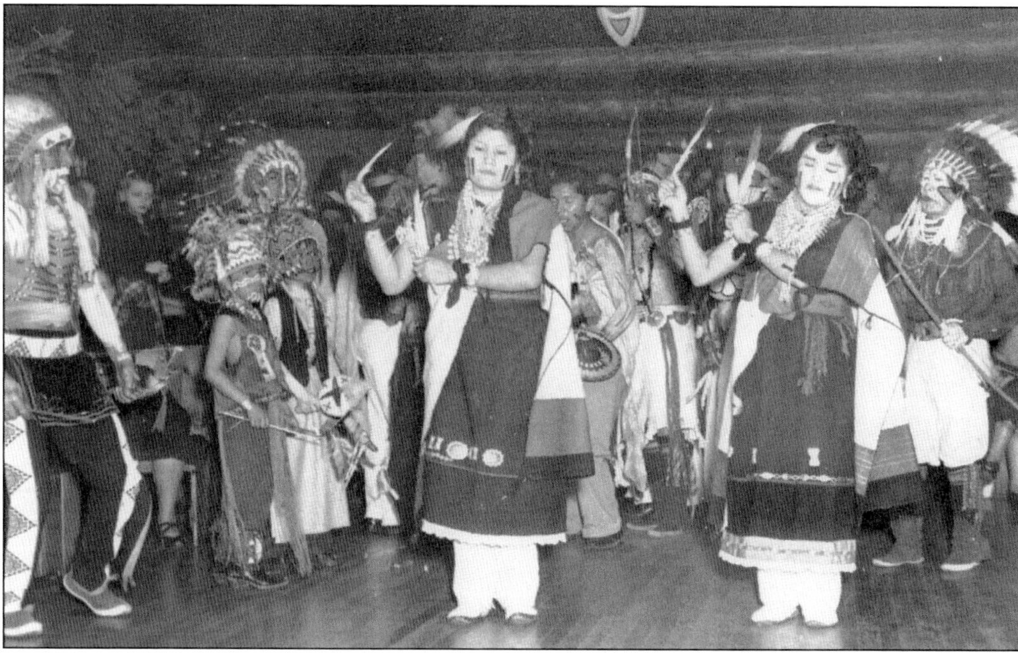

A number of Hopi dancers perform at the dedication of the American Legion's John Ivens Post. Hopi Sammy Pemahinya is pictured right during the event. The dedication of the Tusayan American Legion Hut was held on April 12, 1953, in the building once occupied by Tusayan icon George Reed. (Courtesy of American Legion Post No. 42.)

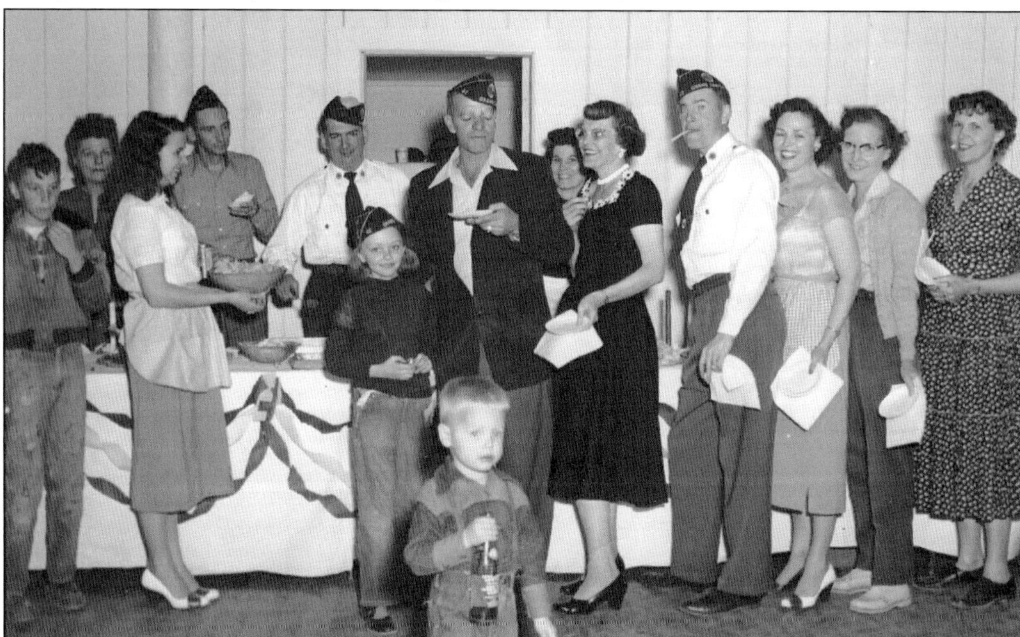

Pictured are Douglas Frank Jr., Bessie Reed, Mary Hoover, J. J. Reed, Buford Belgard, Donnie Scheiere, Doug Frank, Nora Greening, Leanore Gibson, Ernie Greening, Myra Belgard, Ruth Payne, and Jo Scheiere at the April 12, 1953, dedication of the Tusayan American Legion Hut just outside the Grand Canyon National Park. (Courtesy of American Legion Post No. 42.)

Nine

Helicopters and Airplanes

Flights over the Grand Canyon have long been a favorite among visitors to the South Rim. In the village of Tusayan, swooping airplanes and helicopters can often be seen overhead. The area's first flights began in the late 1940s with the arrival of Ed Montgomery, owner of the Arizona Helicopter Service. Montgomery owned a fleet of Bell Model 47 helicopters, which he would use for various business endeavors. In 1950, Montgomery leased an area of land that was once the home of the original Tusayan Bar, where he offered summer sightseeing tours. The air tour company closed after a couple of years, however, in favor of Montgomery's more lucrative business pursuits.

In 1952, one year before construction began on the new highway through Tusayan, plans were announced for a new all-weather airport at the Grand Canyon. Construction on the government-built facility wouldn't begin, however, until 1964. Two other airports existed at the time, one south of the national park in Valle and one in the area of Red Butte. The land for the new airport was fixed primarily on national forest property, though a portion of the site was located on land belonging to R. P. Thurston. Always eager to further business pursuits in the area, the Thurston family worked with government officials to complete the airport facility.

Contractor Elling Halvorson, who came to the South Rim in 1964, soon became a major player in the growing air tourism industry and a well-known businessman in the Tusayan area. Halvorson first came to the South Rim with Halvorson Lents Construction to work on the Park's trans-canyon water pipeline. When not using the company's helicopters to work on the pipeline project, they were used for sightseeing tours. Halvorson's business would go on to become Papillon Grand Canyon Helicopters. With further property acquisitions, Halvorson soon expanded his business dealings in the area with the addition of a tourist center, Grand Canyon Best Western Squire Inn (co-owned with businessman John Seibold), and other holdings. Seibold was also the founder of Scenic Airlines. He and Halvorson would also go into business together as co-owners of Grand Canyon Airlines, called one of the world's oldest air tour companies.

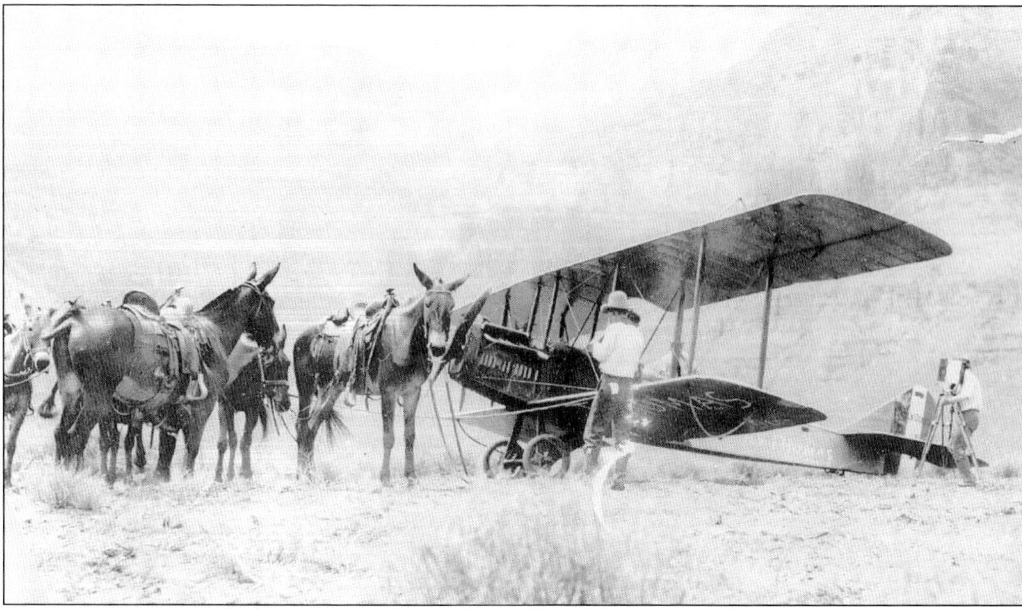

Pictured is the only airplane to land at the Grand Canyon's Plateau Point, according to historians with the National Park Service. Pilot R. V. Thomas manned the airplane in this August 8, 1922, photograph, and he is pictured with a number of Fred Harvey mules on the left. (Fred Harvey Collection; courtesy of the National Park Service.)

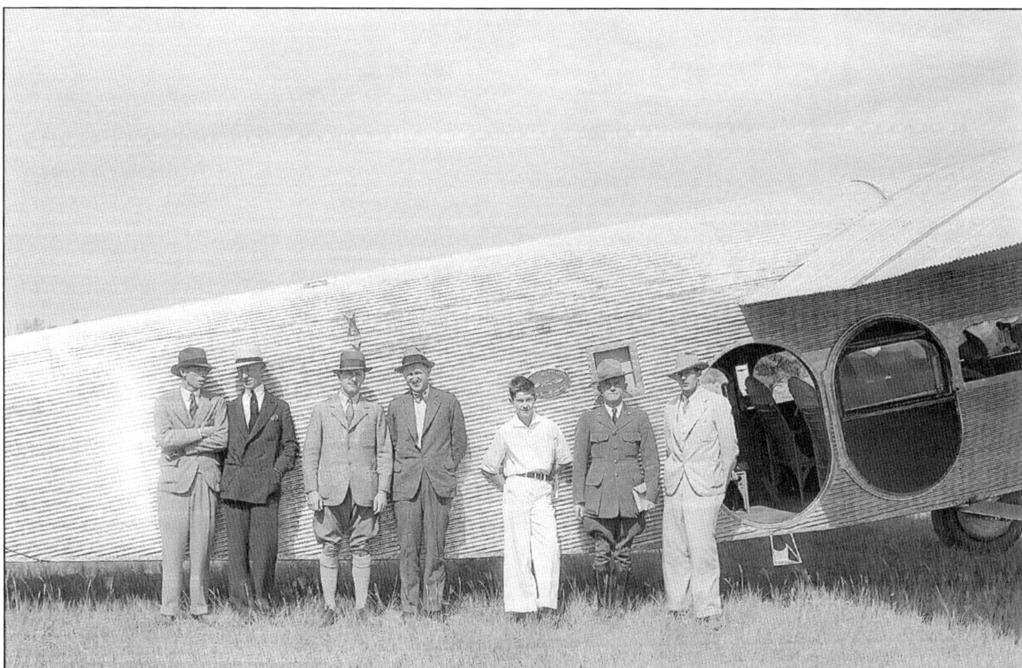

This July 10, 1932, photograph shows a number of area officials as they stand by a Ford Tri-Motor airplane NC-5092, which was owned by Grand Canyon Airlines. Officials in the picture are indentified as Harvey, Ruckstell, Edwards, national park director Albright, superintendent Tillotson, and Thornburg. (Courtesy of the National Park Service.)

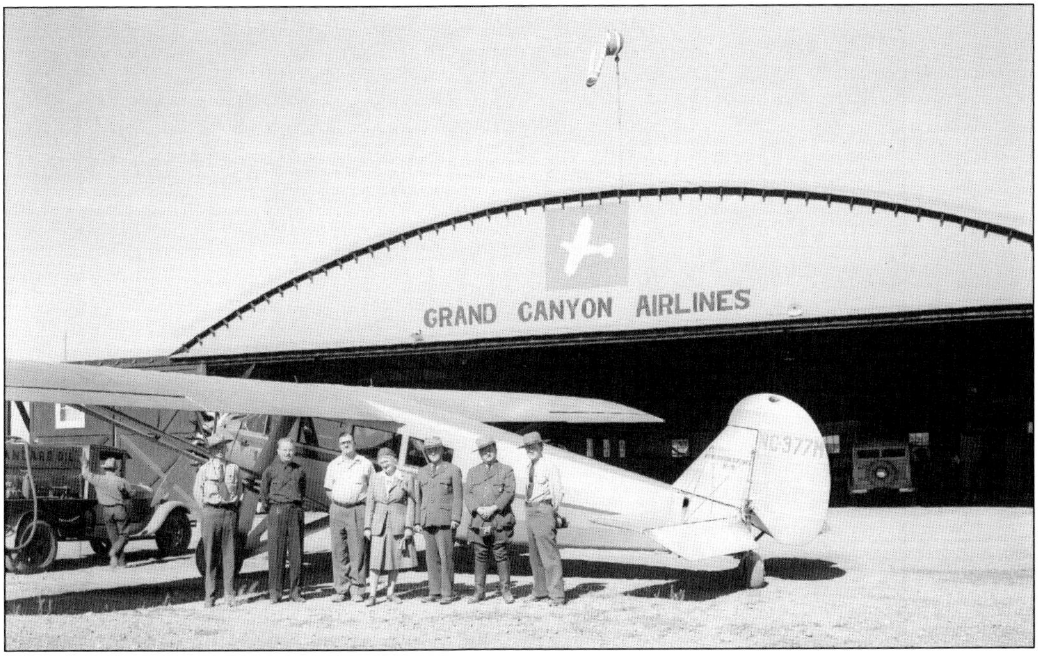

Grand Canyon National Park personnel are pictured as they stand outside of the Red Butte airport, located south of the national park, around 1934. The group is pictured standing by a Travel Air A-6000-A at the hangar for Grand Canyon Airlines. Red Butte is also known as a sacred location for the Havasupai people. (Courtesy of the National Park Service.)

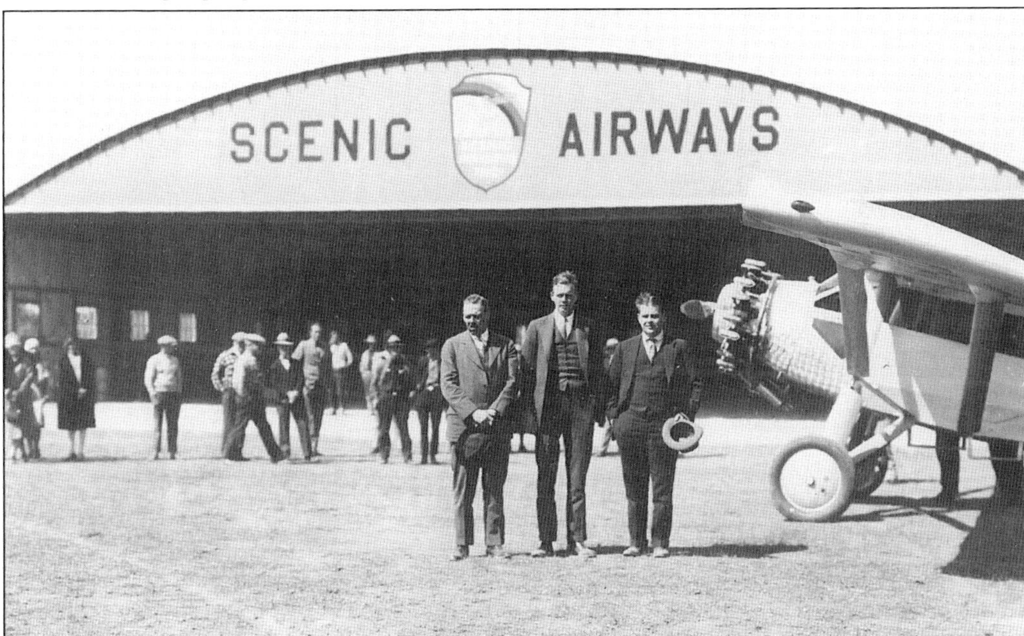

Aviator Charles Lindbergh, pictured with two of his backers, visited the Grand Canyon area on April 20, 1928. Lindbergh is pictured standing in front of the hangar for Scenic Airways, another air tour operator that flew visitors over the Grand Canyon National Park. (Fred Harvey Collection; courtesy of the National Park Service.)

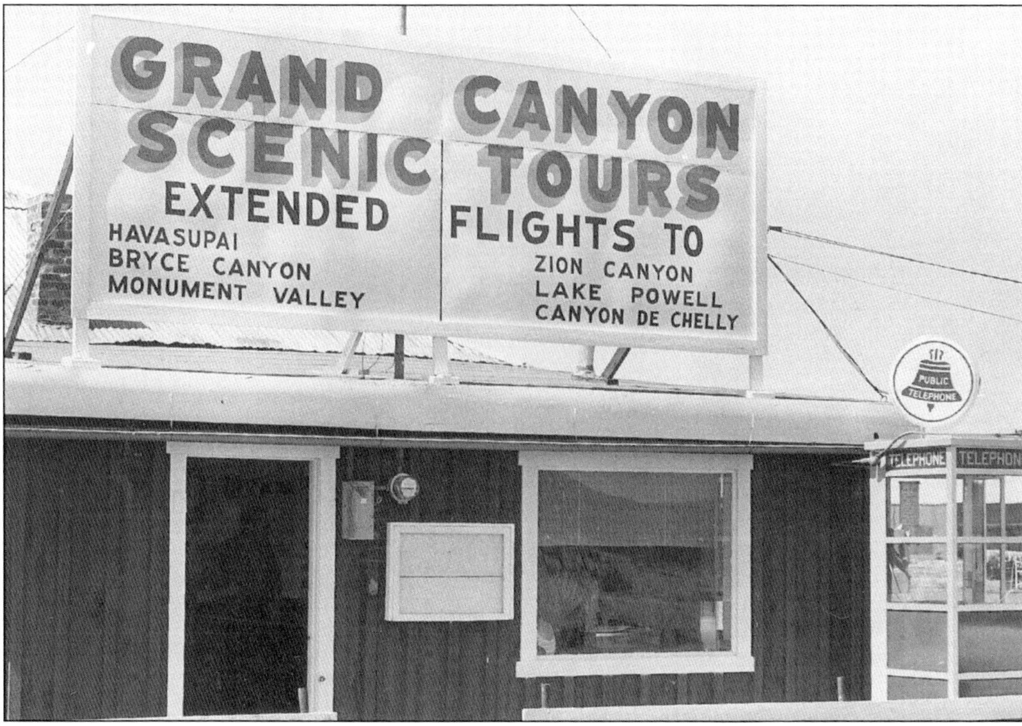

The offices for Grand Canyon Airlines are pictured around the 1950s. Scenic tours were offered over the Havasupai reservation, Bryce, Lake Poweel and a number of other locations. The first air tour to take off from Tusayan consisted of two passengers, Bess Thurston and Will Rogers Jr. (Courtesy of the Williams Public Library.)

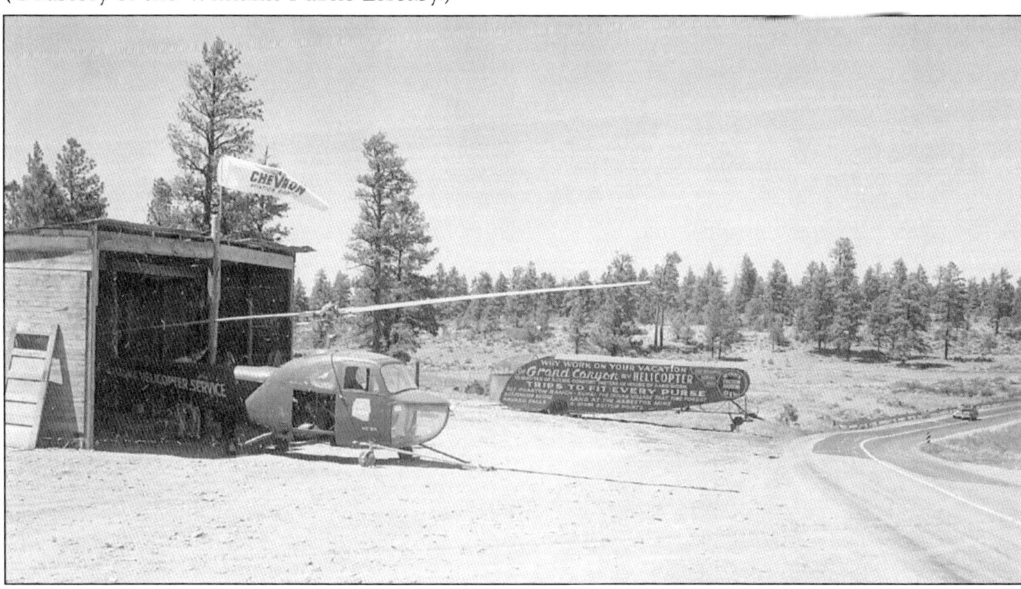

The Arizona Helicopter Service is pictured here in the summer of 1950. The service was located at Tusayan Camp, located south of the Grand Canyon National Park. The camp was located on old Highway 64 in what is now known as Tusayan's Canyon Pines Mobile Home Park. (Photograph by J. M. Eden; courtesy of the National Park Service.)

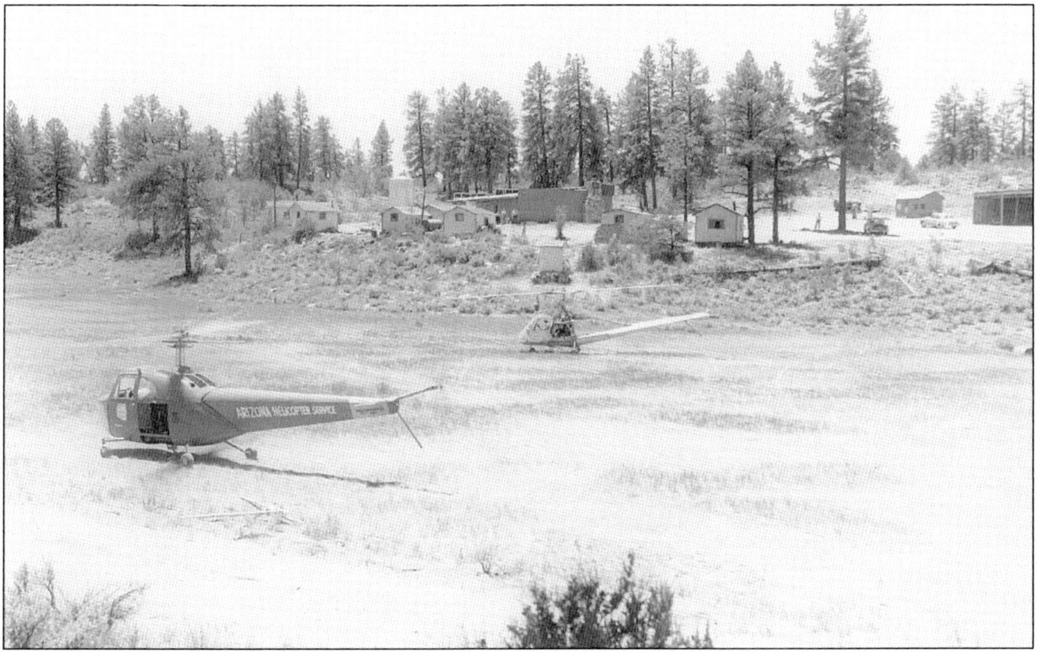

Another view of the Arizona Helicopter Service's tourist operations, which would fly visitors to the Grand Canyon over the national park, as seen in the summer of 1950. An official Grand Canyon airport would not become a fixture in the Tusayan area for another 14 years. (Photograph by J. M. Eden; courtesy of the National Park Service.)

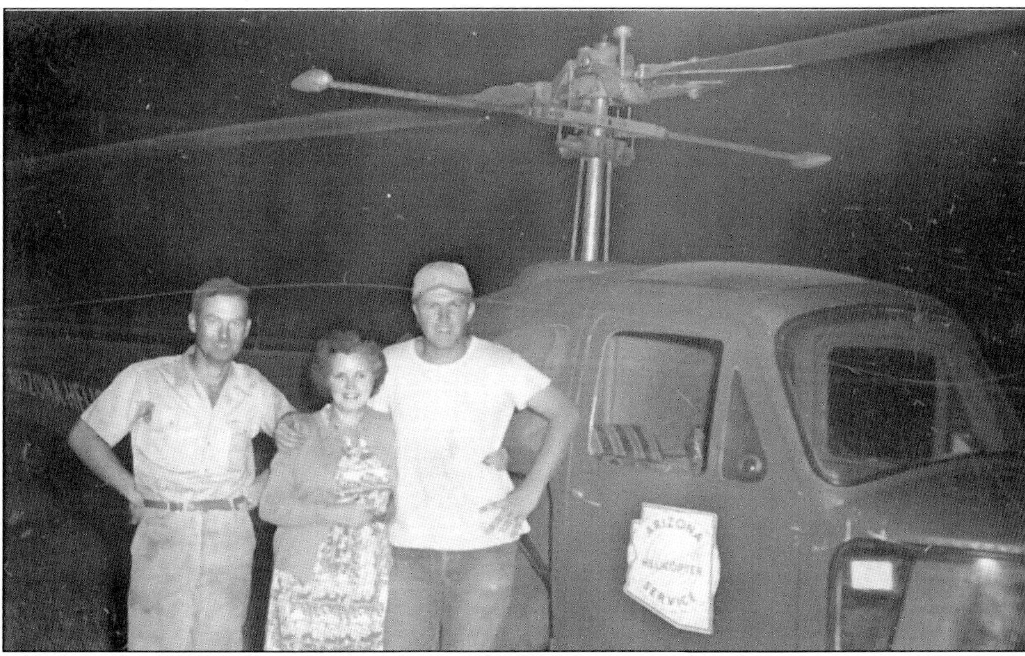

This June 1950 photograph shows Arizona Helicopter Service pilot Red Carson (right), Mrs. Ed Hudson, and Ed Hudson Jr. The group is pictured following the rescue of Ed Hudson Jr., who lost his boat in the Grand Canyon. They are pictured at the Arizona Helicopter Service operating base. (Photograph by J. M. Eden; courtesy of the National Park Service.)

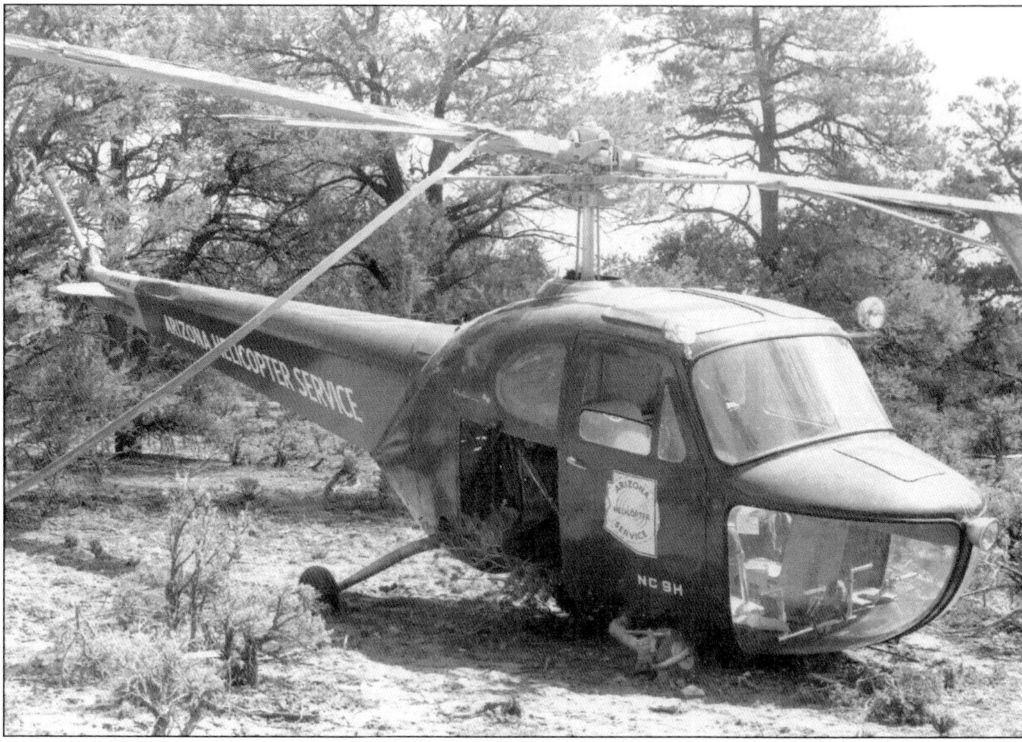

This original Bell 47 helicopter is pictured after it crashed in 1948. The helicopter went down while en route to the Hualapai hilltop from the airport at Red Butte. The aircraft was attempting to deliver a Quonset hut church to the Havasupai tribe when the accident occurred. Another aircraft finished the delivery roughly a week later. (Photograph by J. M. Eden; courtesy of the National Park Service.)

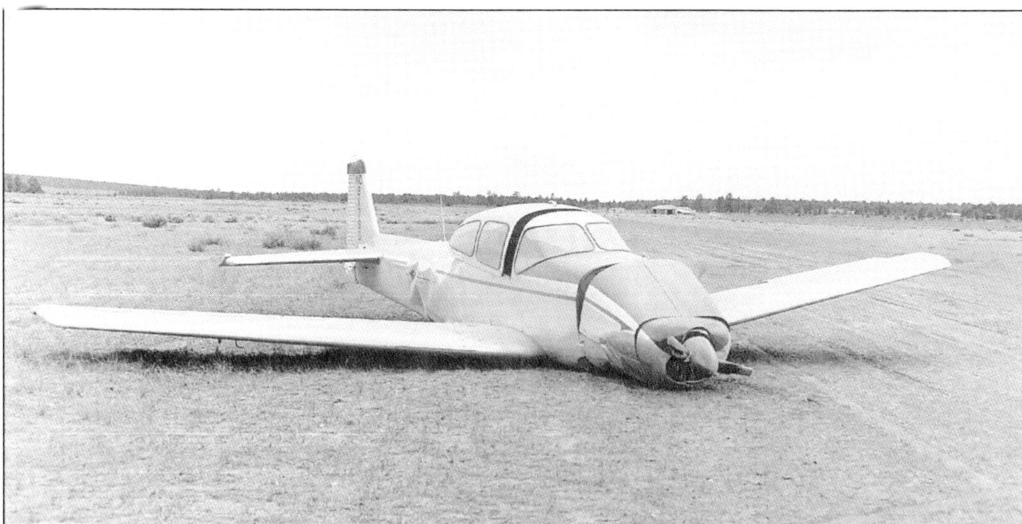
This 1949 photograph shows a four-seat airplane that was owned by Barry Goldwater of Phoenix, Arizona. The airplane crashed while attempting to take off from the Red Butte Airport. It went down at roughly 1:30 p.m. on April 17. (Photograph by J. M. Eden; courtesy of the National Park Service.)

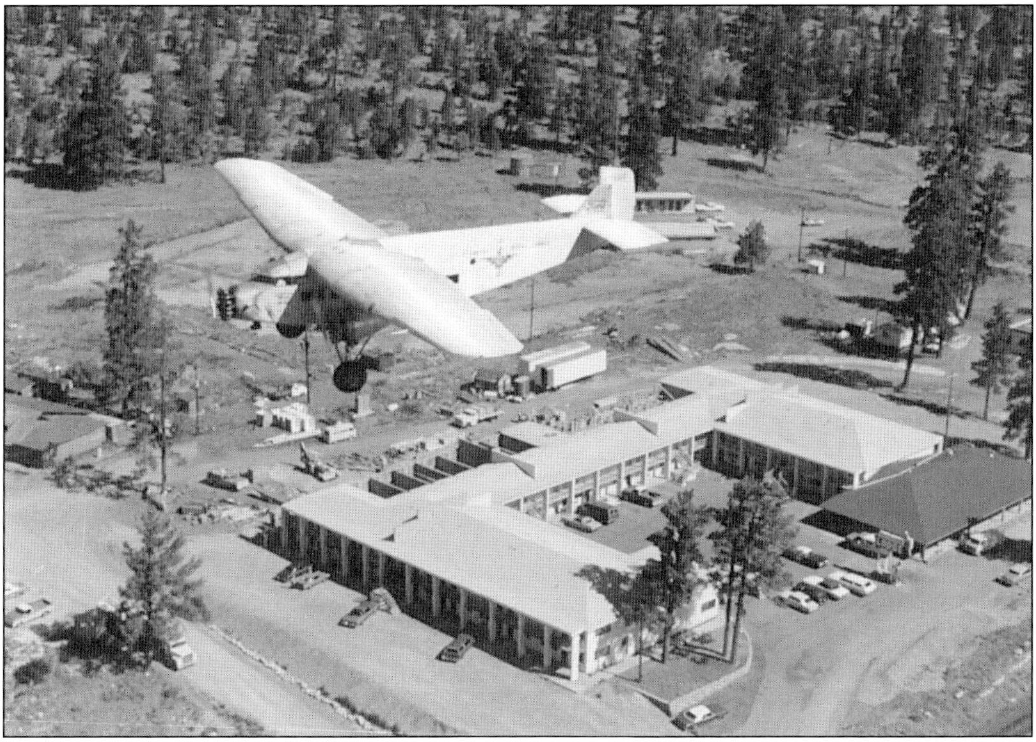

Pictured in this late 1970s photograph is a Ford Tri-Motor airplane as it soars over the Red Feather Lodge in Tusayan. The lodge, owned by the Thurston family, has undergone a number of renovations over the years since it was first built. A restaurant addition can be seen in the photograph as well, which remains a part of the complex. (Courtesy of Clarinda Vail and the Thurston family.)

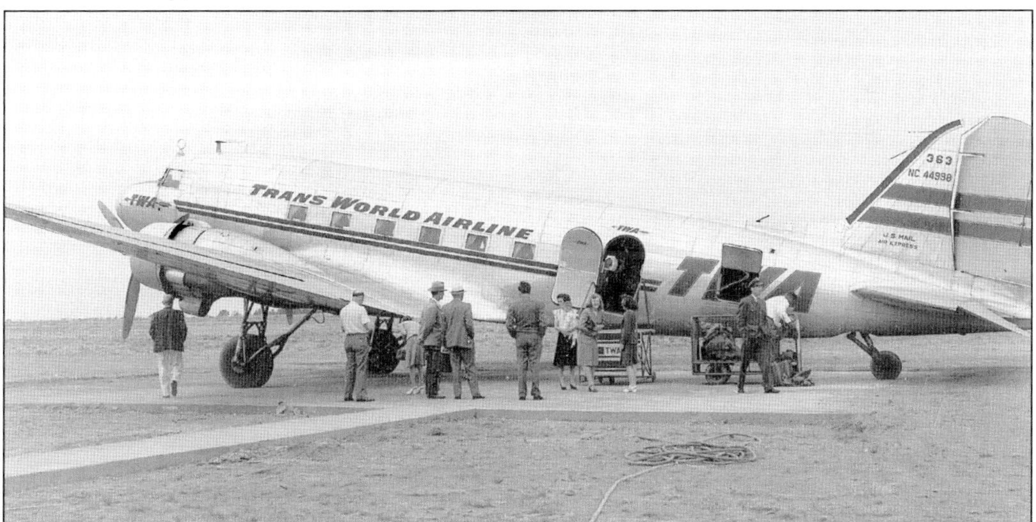

Pictured is the first scheduled landing of a westbound TWA flight at the airport in Valle, located south of Tusayan village. The airplane flew in to the airport at 7:00 a.m. on July 5, 1947. Crewmembers and aviation officials are pictured standing next to the jet after it landed. (Photograph by J. M. Eden; courtesy of the National Park Service.)

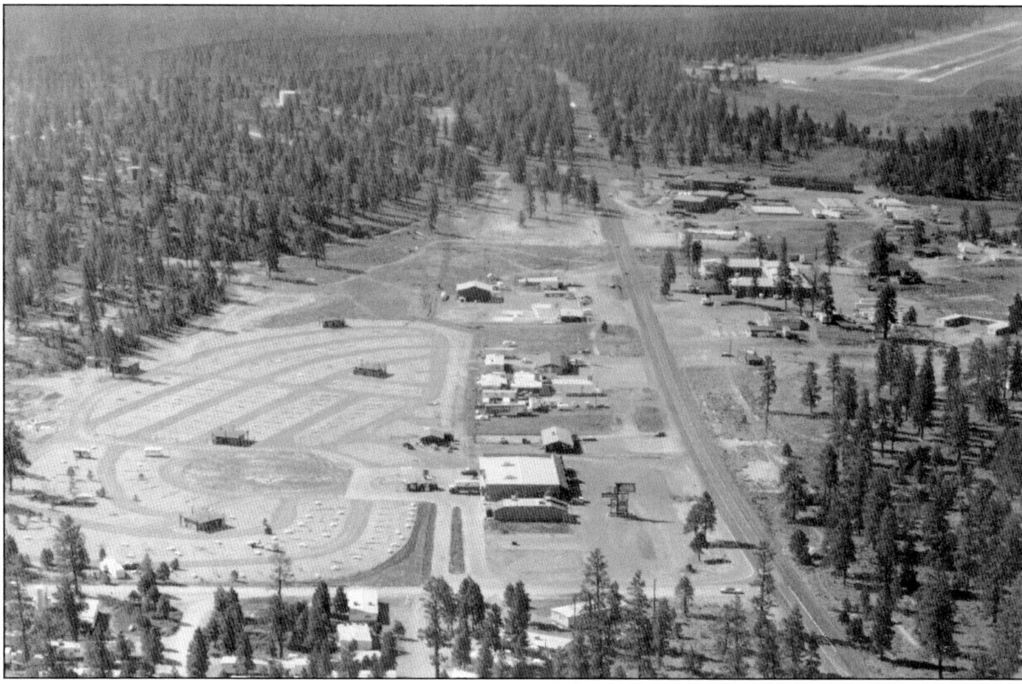

This aerial photograph shows the Tusayan area as it appeared in the mid- to late 1970s. The photograph was taken during a congressional effort made by Tusayan residents to get water from the Grand Canyon National Park. A number of the amenities one sees in the area today were not yet constructed. (Courtesy of Clarinda Vail and the Thurston family.)

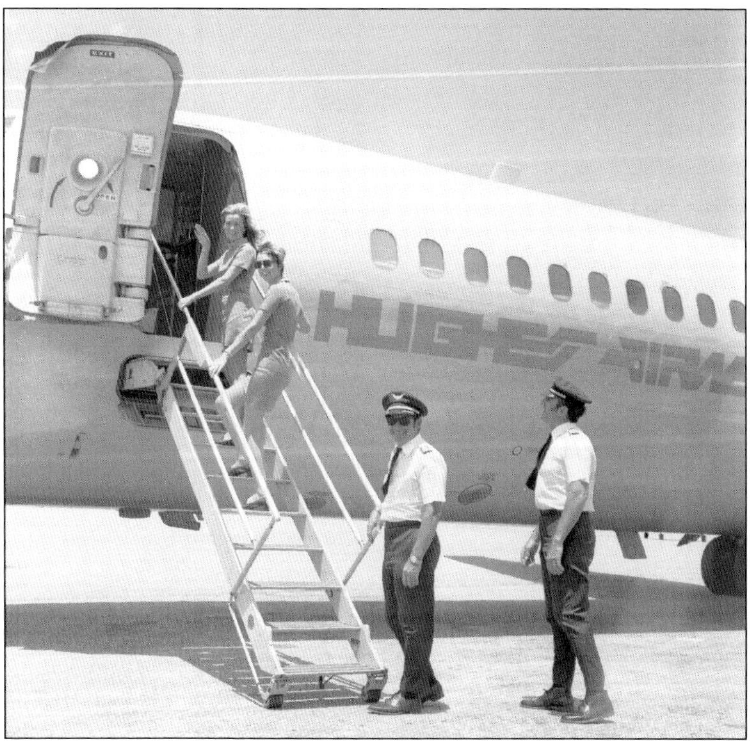

The first jet service to the Grand Canyon Airport, provided by Hughes Air West, can be seen in this July 1, 1972, photograph. Today a number of flights depart and arrive at Grand Canyon Airport daily. Air Force One, as well as other assorted government aircraft, has landed at the airport over the years. (Photograph by Rayner; courtesy of the National Park Service.)

Ten

Tourism and More

Tourism has always been the backbone of the Tusayan area. Without it, many of those who made the small South Rim village what it is today would not have come, or at least not spent their lives there. It is the beauty, the grandeur, and sheer power of the Grand Canyon that keeps visitors coming to the park year after year. Those same attractions hold true for those who live in the village of Tusayan.

Visitor amenities continue to evolve in Tusayan to this day, as they have evolved since George Reed's homesteading days. Tourism in the area boomed with the completion of Highway 64 in the mid-1960s and the addition of the Grand Canyon Airport. Hotels, restaurants, air tours, land tours, curio shops, a grocery store, and employee housing were quick to spring up in the area. Fast food restaurants, such as McDonald's and Taco Bell, as well as others, further added to the amenities offered to visitors in the area.

The IMAX Theater is by far one of the largest structures in the village of Tusayan. The theater, which opened in 1984, was built on the site of the Western Village. The film originally showed *Grand Canyon—The Hidden Secrets*, a 35-minute production that soon became a popular hit for travelers to the national park.

Aside from accommodating the millions who travel to the canyon annually, Tusayan was also an attractive locale for miners who once flocked to the area in search of valuable minerals. A number of Grand Canyon notables, including the Kolb brothers and John Hance, tried their hand at mining in the area, though rarely with much success. The discovery of high-grade uranium deposits in 1951, however, created the first notable population boom in the Tusayan area. In order to house their employees, the owners of the Golden Crown Mining Company bought 10 acres of land, which they fashioned into a campsite for their workers. Both the mine and campsite were later sold. The Orphan Mine ceased operations in 1969. Employee housing remains in and around Tusayan area, though these days the residents work almost entirely in the tourism industry.

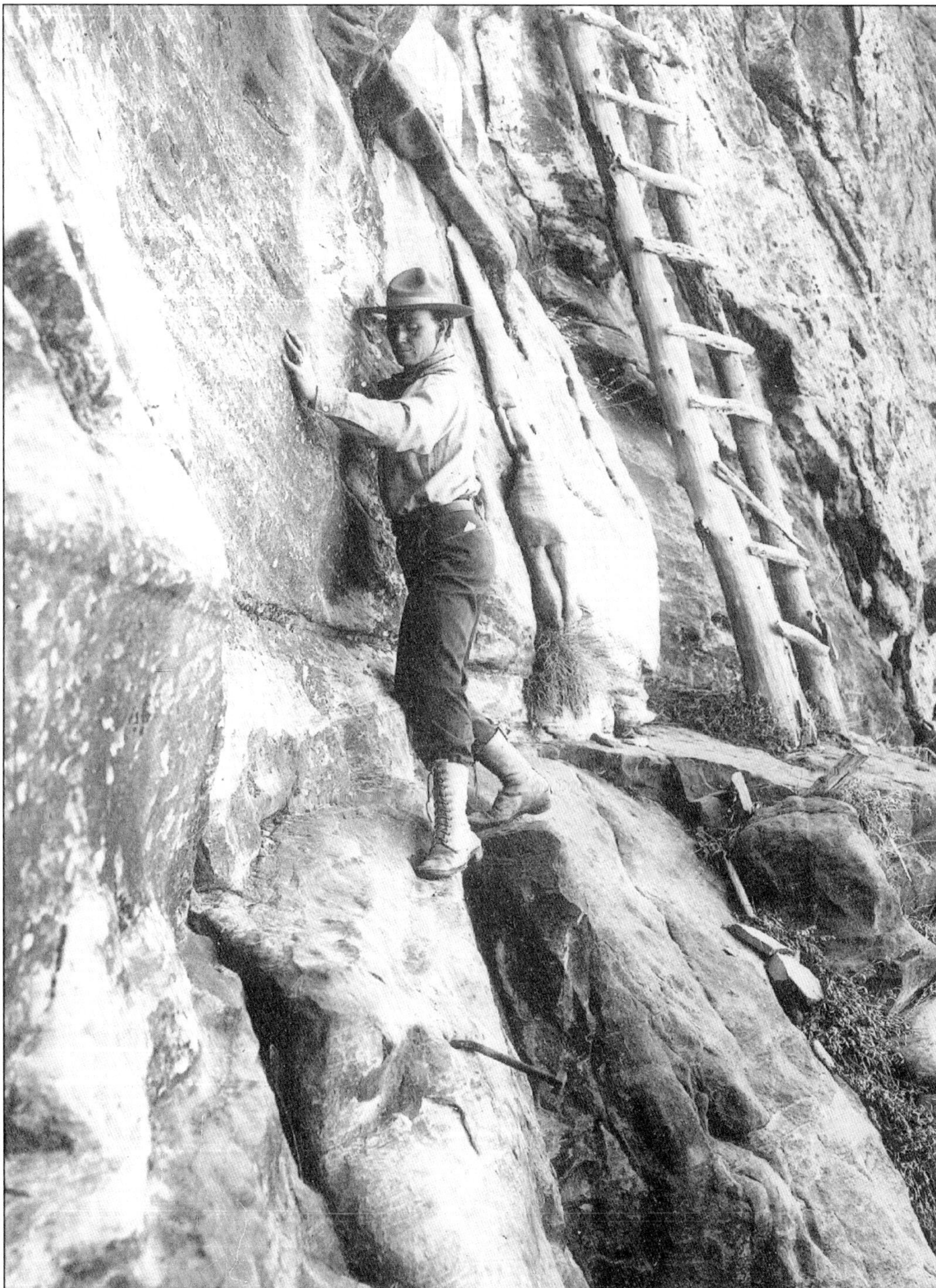

Ellsworth Kolb negotiates a ladder and rough terrain in this 1913 photograph. Kolb is making his way along a route built through the Coconino sandstone on the famous Hummingbird Trail. The route was built in order for miners to gain access to Dan Hogan's Orphan Copper Claim. (Photograph by the Kolb brothers; courtesy of the National Park Service.)

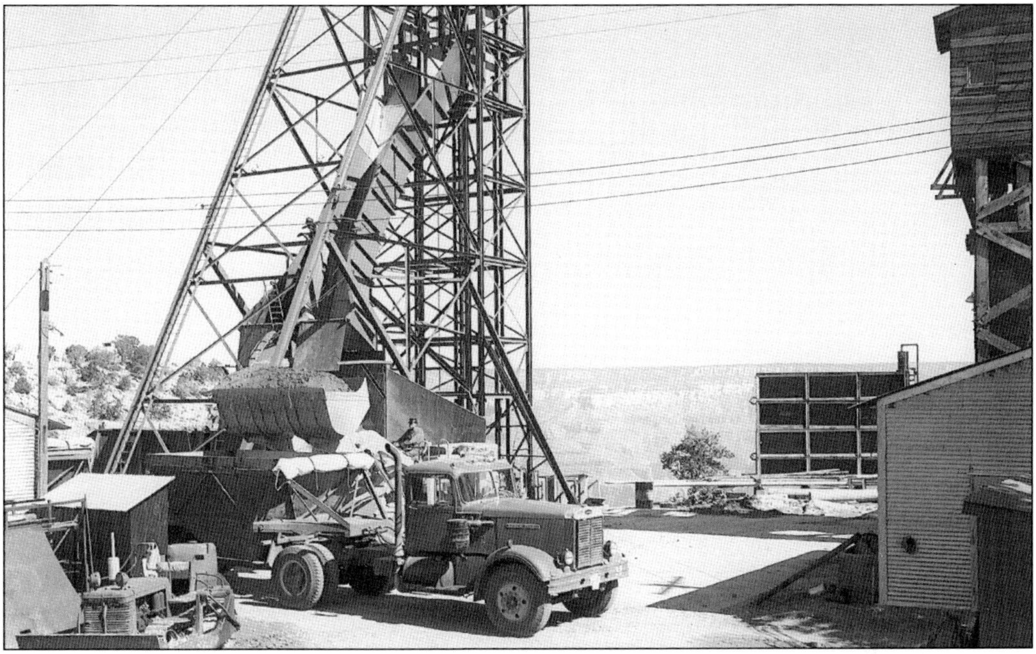

Besides the lucrative tourist trade, many came to the Tusayan, Grand Canyon area to seek employment in the mining industry. An ore truck can be seen in this March 21, 1963, photograph as it is loaded by a head frame at the Orphan Mine. The mine is located along Hermit Road, also known as Rim Drive. (Photograph by Blaisdell; courtesy of the National Park Service.)

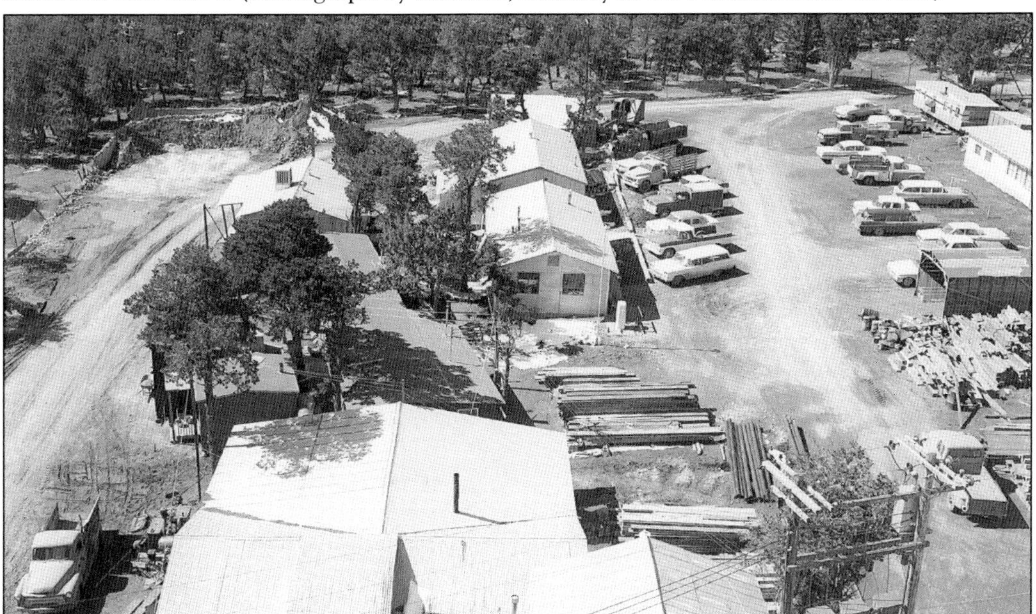

This March 21, 1963, photograph was taken from the top of the head frame located at the Orphan Mine on the Grand Canyon's South Rim. The view faces south and looks down on the buildings and parking areas that were a part of the mine. Many miners who worked in the area would live in camps located in Tusayan village. (Photograph by Blaisdell; courtesy of the National Park Service.)

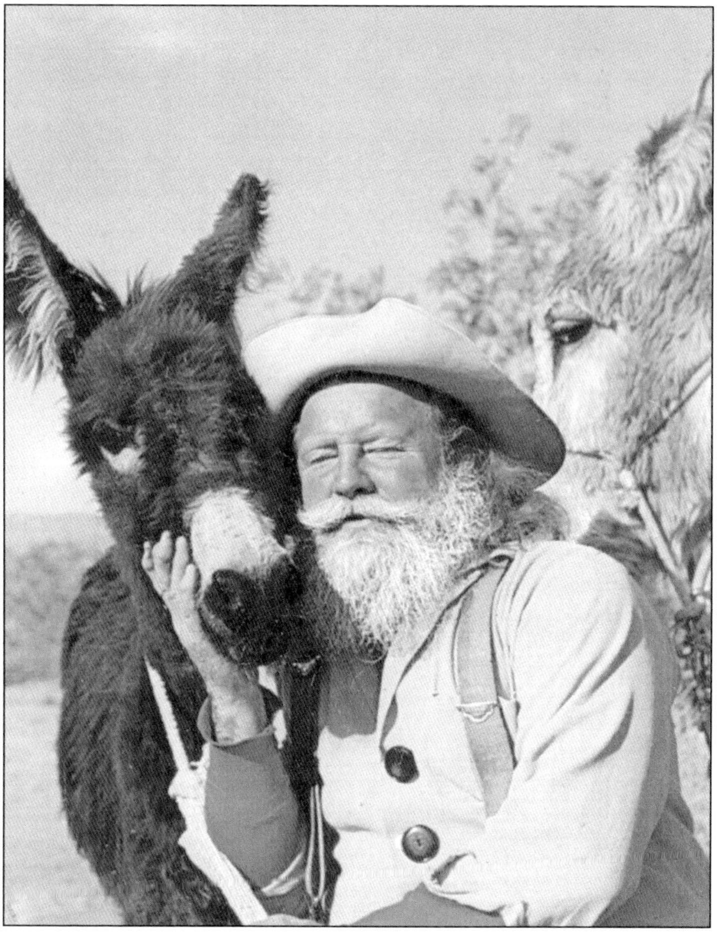

Badwater Bill can be seen with a couple of his furry companions in this 1960s photograph. Bill was a staple of the Tusayan community for a number of years, having moved to the area from Death Valley in California. In both locations, Badwater Bill was a popular attraction for tourists in the area. (Courtesy Clarinda Vail and the Thurston family.)

This sign for the Grand Canyon is said to have once been located near the community of Ash Fork, located roughly 90 minutes away from the South Rim. While no longer there, many in the area recall the sign as they drove through northern Arizona from Ash Fork to Williams. (Courtesy of the Williams Public Library.)

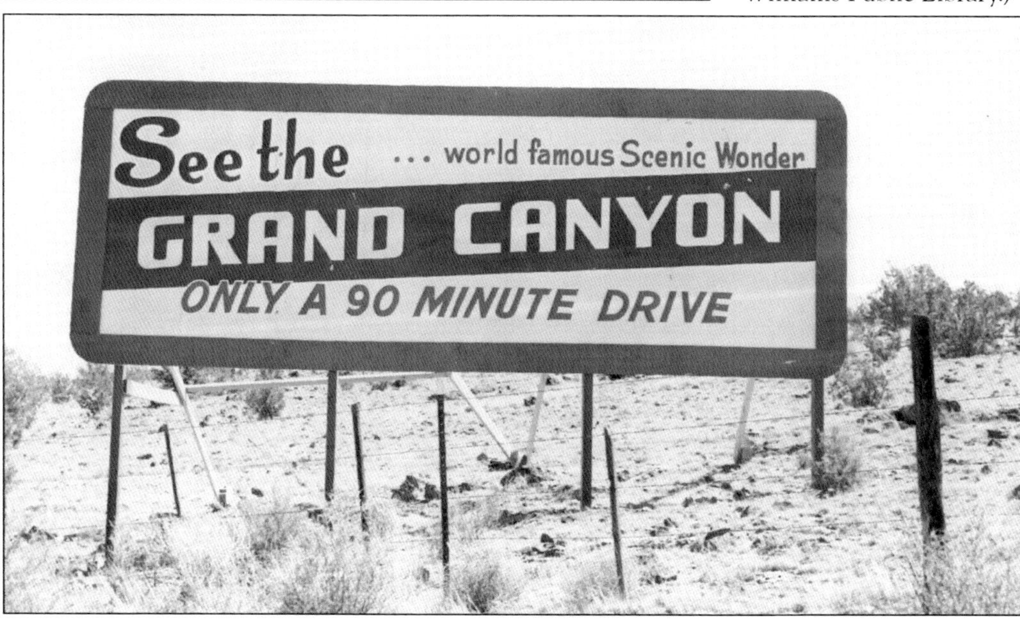

Pictured is a brochure for Moqui Lodge that boasted luxury accommodations for its visitors. The lodge offered 100 rooms and a number of dining choices for guests. The brochure also listed the elevation, at 7,000 feet, and "air conditioning by nature." Besides other accommodations, the lodge also offered a salon. (Courtesy of Thomas Ratz.)

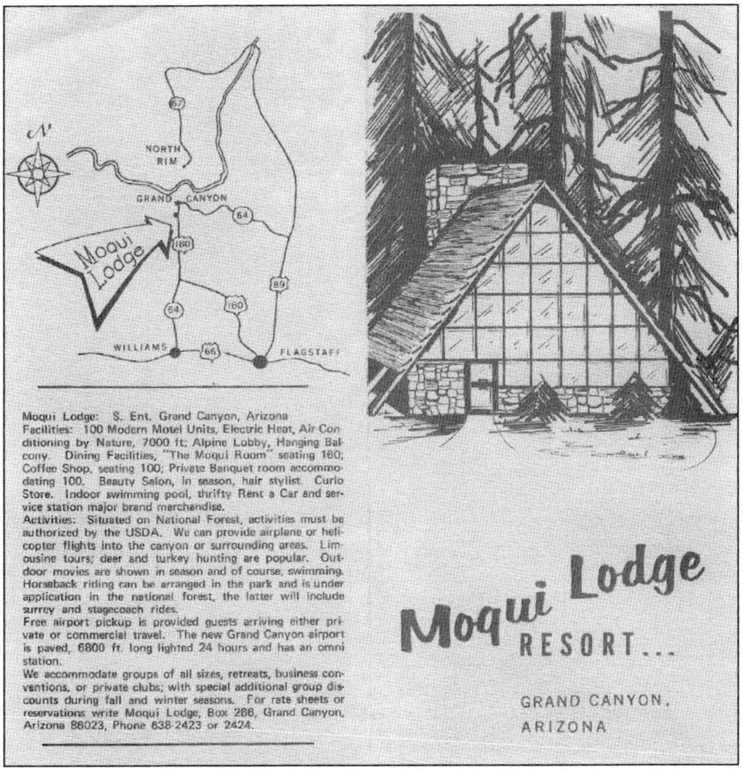

N
NORTH RIM
GRAND CANYON
Moqui Lodge
WILLIAMS
FLAGSTAFF

Moqui Lodge: S. Ent. Grand Canyon, Arizona
Facilities: 100 Modern Motel Units, Electric Heat, Air-Conditioning by Nature, 7000 ft; Alpine Lobby, Hanging Balcony. Dining Facilities, "The Moqui Room" seating 160; Coffee Shop, seating 100; Private Banquet room accommodating 100. Beauty Salon, in season, hair stylist. Curio Store. Indoor swimming pool, thrifty Rent a Car and service station major brand merchandise.
Activities: Situated on National Forest, activities must be authorized by the USDA. We can provide airplane or helicopter flights into the canyon or surrounding areas. Limousine tours; deer and turkey hunting are popular. Outdoor movies are shown in season and of course, swimming. Horseback riding can be arranged in the park and is under application in the national forest, the latter will include surrey and stagecoach rides.
Free airport pickup is provided guests arriving either private or commercial travel. The new Grand Canyon airport is paved, 6800 ft. long lighted 24 hours and has an omni station.
We accommodate groups of all sizes, retreats, business conventions, or private clubs; with special additional group discounts during fall and winter seasons. For rate sheets or reservations write Moqui Lodge, Box 266, Grand Canyon, Arizona 86023, Phone 638-2423 or 2424.

Moqui Lodge
RESORT...
GRAND CANYON, ARIZONA

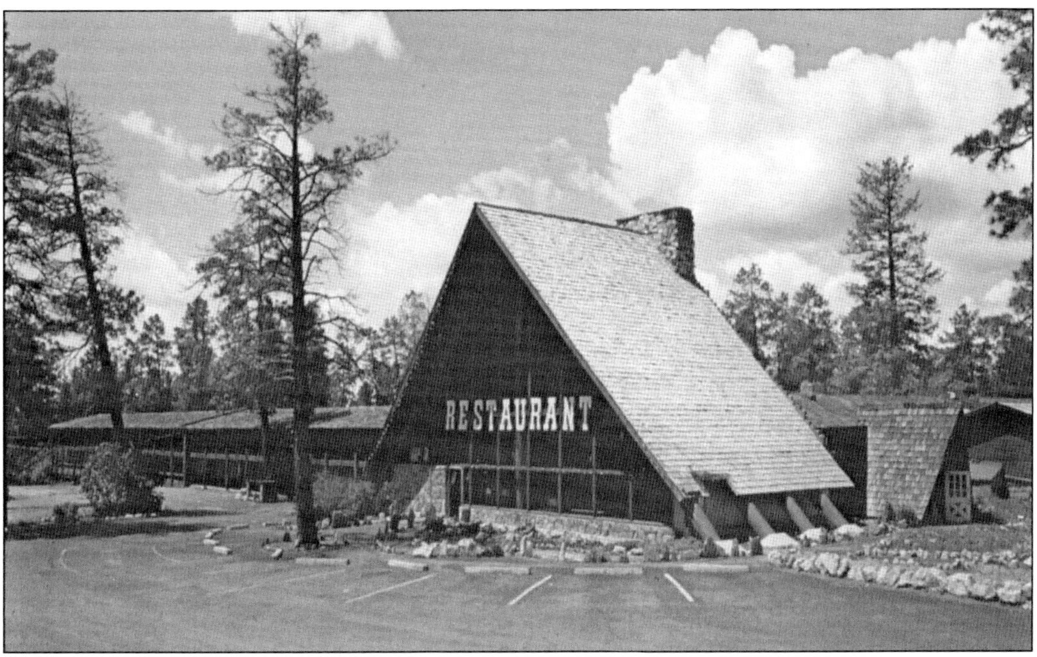

Moqui Lodge can be seen in this photograph during its prime. The lodge sat empty for a number of years before it was torn down. Moqui Lodge was a popular destination for those visiting Grand Canyon. Its restaurant was also a popular spot for locals in the Tusayan area. (Courtesy of Thomas Ratz.)

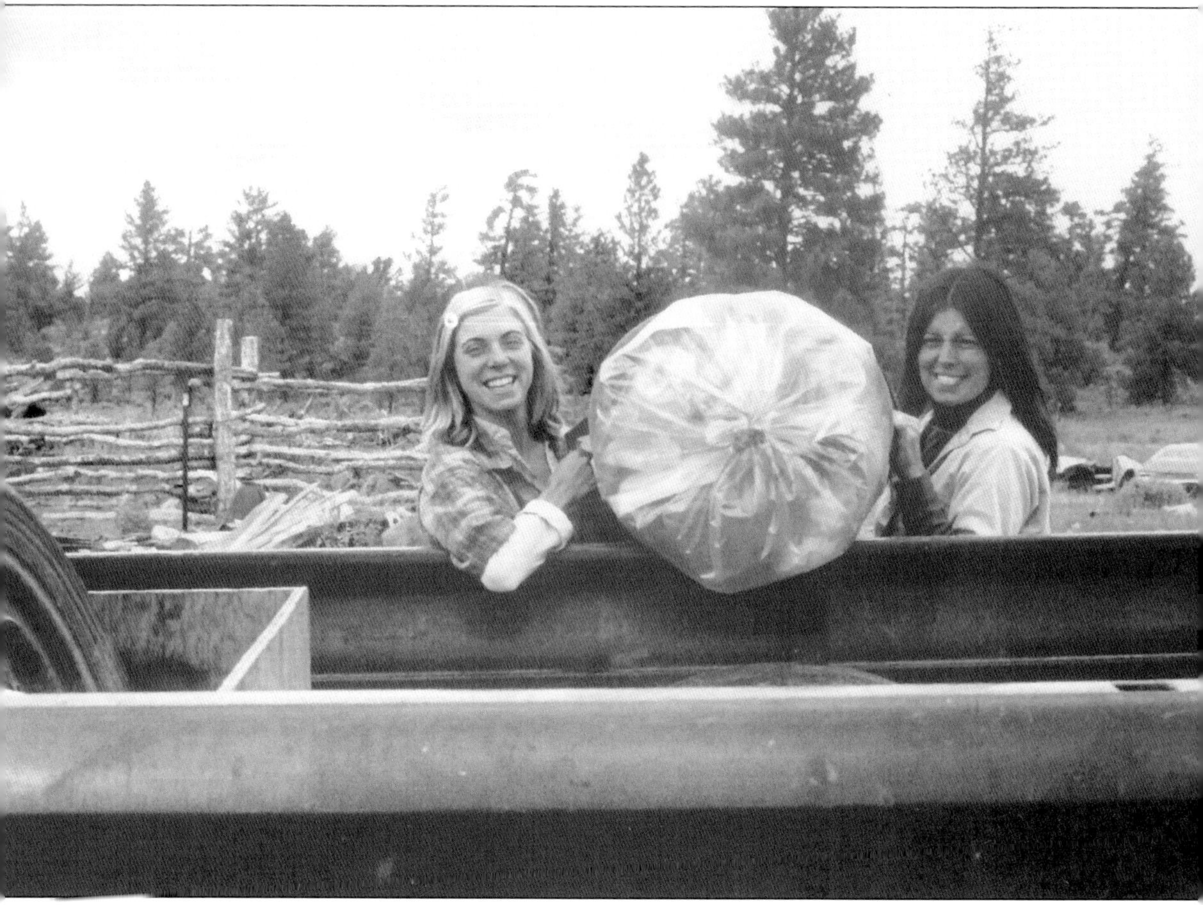

Local residents Chris Brickley and Michelle Ketering are pictured as they load a bundle of trash into the back of a truck. The two women began the Super Trash hauling company in the 1975 to help those living in the area to dispose of their rubbish. (Courtesy of Clarinda Vail and the Thurston family.)

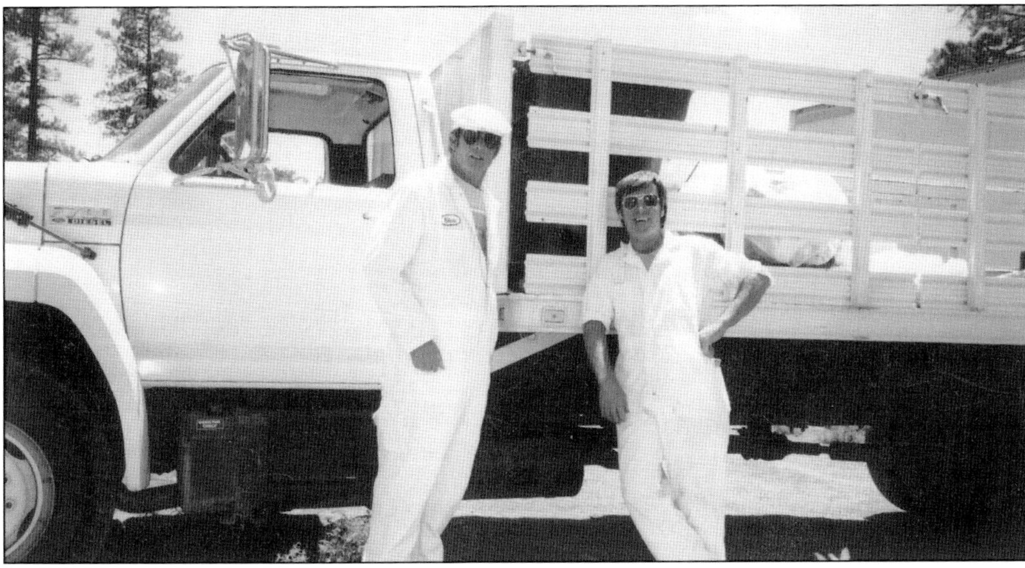

Chris Crossland (left) and Tom Maier stand before a garbage truck in the Tusayan, Grand Canyon area in the 1980s. The two are sporting their new uniforms after beginning their new contract as the first recycling company within the Grand Canyon National Park. (Courtesy of Clarinda Vail and the Thurston family.)

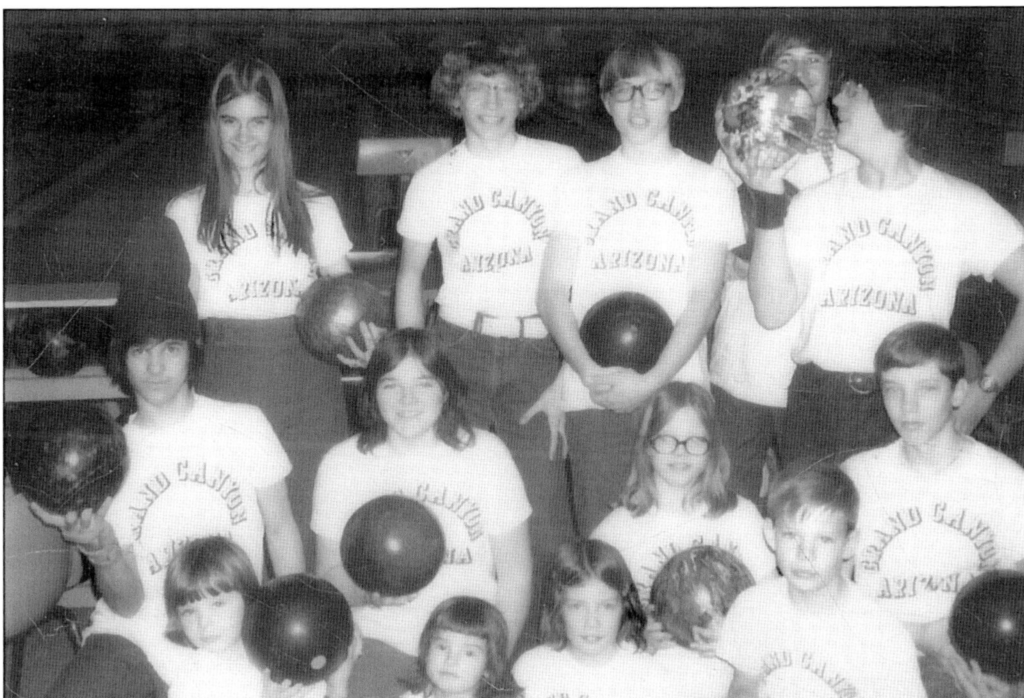

Members of the youth bowling league of Tusayan can be seen in this early 1970s photograph. Bonnie Thurston, along with Bill and Shirley Back, organized the youth league. Bill Back was employed as a department of public safety officer in the area. He is also known as one of the only ones to bowl at least two 300 games at the Squire Inn. (Courtesy of Clarinda Vail and the Thurston family.)

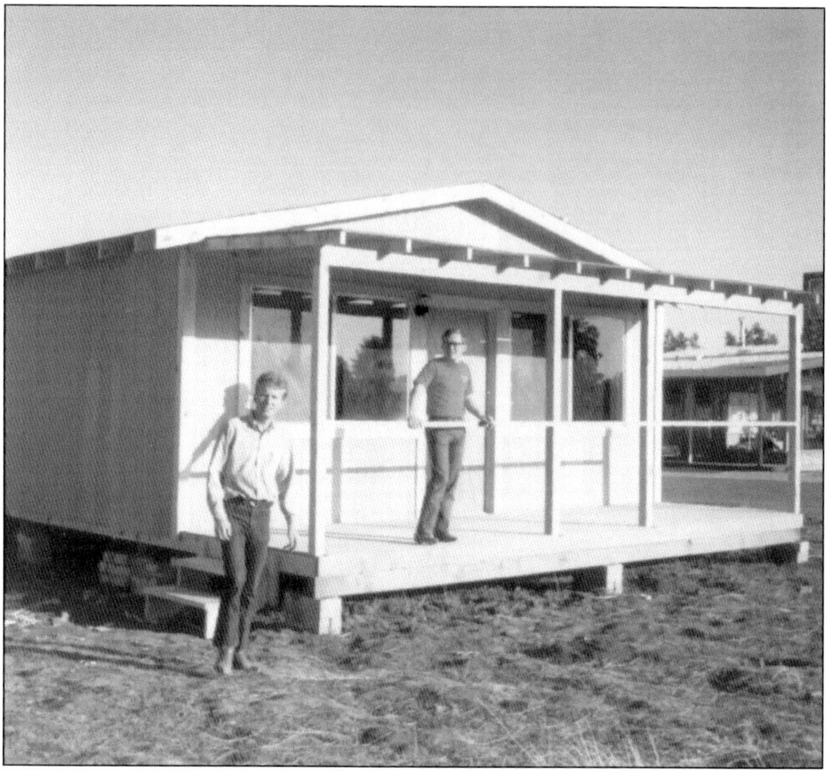

A number of new businesses began to open in the Tusayan community in the 1970s and 1980s, including the Village Sports Den. The business was owned by Clyde Dillon and Norm Johnson, pictured above around 1971. The sporting goods store, part of a franchise from Utah, sold and rented hiking equipment, among other items. (Courtesy of John Dillon.)

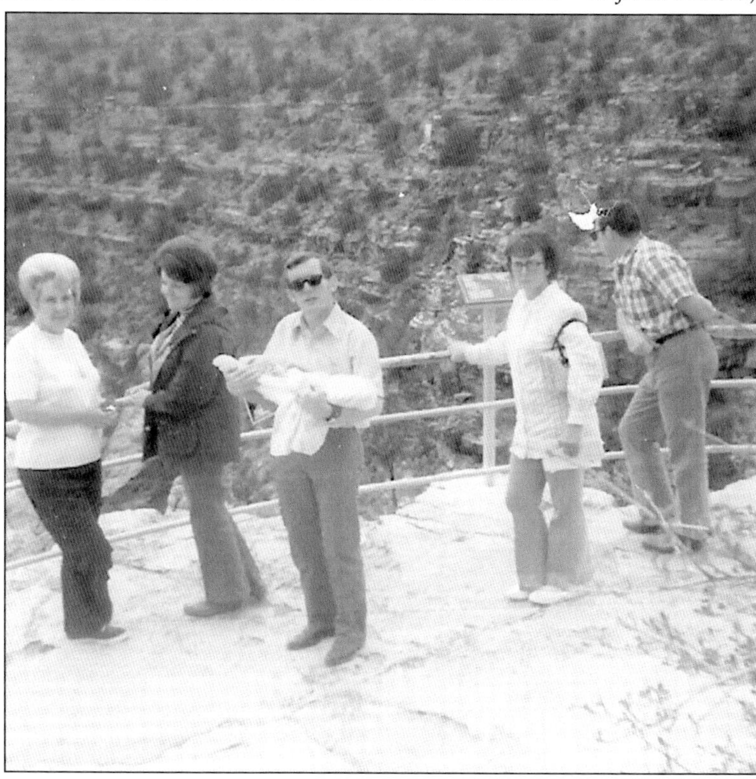

Helen Belnap, Marty Dillon, Clyde Dillon (pictured holding his son John Dillon), Dona Dillon, and Fay Dillon (grandpa) can be seen as they visit Mather Point in 1972. Besides owning a business in Tusayan, and eventually closer to the South Rim as well, the Dillon family also had a number of other business interests throughout northern Arizona. The family eventually settled in the Flagstaff area. (Photograph by Bob Belnap; courtesy of John Dillon.)

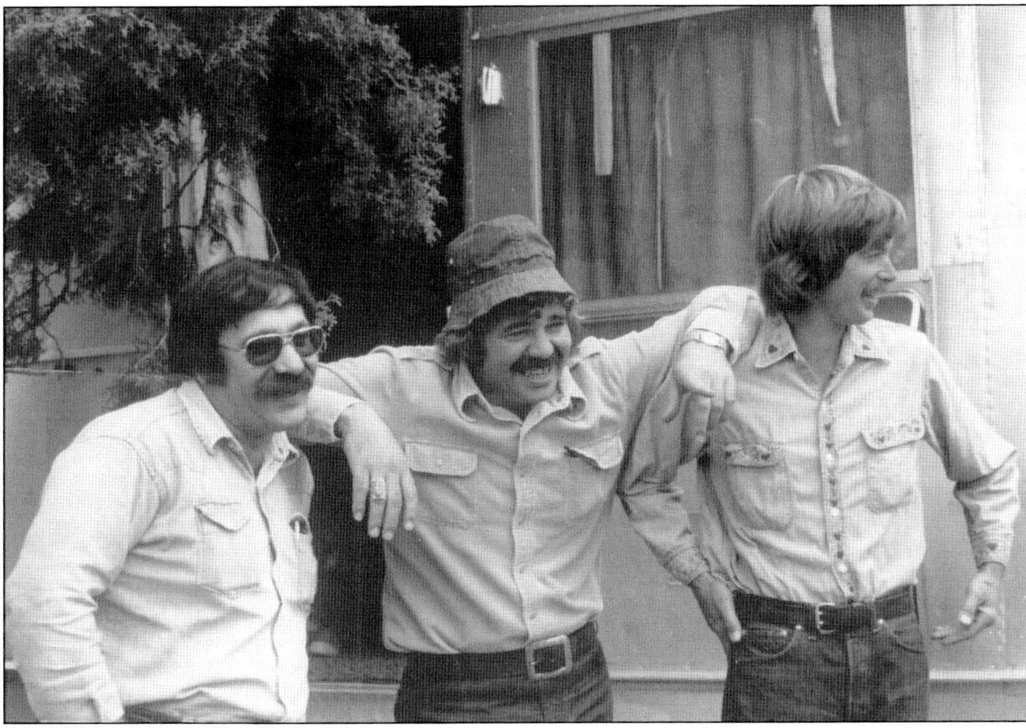

Bob Sutton (who ran the Super Trash company out of Tusayan), Boyce McClung, and Michael Vedekeya are pictured in Grand Canyon National Park in the 1970s. The three were employed with the Fred Harvey Company and were well known in the area. (Courtesy of Clarinda Vail and the Thurston family.)

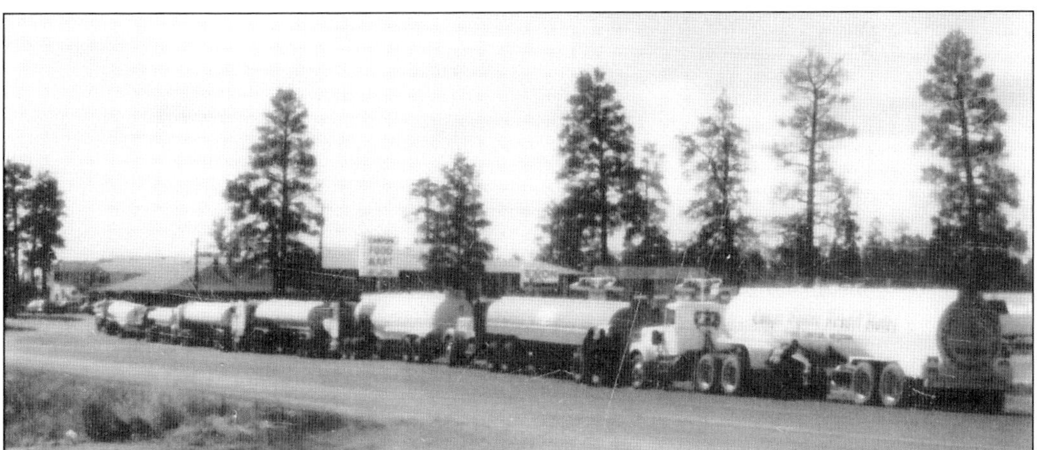

Water trucks can be seen participating in this 1970s Fourth of July parade, which was held every Independence Day in the Tusayan area. Parades once consisted primarily of water trucks, which played a big part in the area's history as water was hauled in from a number of local sources. (Courtesy of Clarinda Vail and the Thurston family.)

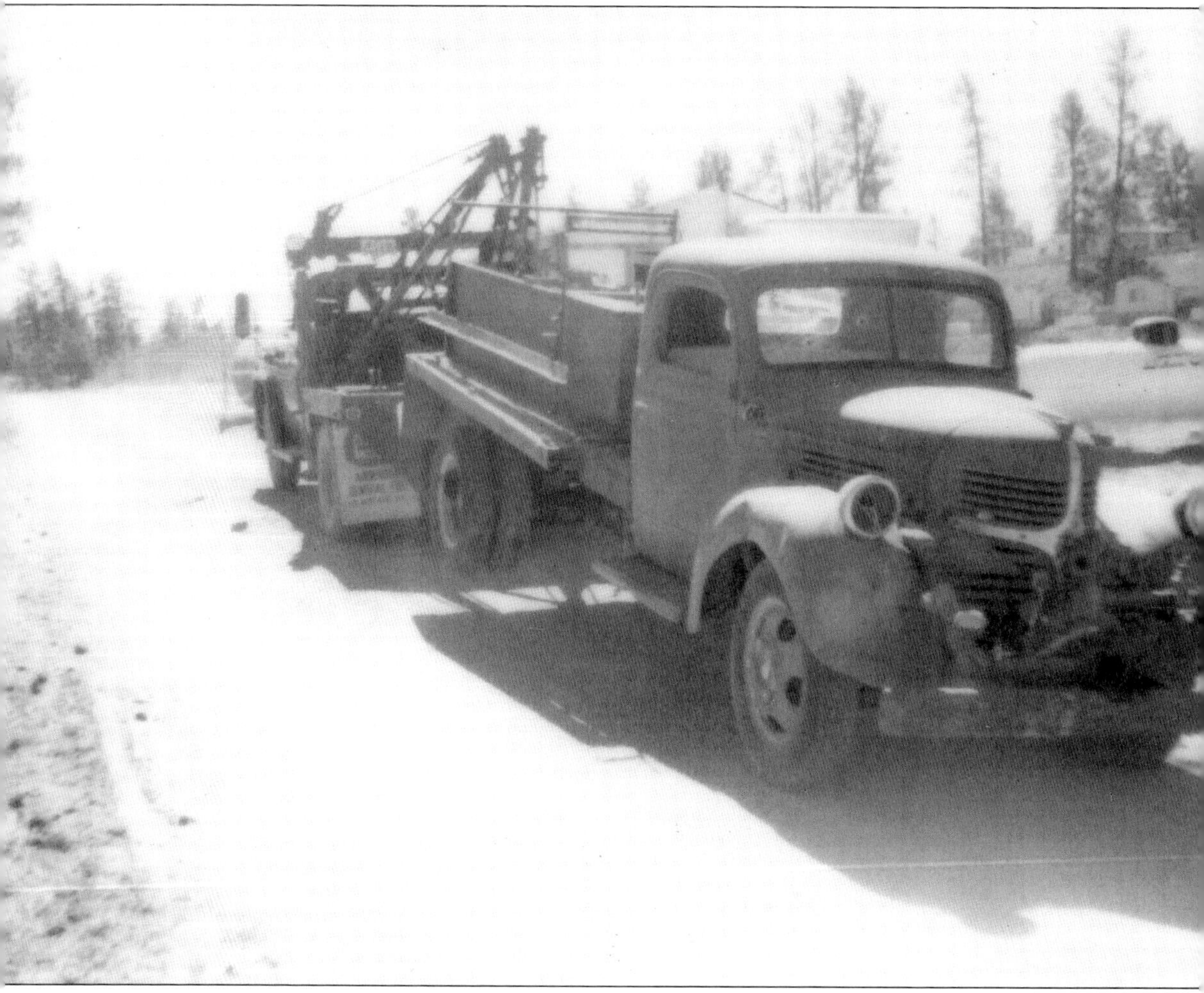

Pictured is an old fire truck used by Moqui Lodge and donated to the Tusayan community. The community's first fire truck, which never really worked, according to residents, is pictured as it is hauled away by Tom Maier in the 1980s. (Courtesy of Clarinda Vail and the Thurston family.)

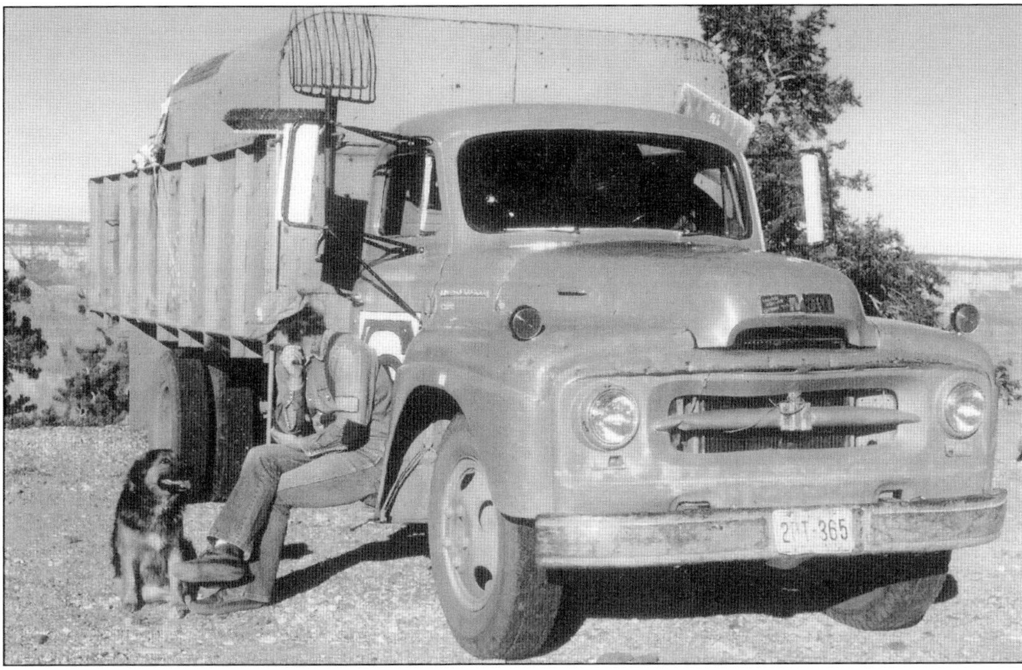

Tusayan resident Bob Sutton can be seen in this 1970s photograph on the South Rim of the Grand Canyon. He is pictured with "Old Clark," the name for the truck he hauled throughout the national park and Tusayan village area. His dog, commonly called the mayor of Tusayan, was named Papillon. (Courtesy of Clarinda Vail and the Thurston family.)

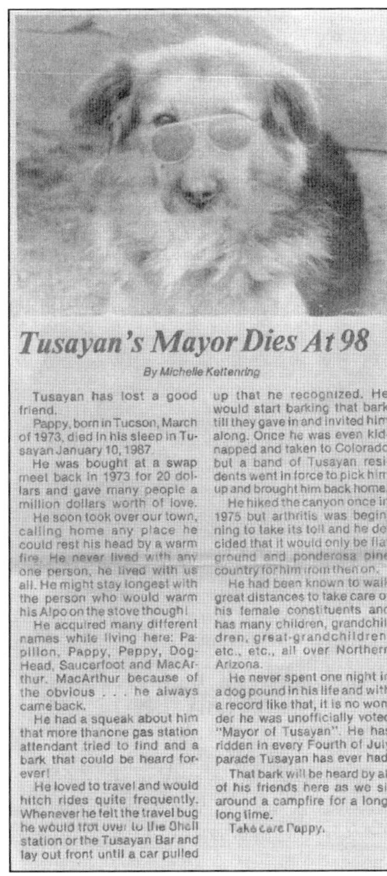

Tusayan's Mayor Dies At 98

By Michelle Kettenring

Tusayan has lost a good friend.

Pappy, born in Tucson, March of 1973, died in his sleep in Tusayan January 10, 1987.

He was bought at a swap meet back in 1973 for 20 dollars and gave many people a million dollars worth of love.

He soon took over our town, calling home any place he could rest his head by a warm fire. He never lived with any one person, he lived with us all. He might stay longest with the person who would warm his Alpo on the stove though!

He acquired many different names while living here: Papillon, Pappy, Peppy, Dog-Head, Saucerfoot and MacArthur. MacArthur because of the obvious . . . he always came back.

He had a squeak about him that more thanone gas station attendant tried to find and a bark that could be heard forever!

He loved to travel and would hitch rides quite frequently. Whenever he felt the travel bug he would trot over to the Shell station or the Tusayan Bar and lay out front until a car pulled up that he recognized. He would start barking that bark till they gave in and invited him along. Once he was even kidnapped and taken to Colorado but a band of Tusayan residents went in force to pick him up and brought him back home.

He hiked the canyon once in 1975 but arthritis was beginning to take its toll and he decided that it would only be flat ground and ponderosa pine country for him from then on.

He had been known to walk great distances to take care of his female constituents and has many children, grandchildren, great-grandchildren, etc., etc., all over Northern Arizona.

He never spent one night in a dog pound in his life and with a record like that, it is no wonder he was unofficially voted "Mayor of Tusayan". He has ridden in every Fourth of July parade Tusayan has ever had.

That bark will be heard by all of his friends here as we sit around a campfire for a long, long time.

Take care Pappy.

Papillon, the famed Tusayan canine, was featured in a *Grand Canyon News* article around the time of his death. Born in 1973 and alive until 1987 (98 in dog years), Papillon reportedly passed away in his sleep. (Courtesy Clarinda Vail and the Thurston family.)

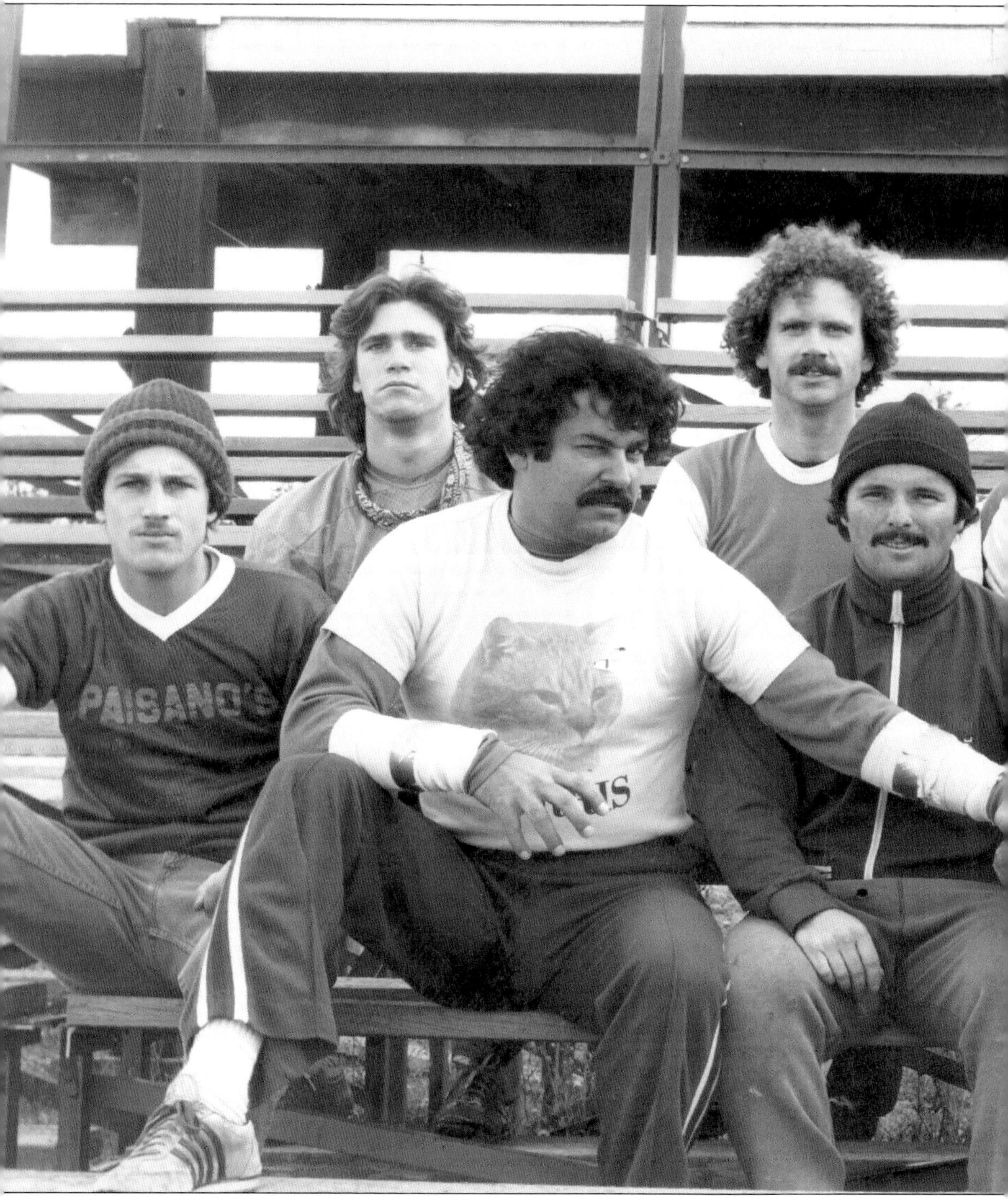

Members of the Paisano's Fred Harvey football team can be seen in this 1979 photograph. Many members of the Tusayan community, as well as within the national park, often participate in adult sporting leagues within the area. The Paisano's are pictured on Guthrie Field, located within the park between Grand Canyon School and the Grand Canyon Recreation Center. The Xanterra

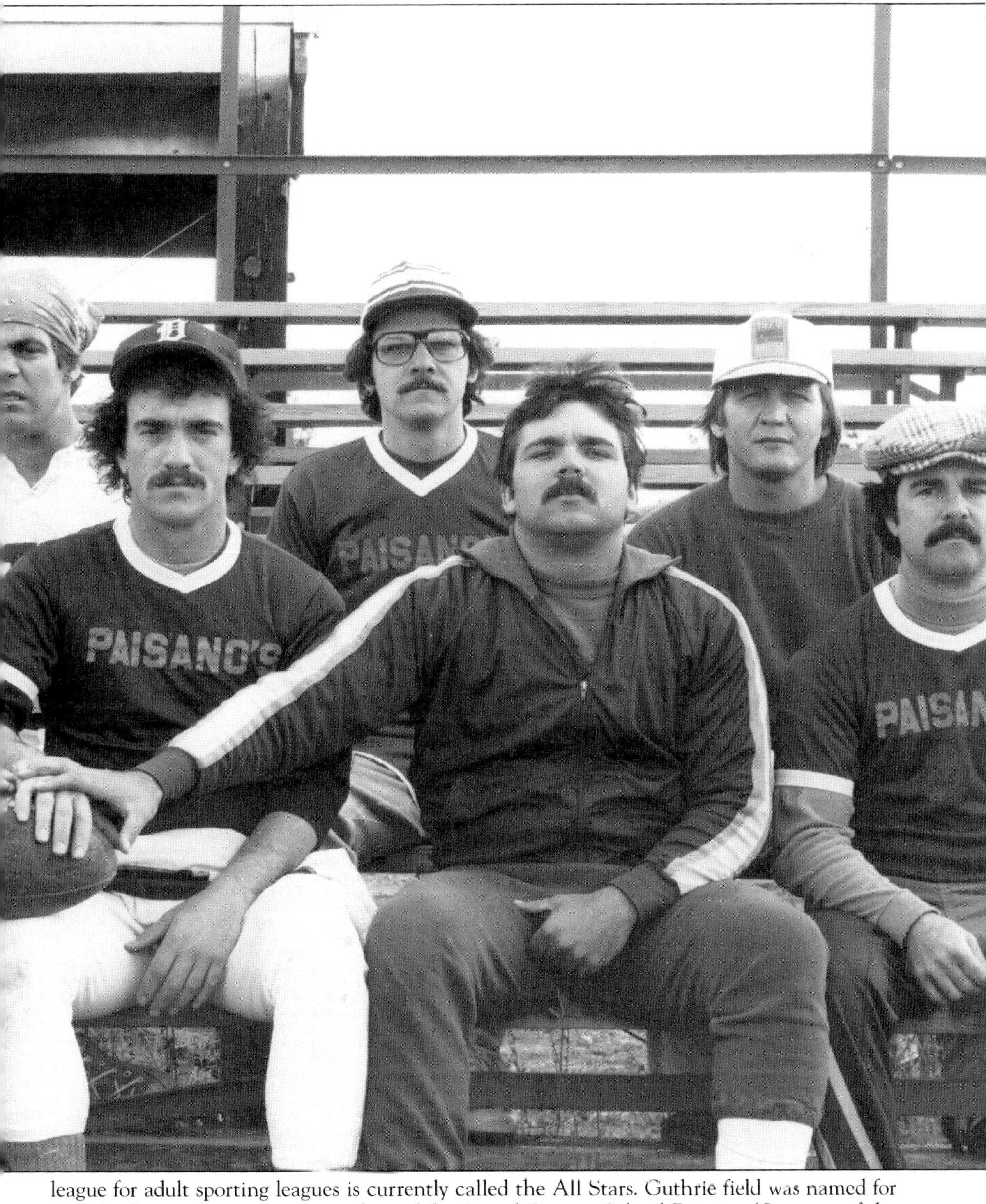

league for adult sporting leagues is currently called the All Stars. Guthrie field was named for Carl Guthrie, a former superintendent of the Grand Canyon School District. (Courtesy of the National Park Service.)

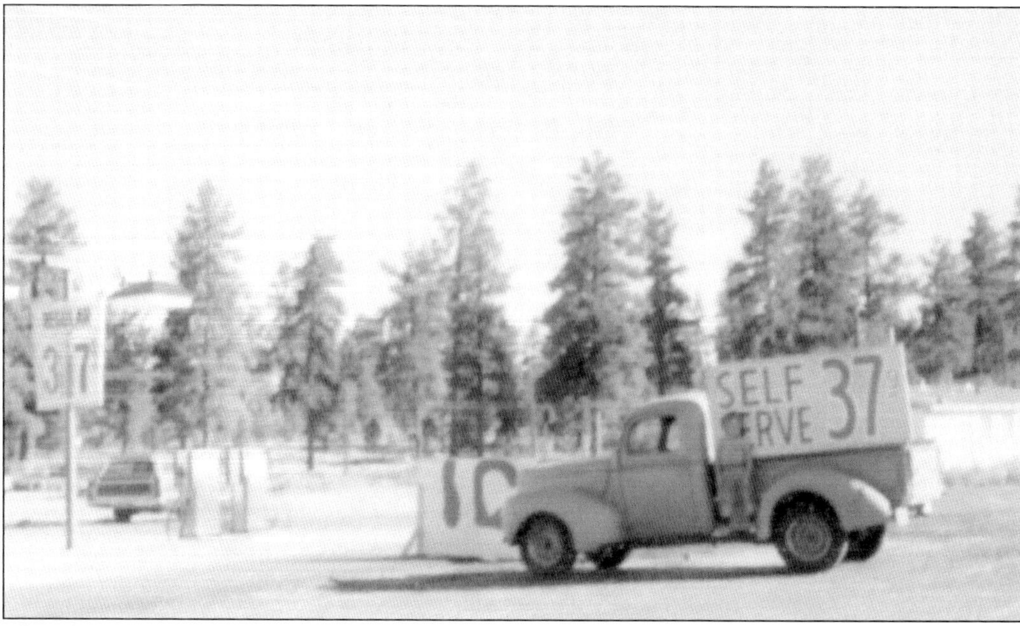

This photograph was taken in the early 1970s in front of the gas station built by Bill and Bonnie Thurston. Their son John Thurston can be seen on the running board of a 1940 Ford truck that was once used at the Grand Canyon Airport in the Red Butte area. (Courtesy of Clarinda Vail and the Thurston family.)

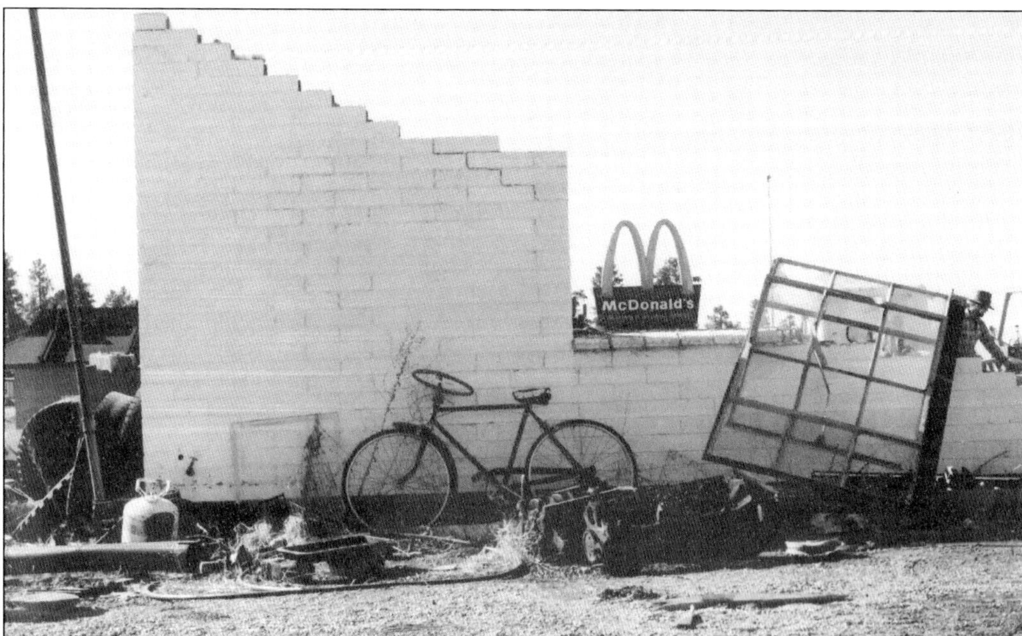

The bicycle belonging to Tusayan resident Rich McNeal's can be seen in this late 1970s photograph, complete with a steering wheel instead of handlebars. The photograph was taken during the demolition phase of the gas station that once belonged to the Thurston family. (Courtesy of Clarinda Vail and the Thurston family.)

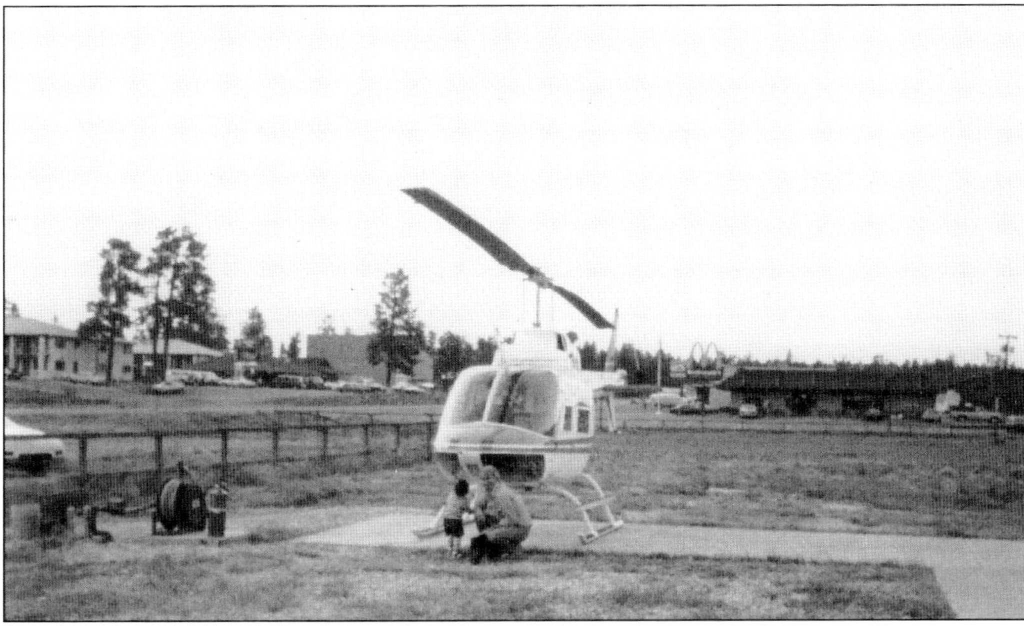

Local Tusayan resident Dan O'Connell introduces his son Patrick to one of the helicopters owned by Madison Aviation. The O'Connell family attended the official kickoff festivities for the tour company, which started around 1982 in the village of Tusayan. O'Connell managed the new company for Madison Aviation. These days, tours are operated from the airport and not from the community itself. (Courtesy of Clarinda Vail and the Thurston family.)

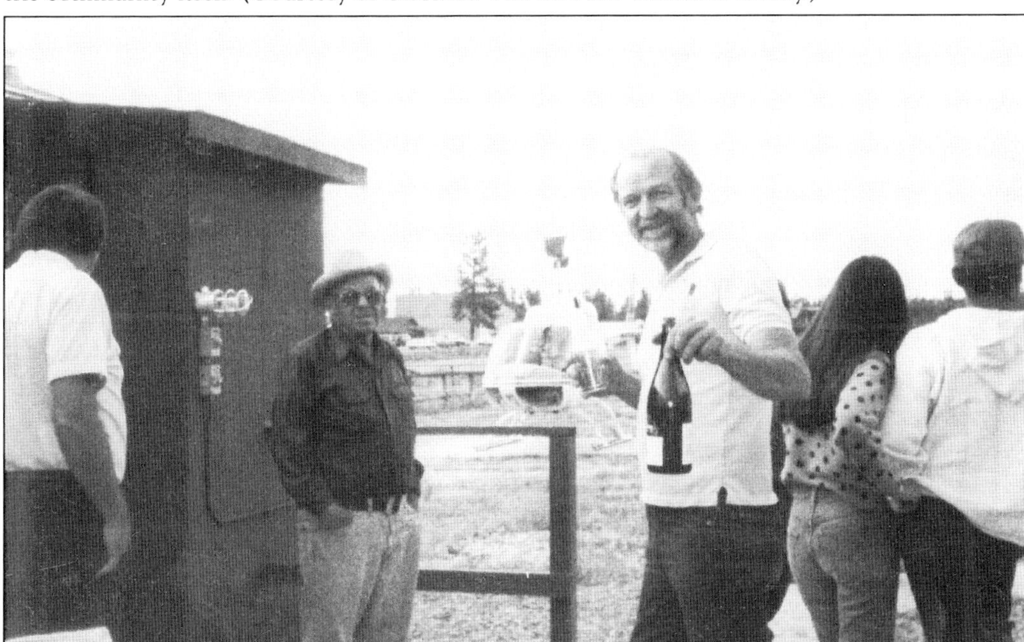

Bill Thurston, seen in a hat and sunglasses, is pictured with Joe Babbitt and a number of other attendees as they celebrate the opening of Madison Aviation in the village of Tusayan. Babbitt is holding a bottle of champagne to commemorate the event. (Courtesy of Clarinda Vail and the Thurston family.)

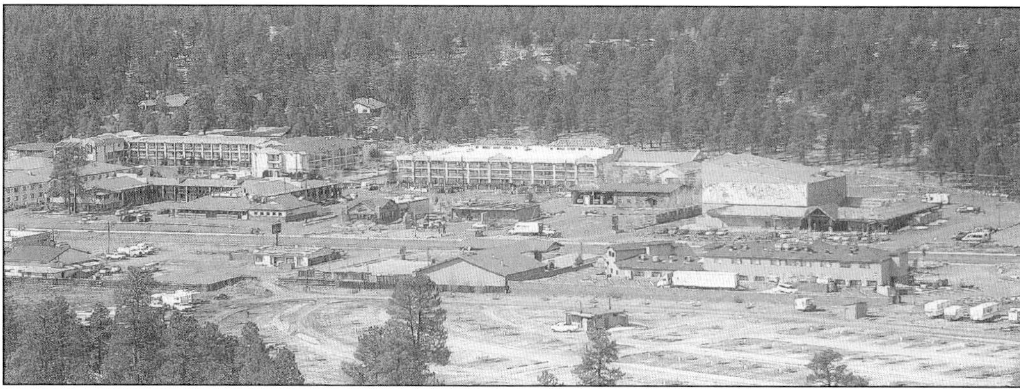

Pictured is an aerial view of Grand Canyon's Tusayan village as it appears today. This is what travelers see on the final leg of an air tour over the national park. A number of air tour operators can be found in and around the Grand Canyon Airport at the south end of the community. (Courtesy of the author.)

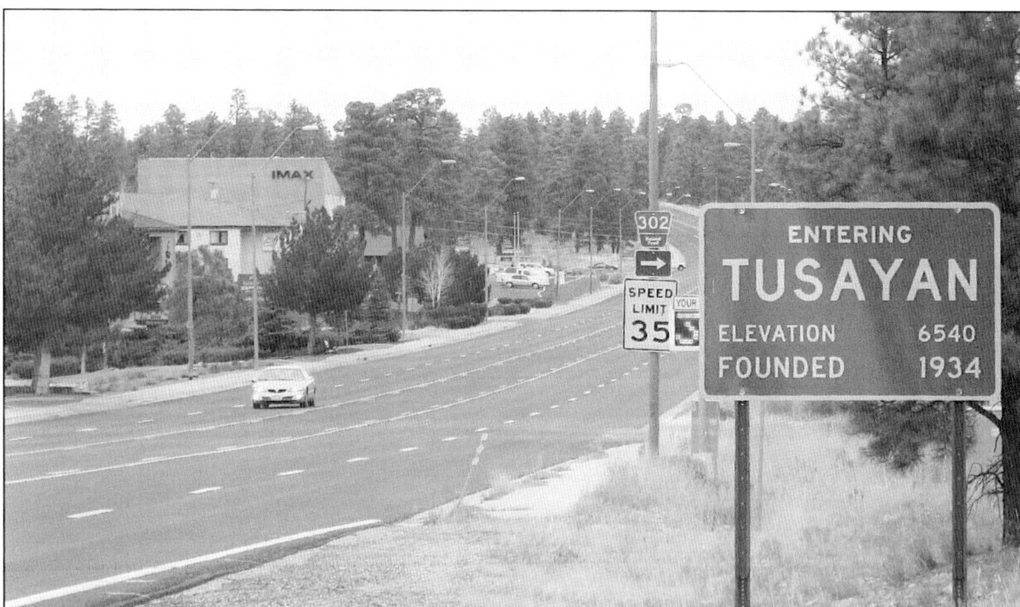

This sign for Tusayan was put in place in 1987 when construction was completed on Highway 64, turning the road from two lanes to five lanes. A lighting district was formed to bring lights to the area in order to make crossing the street at night safer for residents and visitors to Tusayan village. Residents voted to incorporate the small South Rim community in March 2010. (Courtesy of the author.)

Bibliography

Cleeland, Teri A. *Cultural Resources Management Report No. 10: People and Places of the Old Kaibab.* USDA Forest Service Southwestern Region, 1990.

Lauzon, Hubert. "The Ol' Pioneer." Grand Canyon, Arizona: Newsletter of the Grand Canyon Pioneer Society, 1992.

Richmond, Al; Belgard, Buford; Hoover, Mary K. *History of the John Ivens Post No. 42: the First 75 Years.* Grand Canyon, Arizona: The American Legion, 1998.

Warren, Ronald L. "Tusayan: Then and Now." Williams, Arizona: *Williams-Grand Canyon News*, 1994.

Williams-Grand Canyon News. "Thurston Family Pioneered the Community of Tusayan." Williams, Arizona: 1994.

About the Author

Having lived in Williams, just south of the Grand Canyon, for 16 years, Patrick Whitehurst has written numerous stories about northern Arizona for local publications in his role as associate editor of the *Grand Canyon News*. His stories range from news reporting to humor columns. Whitehurst is a graduate of Northern Arizona University with a degree in journalism. His first book, *Williams*, was published by Arcadia Publishing in 2008.